Henry Fielding's Novels
and the Classical Tradition

Henry Fielding's Novels and the Classical Tradition

Nancy A. Mace

Newark: University of Delaware Press
London: Associated University Presses

© 1996 by Associated University Presses, Inc.

All rights reserved. Authorization to photocopy items for internal or personal use, or the internal or personal use of specific clients, is granted by the copyright owner, provided that a base fee of $10.00, plus eight cents per page, per copy is paid directly to the Copyright Clearance Center, 222 Rosewood Dr., Danvers, Mass. 01923. [0-87413-585-0/96 $10.00 + 8¢ pp, pc.]

Associated University Presses
440 Forsgate Drive
Cranbury, N.J. 08512

Associated University Presses
16 Barter Street
London WC1A 2AH, England

Associated University Presses
P.O. Box 338, Port Credit
Mississauga, Ontario
Canada L5G 4L8

The paper used in this publication meets the requirements
of the American National Standard for Permanence of Paper
for Printed Library Materials Z39.48-1984

Library of Congress Cataloging-in-Publication Data

Mace, Nancy A., 1951–
    Henry Fielding's novels and the classical tradition / Nancy A. Mace.
      p.   cm.
    Includes bibliographical references and index.
    ISBN 0-87413-585-0 (alk. paper)
    1. Fielding, Henry, 1707–1754—Knowledge—Literature.
2. Classical literature—Appreciation—England—History—18th century. 3. English fiction—Classical influences. 4. Fiction-
-Technique. 5. Rhetoric, Ancient. I. Title
PR3458.L5M33   1996
823'.5—dc20   95-42482
                                                        CIP

PRINTED IN THE UNITED STATES OF AMERICA

For Robert D. Hume
and John T. Harwood

Contents

List of Tables / 9

Preface / 11

1. Classical Learning and Novel Readers, 1701–1750 / 17
2. Fielding, the Classical Scholar / 39
3. Classical Epic and the "New Species of Writing" / 61
4. Classical Allusion and the Judgment of Character / 77
5. The Ancients, the Moderns, and the English Novel / 105

Postscript: Literary Politics in the Mid-Eighteenth Century and the Genealogy of the Novel / 129

Appendix A: Tables for Chapter 1 / 137

Appendix B: Tables for Chapter 2 / 152

Appendix C: Tables for Chapter 3 / 157

Notes / 161

Bibliography / 181

Index / 191

Tables

Table 1.1	Authors and Works Covered in the Curriculum of the Upper School at Eton (1766)	22
Table 1.2	Authors Recommended in Six Guides to Classical Learning	24
Table 1.3	Latin Authors with the Highest Number of Editions in the *ESTC*	33
Table 1.4	Greek Authors Represented by the Largest Number of Editions in the *ESTC*	35
Table 1.5	Total Loans for Individual Latin and Greek Authors at Cathedral Libraries	38
Table 2.1	Greek and Latin Authors Named Most Frequently in the Baker Catalog	41
Table 2.2	Latin Authors Cited Most Frequently in Fielding's Periodicals	52
Table 2.3	Greek Authors Cited Most Frequently in the Periodicals	53
Table 2.4	Latin and Greek Authors Cited Most Frequently in the Periodicals	53
Table 3.1	Number of References to Latin Authors Mentioned Most Frequently in Fielding's Novels	63
Table 3.2	Number of References to Greek Authors Mentioned Most Frequently in Fielding's Novels	64
Table 3.3	Latin and Greek Authors Most Frequently Mentioned in Fielding's Novels	64
Table A-1	Latin Authors Recommended in Six Guides for a Gentleman's Reading	137
Table A-2	Latin Authors in the *ESTC*	140

Table A-3	Greek Authors in the *ESTC*	143
Table A-4	Latin Editions with the Greatest Number of Issues in the *ESTC*	147
Table A-5	Greek Editions with the Greatest Number of Issues in the *ESTC*	150
Table B-1	Latin Authors in *The Champion*	152
Table B-2	Greek Authors in *The Champion*	153
Table B-3	Latin Authors in *The True Patriot*	153
Table B-4	Greek Authors in *The True Patriot*	153
Table B-5	Latin Authors in *The Jacobite's Journal*	154
Table B-6	Greek Authors in *The Jacobite's Journal*	154
Table B-7	Latin Authors in *The Covent-Garden Journal*	155
Table B-8	Greek Authors in *The Covent-Garden Journal*	156
Table C-1	Latin Authors in *Jonathan Wild*	157
Table C-2	Greek Authors in *Jonathan Wild*	157
Table C-3	Latin Authors in *Joseph Andrews*	158
Table C-4	Greek Authors in *Joseph Andrews*	158
Table C-5	Latin Authors in *Tom Jones*	158
Table C-6	Greek Authors in *Tom Jones*	159
Table C-7	Latin Authors in *Amelia*	159
Table C-8	Greek Authors in *Amelia*	160

Preface

Henry Fielding's references to classical literature challenge some of the common assumptions about his audience, his sources, and his relationship to other novelists that have dominated criticism of his fiction since the publication of Ian Watt's *Rise of the Novel* thirty-five years ago. Like Watt, most scholars have maintained that Fielding tailored his novels primarily to middle-class readers, many of whom were women and others untrained in the classics; therefore, they stress his ties to the romance and other "modern" genres, belittling or ignoring his use of ancient literature as ornament designed to appease his learned critics.[1] They support this position by noting that Fielding's learned contemporaries often ignored his novels or mocked his references to antiquity as pretension, and they also cite the example of such other fiction writers as Defoe and Richardson, who rejected the classical past as they wrote novels suitable to the taste of the new body of readers created in the eighteenth century.[2] Consequently, because Fielding's use of the classical tradition sets him apart from other early novelists, historians of the novel have argued that it is one of the flaws of the fiction.[3]

While Fielding's use of the classics is important in understanding his work and the genealogy of his fiction, it also provides a gauge by which we can measure the larger issue of the importance of the classics in eighteenth-century literature as a whole. Because recent scholarship has concentrated on the role played by the eighteenth century in the development of modern critical thought, it has often downplayed the extent to which many eighteenth-century authors still admired the ancient classics even as they praised modern developments in science, technology, and literature. By looking closely at a prolific author who was actively engaged in the intellectual and social debates of his times, we can examine in microcosm the interplay between the ancient and the modern worlds, considering whether the two are as incompatible as we have often assumed.

Despite the potential ramifications of the classical references on these issues, critics have paid surprisingly little attention to Fielding's use of ancient literature. Aside from Bernard Shea's 1952 Harvard dissertation, no

one has dealt with Fielding's classics in a full-length study
is limited because he does not consider the classical lea.
audience or explain why he chooses to compare certain nov
ancient works—for example, *Joseph Andrews* with the *Odyssey*. ᴄ
and Charles Knight have done useful surveys of the refere·
and Aristophanes, but neither has explored extensively w¹
from these authors or how such influences affect our
Fielding's work.⁵ Most of the criticism related to Fieldin
has focused exclusively on the influence of Lucian. Extrapᴄ
article written in 1936 that suggested some tenuous connections betwᴄ
Fielding and the Greek satirist, Henry Knight Miller and Christopher
Robinson have argued at length that this writer was the most important classical influence on Fielding.⁶ Scholars have, therefore, used Lucian to support positions about Fielding's sources in satire, his characterization, his use of quotation, and his narrative stance.⁷ Because none of these treatments carefully considers the place of Lucian in the eighteenth-century canon, Fielding's probable knowledge of him in the original, or the number of direct references to him, however, we must reconsider this commonplace.

These studies have left many questions about Fielding's use of the classical tradition unanswered. Are his references designed to guide his audience, or are they merely ornamental, as many critics have assumed? What can the classics reveal about Fielding's audience? Do they demonstrate that Lucian influenced Fielding profoundly, or do they indicate that other classical writers are more prominent? Finally, how does this information change our interpretation of his genre, his characters, his narrator, and his role in the early development of the novel and in the intellectual debates of his time?

In order to answer these questions, I move beyond a simple study of Fielding's sources and influences on his work to examine how Fielding appropriates classical texts as a system of signs intelligible to him and certain segments of his audience. He makes assumptions about his readers' knowledge and outlook, and he then exploits those assumptions for literary purposes. Thus, he develops and manipulates various codes—part of the transaction between the reader and the writer, between the author and his audience. In order to delineate the significance and extent of this shared knowledge, I begin by examining the classical training of Fielding's potential readers and the ancient authors with whom they were familiar. Against this background, I review what we know about Fielding's learning in the classics and examine the direct evidence of Lucian and other classical authors in his work. This information is then applied to specific issues that have interested critics: his genre, his characterization, and his narrator. Finally, I explore how Fielding views the controversy between the ancients and the moderns and what his position means to his career as a novelist.

As my research demonstrates, Fielding's allusions to classical literature are an integral part of the language he shared with certain parts of his audience; consequently, they affect both his literary technique and his concept of genre. They indicate that he addressed not a single audience but multiple ones, and that he could exploit his readers' knowledge of a small body of authors, among whom Horace, Homer, and Virgil figure prominently, while Lucian is conspicuously missing. Despite the assumptions of Fielding critics, a survey of the classical allusions and quotations in Fielding's novels reveals that Lucian did not influence Fielding as profoundly as Horace, Aristotle, and the epic poets. An understanding of these authors and the role they played in eighteenth-century literature provides new insights about Fielding's concept of genre, his characterization, and his narrative stance; it also suggests that Fielding's novels developed from different origins than those of his contemporaries Defoe and Richardson, revealing that we should reassess theories of the novel that posit a single modern source for the genre and should reconsider the relationship between classical and modern literature in this century.

In bringing this manuscript to its current state, I have received support from several different sources. I am deeply indebted to Robert D. Hume, who originally suggested this topic and supervised the thesis from which this book grew, and to John T. Harwood, whose insightful comments greatly contributed to improvements in my statistical tables and style. I also want to thank the American Association of University Women Educational Foundation for a dissertation fellowship during the 1988–89 school year, when I was doing much of the initial work on this project. As I wrote the first drafts of this book, I received useful comments from Archie Allen and Nicholas Joukovsky; Martin C. Battestin provided many useful insights to substantial portions of the second chapter. The staff of the Rare Book Room at Pattee Library (The Pennsylvania State University), led by Charles Mann and Sandy Stelts, facilitated my research by obtaining editions that proved important in my work. I also benefited from the expertise of staffs at the British Library, Dr. Williams' Library in London, the Bodleian Library, the Folger Shakespeare Library, and the Public Record Office, London. I wish to express my appeciation to the University of Chicago Press for permission to use material in chapter 2 that appeared earlier in Nancy A. Mace, "Henry Fielding's Classical Learning," *Modern Philology* 88, no. 4 (May 1991): 243–60, © University of Chicago Press, 1991. Finally, I want to thank my parents, the late Sherburne F. Mace and the late Ada L. Mace, to whom I am very grateful for their moral and financial support throughout this project. I would also like to acknowledge the support of my colleagues at the Naval Academy and of my friends and family, especially my husband Raymond Lee Jr., Richard C. Taylor, and my son John Bowen.

Unless otherwise noted, all citations to the works of Henry Fielding are to the Wesleyan edition where available or to the first edition if no volume has been completed in the Wesleyan edition.

Henry Fielding's Novels
and the Classical Tradition

1
Classical Learning and Novel Readers, 1701–1750

> And as for *Greek and Latin* their is so little need to carry that to the *Plow* or *Forge* that it is rather mischievous; a smattering in such kind of learning having too often this ill effect, to make such persons more *pragmatical* in *conversation*, and *less mindful* of their proper *business* as thinking themselves above it, tho' commonly what remains with them of *languages* serves them to little better use, than so much *gibberish*.
> —Francis Brokesby, *Of Education* (1701)

> Upon all which Accounts, I think the Ancients, as well Greeks as Latins, at least such as are allowed on all hands to excell amongst them, in their several Ways, ought to be well studied by a professional scholar.
> —John Clark, *An Essay upon Study* (1731)

> "You are a provoking Man, Doctor," said Mrs. *Atkinson*, "Where is the Harm in a Woman's having Learning as well as a Man?"
> "Let me ask you another Question," said the Doctor. "Where is the Harm in a Man's being a fine Performer with a Needle as well as a Woman? And yet, answer me honestly, Would you greatly chuse to marry a Man with a Thimble upon his Finger? Would you in earnest think a Needle became the Hand of your Husband as well as a Halberd?"
> —Henry Fielding, *Amelia*

The classical learning of Henry Fielding's audience provides some clues to the diverse character of the "classical" and "English" readers so often addressed in his fiction and offers a key by which we can interpret his use of ancient literature. Before we can accurately assess how Fielding used the classical tradition, we must ascertain how much—if anything—his readers knew about the ancient world and what classical authors were most familiar to them. With this information, we can appreciate more fully the responses Fielding expected from his audience and determine whether—like many twentieth-century readers—they considered such displays of learning little more than window dressing. By assessing the opportunities available for classical education in this period, we will be able to learn more about the audience Fielding created for his fiction; particularly we can discover whether he imagined a single ideal reader or anticipated multiple responses to his novels. From a fuller knowledge of the "classical" reader, we can measure Fielding's own grasp of and commitment to the classical tradition—an important issue when we evaluate his claims about the influence of the classics on his conception of the novel.

Obtaining an accurate picture of the authors in the classical canon and the classical learning of novel readers is a more complicated task than it would at first seem. Available studies of classical education in this period focus only on the "public" schools, where information about the curriculum is relatively plentiful and detailed. Because these schools catered to an elite group of young men, however, such accounts create the impression that all eighteenth-century readers shared the same level of classical learning and that they either read the classics in the original or not at all.[1] To understand the variations in classical learning among Fielding's readers, we must explore other evidence about education and reading habits: information about other kinds of schools, handbooks, the records of libraries, and the classical editions listed in the *ESTC*. What do these sources reveal about the classical backgrounds of Fielding's readers? Can they suggest who Fielding's readers were most likely to be? What information do they provide about the classical canon in the eighteenth century?

A review of the evidence indicates that Fielding's audience was less homogeneous than scholars have assumed. He attracted readers with three quite different types of classical training: some had extensive knowledge of classical languages, others a smattering of classics learned from grammars and handbooks, and many a familiarity gained only through translations. Despite the diversity of their knowledge, all appear to have known the same small range of authors fairly well: Latin authors—particularly Horace, Virgil, and Cicero—were popular with all types of readers and were available in both English and Latin. Since eighteenth-century readers seldom read Greek well, if at all, and since many Greek classics were unavailable in translations, the ancient Greek classics—except for the Homeric epics—were almost completely unknown.

Traditional Education at the Public Schools and Universities

Like many other eighteenth-century writers, Henry Fielding was a product of the traditional education offered at the endowed grammar schools, or "public" schools. Because the alumni of these institutions left detailed reports of their experiences there, accounts of their curricula have been a primary source for our knowledge about classical learning in this period; thus, most scholars assume that educated people in the eighteenth century were fluent in Latin and Greek and well read in the classics. When we examine these public schools and the alternatives to them more closely, however, we find that students studied only a handful of ancient authors well and that many emerged from the system with little knowledge of Latin and no Greek. Consequently, even among those trained by the traditional method, the level of classical learning varied widely.

Since Eton was Fielding's alma mater and the model for other classical schools, its curriculum is a good example of the type of classical program followed by the public schoolboy.[2] Although the only surviving eighteenth-century curriculum is an account drawn up around 1766, we can ascertain from it which classical authors Fielding and his contemporaries probably knew best and the extent of their expertise in Latin and Greek.[3] Textbooks published in the first half of the century round out our picture of the curriculum during Fielding's years as a student.

When Fielding attended Eton (1719–25), and indeed throughout the eighteenth century, the life of the student revolved around classical languages, especially Latin. After arriving with some knowledge of Latin accidence, which they had acquired either at a preparatory school or from a private tutor, students concentrated exclusively on the classics, since no other subjects were taught. In the beginning of the century, they spoke Latin in all their classes, at prayers, and in conversation with their peers; not until the middle of the century did English slowly supplant Latin as the medium of instruction. The method by which pupils studied is also significant: they memorized all their Latin and Greek lessons, repeating them for their masters at least twice, and at every level composed Latin themes and poetry, since ancient authors served as models of style. Upperclassmen also declaimed in Latin once a week and even learned Greek through the medium of Latin. After such a thorough grounding in the language, students were theoretically fluent and able to recall large portions of their reading in classical authors.[4]

The curriculum also indicates which classical authors they studied most often. Boys spent their first two years memorizing William Lily's *Short Introduction of Grammar*, which had been compiled in the sixteenth century and was used in various versions at Eton and many other schools for the next three hundred years.[5] Its popularity is evident from the number of editions published; for the first half of the eighteenth century alone, the *Eighteenth-Century Short Title Catalogue* lists forty-seven editions or variations of Lily.[6] Because Lily introduces Latin authors through short quotations illustrating grammatical rules, it offers useful information about the Latin tags known to every schoolboy, which would have been deeply ingrained into each student as he learned the book a page or two at a time.[7] Of the forty-two authors quoted by name, the most frequently cited are Virgil (153 times), Terence (104), Cicero (66), Ovid (55), Horace (45), Plautus (20), Juvenal (17), and Sallust (17); they represent 477 of the 596 quotations (or 80 percent).[8] Readings from Phaedrus supplemented the grammar lessons in these classes.

Greek instruction began when students moved on to the third form, where they used William Camden's *Institutio Graecae grammatices compendiaria, in usum regiae scholae westmonasteriensis*, the royal Greek grammar adopted by Eton in 1600 and used virtually unchanged until the nineteenth century.[9] The twenty editions listed in the *ESTC* in the first half of the eighteenth century attest to its popularity. Unlike Lily, which is replete with quotations of Latin authors, Camden's grammar contains only twelve identified citations, four of which come from Homer; thus, although it indicates that Homer was the best-known Greek writer, it also suggests that students acquired a much smaller stock of Greek tags than Latin ones.[10] While they learned Greek, students continued their Latin studies by construing and reciting Ovid, Terence, the Latin Testament, and the Church Catechism in Latin.

Boys in the upper school devoted their class sessions to three activities: construing and translating Latin and Greek authors, reciting what they had construed, and composing Latin and Greek themes and poetry. Several of the textbooks from which they read and memorized passages were anthologies of Greek and Latin writers, but the most important of these was the *Epigrammatum Delectus*, which is another source of stock quotations. It begins with five books of Martial's epigrams, followed by shorter sections containing tags from major Latin authors; the longest sections concentrate on selections from Horace, Seneca, Virgil, Terence, and Ovid.[11] Although Greek authors do appear in the section entitled "sententiae breves," these quotations indicate that Latin was the predominant classical language; often sayings attributed to Greek writers are given only in Latin, and a Latin translation always accompanies those Greek quotations in the original. The only Greek writers mentioned with any frequency are Homer (eighteen times), Plutarch (thirteen), Aristotle (eight), and Diogenes (eight). Clearly such anthologies indicate that students did not read Greek well and were familiar with few Greek authors.

Several other anthologies mentioned in the curriculum for the upper school and elsewhere supplement this information about students' reading in the classics. The 1766 curriculum mentions *Electa Minora Ex Ovidio, Tibullo, et Propertio*, which is primarily a collection of Ovid's shorter poems; the final third of the book has selections from Propertius and Tibullus. *Poetae Graeci* contains excerpts from Hesiod, Theocritus, Moschus, Bion, Musaeus, Theognis, Phocylides, and Pythagoras. Although *Scriptores Romani* includes readings from Livy, Tacitus, Velleius Paterculus, and Pliny the Younger, the

1766 curriculum suggests that pupils concentrated almost exclusively on the passages from Cicero.[12] One collection published for the use of Eton during Fielding's youth but not mentioned in 1766 was *Poikile Historia*, which includes readings from Aelian, Polyaenus, Aristotle, Dionysius of Halicarnassos, Maximus Tyrius, and Herodotus. Another is *Treis tragodiai*, published for Westminster in 1729, which contains Aeschylus's *Choephoroi* and both Sophocles' and Euripides' *Electra*.[13] These books offer longer selections and a longer list of authors than those in anthologies and grammars, but they also attest to the preference for Latin over Greek writers.

The curriculum reveals how much time students in the upper school spent reading such anthologies and full texts of other classical authors; table 1.1 presents a list of the major authors covered in the upper school and the number of class sessions spent on each.

From this list and other evidence, we can see that Horace was preeminent—clearly the writer that most students knew best by the end of their schooling. In fact, the author of the 1766 curriculum says that boys in the fifth and sixth forms repeated the odes yearly in their classes and that they "become perfect in them."[15] M. L. Clarke estimates that, according to this course of study, a student would also have read the *Aeneid* twice and Homer's *Iliad* one and a half times by the end of the sixth form.[16] The list is striking because it emphasizes Latin authors over the Greek and poets over prose writers; it also shows that the average public school boy knew a few classical masterpieces well: he memorized Virgil, Horace, Homer, and Ovid, but only learned short selections from Cicero and the authors in the anthologies. Although he read Lucian, he spent no time committing him to memory.

Even when a boy was exposed to an education like this, how effective was it in instilling a desire to read more deeply in the classics? More important, did students retain what they had learned from this traditional curriculum? Certainly their intensive exposure to Latin meant that they could read and to some degree converse in Latin; however, the system was subject to abuses, and many boys finished school without learning much Latin or Greek. Even though this curriculum familiarized students with some of the masterpieces of ancient literature and provided them with a stock of classical quotations, many cheated their way through school by using "old copies" to construct the required Latin themes.[17] Steele alludes to this practice when he criticizes the high repute of Latin and Greek—

> which puts the Youth upon such Exercises as many of them are incapable of performing with any tolerable Success. Upon this Emergency they are succour'd by the allow'd Wits of their respective Colleges, who are always ready to befriend them with two or three hundred *Latin* or *Greek* Words thrown together, with a very small Proportion of Sense.[18]

Table 1.1. Authors and Works Covered in the
Curriculum of the Upper School at Eton (1766)

Author or Work	Fourth Form		Remove		Fifth Form		Sixth Form		Total
	C	R	C	R	C	R	C	R	
Horace									
Odes	0	0	2	1	0	0	0	0	3
Odes (Sum.)	0	0	0	0	7	2	7	2	18
Epis., Sat., Ars	0	0	0	0	2	1	1	1	5
Virgil	0	0	2	1	2	1	2	1	9
Ovid									
Electa	2	1	1	0	2	0	0	0	6
Metamor.	2	1	0	0	0	0	0	0	3
Camden	3	3	2	0	0	0	0	0	8
Poet. Graec.	0	0	2	1	1	1	1	1	7
Homer	0	0	0	0	2	1	2	1	6
Farnaby									
Index	2	2	0	0	0	0	0	0	4
Greek Testament	1	1	0	0	1	0	1	0	4
Lucian	0	0	0	0	2	0	2	0	4
Aesop	2	0	0	0	0	0	0	0	2
Caesar	2	0	0	0	0	0	0	0	2
Cicero	0	0	0	0	1	0	1	0	2
Epig. Del.	0	0	0	0	0	0	1	1	2
Pomp. Mela	0	0	2	0	0	0	0	0	2
Terence	1	1	0	0	0	0	0	0	2
Nepos	0	0	1	0	0	0	0	0	1

Note: "C" stands for sessions spent construing, "R" for those spent repeating previous lessons. Normally, in one repetition class students would repeat two lessons previously construed. Horace was covered in the fifth and sixth forms in the summer, replacing one Greek Testament lesson, one Cicero, two Virgil, two Lucian, one in *Poetae Graeci*, two in the *Epigrammatum Delectus*, and two in *Electa Ex Ovidio*.[14]

Although in later years they may have imperfectly recalled a few tags memorized from Lily, pupils who resorted to such aids learned virtually nothing of the classics and would recognize references to very few classical authors.

From the pedagogical and periodical literature of the early eighteenth century, we also glimpse the system's failures with students of low aptitude. For example, John Locke complains of men who are "made spend many Hours of their precious time uneasily in *Latin*, who, after they are once gone from School, are never to have more to do with it, as long as they live."[19] Isaac Watts also describes the disappointing results produced by a grammar school education: "When they leave the school they usually forget what they have learned, and the chief advantage they gain by it is to spell and pronounce hard words better when they meet them in english."[20] Such criticisms suggest that this system did more than foster classical ignorance; while it produced some who had a lifelong interest in ancient literature, it left many with a total aversion to classical learning.

Because many parents did not want to expose their sons to the corrupting influences of the public schools or lacked the financial resources to send them there, other possibilities were available for those who wanted to prepare their children for the universities. Wealthy parents often hired a private tutor, who would offer a classical curriculum similar to the public schools', or they would send their sons to a private classical school, usually run by one scholar in his own home. Here the master accepted that the classics were the basis for education but used different methods from those of the larger, more traditional institutions. The quality of the education at these schools depended on the training of the man who ran them. Some, such as those directed by distinguished scholars like Michael Maittaire (1668–1747), who edited several Latin texts published by Tonson and Watts, and Robert Ainsworth (1666–1743), author of the popular Latin dictionary, gave their students a first-class classical education. Others provided them with little more than the rudiments. We can assume, however, that students who attended these private classical academies covered the same authors as pupils in the larger schools, and the results would have been much the same.[21]

After a student had passed through one of these institutions, he usually went to Oxford or Cambridge, where he presumably built on the foundation established at public school. During the eighteenth century, however, the universities stressed logic and ethics and had no formal classes in ancient literature. Although various prizes and scholarships were awarded in classics, the universities required no real knowledge of Latin or Greek for a degree; even the practice of speaking Latin was dying out—first at meals and, by the middle of the century, in lectures themselves. Both universities considered the chairs in Latin and Greek little more than sinecures; for example, in the first half of the century only two of the ten men who held the Greek professorships at Oxford and Cambridge were distinguished classical scholars.[22] Consequently, the universities subtly discouraged further study in the classics, thus guaranteeing that most students would lose much of their early classical learning and would progress no farther in their classical studies.

Although the universities did not formally teach ancient literature, students sufficiently interested in the classics did pursue their own course of study by consulting the handbooks that proliferated throughout the century. Because these guides recommend specific classical works and authors, they offer reliable evidence of the ancient writers most familiar to readers with the broadest classical learning. When we compare the lists given in six of the best-known handbooks—Francis Brokesby's *Of Education* (1701), Henry Felton's *Dissertation on Reading the Classics* (1713), Anthony Blackwall's *Introduction to the Classics* (1719), Daniel Waterland's *Advice to a Young Student* (1730), John Clarke's *Essay upon Study* (1731), and John Boswell's *Method of Study: or, An Useful Library* (1737)—we discover those classical authors generally acknowledged to be most worthwhile.[23] Although each handbook reflects the biases of its author—for example, Clarke clearly favors historians and recommends only a handful of poets—these works provide a clue to a gentleman's outside reading in classical authors. Overall, the handbooks mention forty-one Latin and forty-eight Greek writers.[24] Table 1.2 presents those authors who appear in at least five of the six handbooks.

Table 1.2. Authors Recommended in Six Guides to Classical Learning

Author	Brokesby	Felton	Blackwall	Waterland	Clarke	Boswell
Caesar	x		x	x	x	x
Cicero	x	x	x	x	x	x
Horace		x	x	x	x	x
Livy	x	x	x	x	x	x
Sallust		x	x	x	x	x
Suetonius	x		x	x	x	x
Tacitus	x		x	x	x	x
Terence		x	x	x	x	x
Virgil		x	x	x	x	x
Herodotus		x	x	x	x	x
Homer		x	x	x	x	x
Plutarch	x		x	x	x	x
Thucydides	x	x	x	x	x	x
Xenophon	x	x	x	x	x	x
Totals	8	10	14	14	14	14

This compilation shows that even handbooks do not cover substantially more authors than appear in the public school curriculum; instead of selections, however, students are now encouraged to read through writers like Livy, Sallust, Suetonius, Herodotus, and Plutarch in their entirety. The list differs from that of the public schools in that it includes more prose authors (ten) than poets (four), but Latin authors still predominate, outnumbering the Greek nine to five. Because several of the guides advise alternating a Latin with a Greek author, they put more emphasis on skill in Greek than before, indicating that those who pursued their classical studies did improve their knowledge of Greek. Finally, these handbooks suggest that, although young men who followed such guides would have a wide knowledge of many important primary and secondary classical writers, only a small number of classics were part of the accepted canon.

From this survey, we can see that public schools, universities, and other institutions using this model offered a classical curriculum in which students intensely studied a relatively small group of ancient authors. The results of this system of education were not uniform, however, since many who attended such schools remembered only a few Latin tags out of Lily or the anthologies and little or no Greek. Although a few undoubtedly acquired a lifelong love of ancient literature, which they pursued by reading more widely among those works listed in the popular handbooks, many others probably felt hostile toward all classical learning. Fielding undoubtedly attracted readers from both these groups.

While the traditional curriculum did not yield scholars with the same knowledge of ancient literature, other institutions also demonstrate the diverse classical backgrounds of Fielding's readers. Because they had religious objections or lacked the requisite social status or money, many parents chose one of the alternative forms of education available in the eighteenth century: dissenting academies, private or boarding academies, or, in the case of the very poor, charity schools.

ALTERNATIVES TO THE TRADITIONAL CURRICULUM OF THE PUBLIC SCHOOL

Although everyone agreed that classical training was the mark of a gentleman, many objected to the methods used at public schools and argued that the narrow curriculum, emphasizing only the classics, was not useful to those destined to be merchants, professionals, and tradesmen. Still others did not attend public schools because they disliked the emphasis on "heathen" literature and refused to swear to the Thirty-nine Articles. To meet the needs of both these groups, new types of schools were founded in the eighteenth century that offered a more diverse curriculum than traditional schools and reduced the amount of time spent on the classics. A survey of such institutions reveals the unevenness of the classical learning among such students and provides additional evidence that the classics were losing their importance among many readers of eighteenth-century novels.

While public schools and classical academies catered to gentlemen, private academies satisfied the demand for education among the lower middle classes—teachers, artists, merchants, farmers, and craftsmen. Many educators and thinkers in the eighteenth century argued that classical education was unnecessary and even harmful for those destined for such businesses, since it gave them a false sense of superiority and distracted them from their primary responsibilities. For example, Isaac Watts observes that classical learning "will be of very little use to them in all the following affairs of their station."[25] The *Spectator*, which discusses this subject several times, prints one letter (no. 353, 15 April 1712) in which the writer argues, "[I]t would be far more advantageous for the greatest part of them, to be taught such little Practical Arts and Sciences as do not require any great share of Parts to be master of them, and yet may come often into Play during the course of a Man's life."[26] Consequently, the masters of private academies designed curricula that produced businessmen and technicians who had some exposure to a liberal education but little classical literature.[27]

Because so many of these schools existed in the eighteenth century, we cannot easily generalize about their curricula, but they all share certain features. Offering too many subjects for one person to study, most of these academies gave students different courses of instruction from which to choose; pupils could select tracks that led to the university, the navy and mercantile marine, the army, business or law clerking, or to a technical profession. As a result of their diverse curricula, very little Latin and Greek instruction was available, and students could easily avoid the classics entirely. Of twenty-eight schools surveyed by Nicholas Hans in his study of these academies, only fifteen advertised that they taught Latin and nine, Greek. To facilitate instruction, masters who taught ancient languages used new, quicker, "modern" methods; hence, there proliferated interlinear translations, Latin-English versions, and Latin texts in which the word order was rearranged to approximate English. Although students at these schools could be exposed to Latin and get a smattering of Greek, then, the methods used would have made them far more comfortable reading the classics in translations or in Latin-English editions.

While private academies addressed the needs of the lower classes, dissenting academies were founded in the late seventeenth century to offer three to five years of religious training to students barred from the public schools and universities because of their religious beliefs. From their inception until about halfway through the eighteenth century, these academies were much like the public and classical schools, because many of the scholars who ran them were university graduates excluded from traditional appointments by their religious convictions. Thus, in the early academies all discussion was in Latin, and most of the textbooks were identical to those used at Oxford and Cambridge. Since the primary goal of these academies was to train dissenting clergy, however, the percentage of ancient "heathen" literature in the curriculum grew increasingly smaller as these schools offered a more diverse course of study and replaced Latin with English in the classroom.[28] By the time Fielding wrote his novels, then, students from these schools would know little about classical literature, most of it from translations.

The changes in the curricula of the dissenting academies show how much the level of classical learning decreased from the beginning to the middle of the eighteenth century. Descriptions of Kibworth Academy in 1715 by Philip Doddridge and its headmaster, John Jennings, reveal that students studied classical literature only during the first two of their four years.[29] Entering with some Latin, they devoted one hour per week in the first half-year to Latin prose authors; Doddridge mentions Suetonius, Tacitus, Seneca, Caesar, and Cicero. They turned to Latin poets in the second half-year; Doddridge says that they most often read Virgil, Horace, and Terence but sometimes Lucretius, Juvenal, Plautus, or Lucan. Their studies in the third half-year included one hour per week of Theocritus, Homer, and Pindar. Although both accounts of this curriculum mention that students also did Latin exercises and that Jennings required students to speak Latin at fixed times, Doddridge observes that they often consulted translations when they read their classical authors. He also criticizes Jennings for neglecting classics in the course of study. After the first year and a half, pupils no longer formally studied the classics, and Jennings did not expect them to read ancient authors in their leisure. Although they covered several classical authors, students could at best gain a superficial knowledge of the classics, since they devoted relatively little of their time to ancient studies and did not continue them for all four years.

From the *Rules* of Doddridge's Northampton Academy (1750) and from his letters, we can see that students learned even less about classical literature by midcentury.[30] Although they had no formal instruction in the classics, the rules of the academy indicate that students read four classics in their leisure hours—one Latin and one Greek prose author and one Latin and one Greek poet—and recorded their observations in English for their tutors; however, the manuscripts mention no classical authors by name. In his memoirs of Doddridge (1766), Job Orton says that either Doddridge himself or his assistant read classical lectures to the students each evening, but Doddridge found some students sufficiently deficient in Latin and Greek that in 1750 he sought funds to hire an additional tutor who would instruct such pupils in the rudiments of the classical languages.[31] The students had diverse enough backgrounds that Doddridge also substituted English for Latin as the medium of instruction. Such an account reveals that students entered with little or no classical training and could at best achieve only rudimentary knowledge of the classics during their tenure at school.

Although males could choose from a wide variety of schools, women's educational opportunities in this period were more limited, especially since educational theorists agreed that women had no need to learn ancient languages. For example, in *The Ladies Library* Richard Steele admits that women should probably know some languages, but he says, "I do not see the Necessity of a Woman's learning the *ancient* Tongues."[32] When he discusses whether women should study the classics, John Clarke agrees: "But tho' I think it very requisite that *Ladies* should be well accomplished in their own Language, yet I judge it not proper they should be troubled with any more." He argues that only maiden-ladies should be allowed to study learned languages.[33] William Law says that women should not dispute with men in learning because they are reserved for much more (i.e., motherhood).[34] Even Samuel Richardson, who expressed no aversion to female learning, admits, "But, after all, I contend not that women should be taught either of these languages; nor do I hold languages to be learning."[35] Such comments demonstrate that women who studied Latin or Greek faced little encouragement and considerable opposition from society.

Although several educated women distinguished themselves with their classical learning—among them Sarah Fielding and Lady Mary Wortley Montagu—the "learned lady" was a standard satiric target in eighteenth-century literature, indicating that women had little access to classical education.[36] Fielding's portrait of Mrs. Bennet in *Amelia*, a prime example of this satiric type, indicates that he was well aware of the prejudices of his contemporaries.[37] So negative were the connotations of the label that Lady Mary Wortley Montagu, who advocated classical learning for her granddaughters, advised her daughter, Lady Bute, to offer the following warning: "The second caution to be given her (and which is most absolutely necessary) is to conceal whatever Learning she attains, with as much solicitude as she would hide crookedness or lameness."[38] A woman who knew Latin or Greek was considered unmarriageable, if not mad.

Understandably in this hostile environment, there appeared very few accounts of formal instruction in Latin for women or handbooks listing the classics that they should read. The only education for middle- and upper-class women outside of the home was available at the boarding schools, which stressed dancing, musical instruments, crafts, and genteel skills and offered only French as a foreign language. We do know that occasionally a young woman was tutored in Latin at these schools. For example, Charlotte Charke, Fielding's friend during his days in the theater, learned Latin from a tutor in 1710 when she attended a school in Park Street, Westminster, run by a Mrs. Draper, but we do not know what authors she covered in her two years of study or how proficient she became.[39] Other women who learned Latin and Greek were self-taught or received instruction from a father, brother, or other relative.

From handbooks written about education for women, however, we can glean some information about the classical authors a woman might read in translation. John Clarke recommends Echard's *Roman History* (1695–98) and Humphrey Prideaux's *Connections* (1716–18); the only classical works he names are Pope's translation of Homer and Dryden's of Virgil.[40] Daniel Bellamy (1723) imitates Horace and Seneca but suggests only L'Estrange's translations of Seneca and Aesop's *Fables* for a woman's library.[41] When Addison describes the library of Leonora in the *Spectator* (no. 37, 12 April 1711), he mentions Ogilby's translation of Virgil (1659), Dryden's Juvenal, and Seneca's *Morals*; without giving a reason, though, he reveals that he does not think her library at all desirable.[42] Mrs. Chapone recommends Rollin's *Ancient History* (1739) and translations of Virgil and Homer.[43]

The most comprehensive eighteenth-century reading list for women appears in Erasmus Darwin's *Plan for the Conduct of Female Education in Boarding Schools* (1797). Although he argues that women should not learn ancient languages, he compiles an extensive list of translations and commentaries for the female student to read. Under mythology, he recommends Bell's *Pantheon* (1790), the notes attached to Pope's translation of Homer, Ragois's *Instructions sur les Metamorphoses*, containing a summary of each of the stories in Ovid's *Metamorphoses*, the *Metamorphoses* published by Garth (1717), and Bryant's *Mythology* (1774-76). When discussing polite literature, he advises the student to read translations from the ancients and mentions both Homer and Virgil. Finally, he appends a catalog of those volumes a woman should read. In addition to the titles noted above, he mentions Dodsley's version of Aesop's *Fables* (1761), Plutarch's *Lives*, William Smith's translation of Longinus (1739), Spence on Pope's translation of the *Odyssey* (1726), Mrs. Carter's *Epictetus* (1758), Sarah Fielding's *Xenophon* (1762), Cicero's letters to his friends, and Melmoth's translation of Pliny's letters (1746).[44]

From these accounts we can conclude that even at the end of the century most educated women knew the classics only through translations, if at all. Furthermore, if these lists are an accurate indication of what they read, the range of authors with whom they were familiar was decidedly narrow; they would have known Homer, Virgil, and possibly Ovid, but might not have read Horace. Consequently, they would probably recognize allusions to classical myths and epics, although they would not understand quotations from Latin and Greek authors.

While the young men and women who attended private and dissenting academies and female boarding schools acquired a smattering of classical learning, those at the bottom of the social scale learned nothing at all of ancient literature. In most towns and villages poor children could attend dame schools, usually run by old women who charged a few pence a week for each child, where they learned the alphabet, the Lord's Prayer, numbers from the hornbook, and sometimes passages from the Bible. Because instruction was poor and students usually left at an early age, few acquired enough learning to read even English books, much less fiction like Henry Fielding's.[45] At most they learned to read simple texts and do arithmetic.

The most ambitious scheme for the education of the poor was the charity school, supported by the Society for the Promotion of Christian Knowledge (S.P.C.K.), founded in 1696 to provide religious and moral instruction to the children of the poor. In 1706 sixty-four charity schools existed in London, enrolling 1573 boys and 915 girls, and by 1729 the number of schools had increased to 132, with 5225 pupils. Isaac Watts reveals the goals of such schools when he argues that instruction should begin at age eight or nine and should last for three years, which he deems an adequate amount of time for the children to learn all they need for their station in life.[46] The best of these schools offered a "literary curriculum," which focused on the "3 R's" and religious instruction; occasionally students also read Aesop's *Fables* in English and Richard Allestree's *Whole Duty of Man* (1657). After the first quarter of the eighteenth century, however, opponents of the movement like Bernard Mandeville argued that the education provided at these institutions made these children discontented with their lot, forcing the sponsors of the schools to transform many of them into workhouses.[47]

Clearly, the poor did not learn Latin or Greek, and they probably could not read well enough to be part of the audience for Fielding's novels. David Cressy's figures on eighteenth-century literacy support this assumption. Since writing was a skill that one acquired only after one could read, he assumes that people who could sign their names were literate enough to read. From a close study of the admission and discharge records of the Great Yarmouth Children's Hospital, he concludes that literacy among the poorer classes was not widespread. Between 1698 and 1715 just over half the entrants, who ranged in age from five to fifteen, were completely illiterate, and, among those who had acquired some skills associated with literacy, the level of accomplishment varied greatly: in general, the girls knew less than the boys.[48]

Cressy also describes literacy rates for various social groups both in and out of London. Among tradesmen and craftsmen from 1720 to 1729, 8 percent of those in London and 34 percent of those in Norfolk were illiterate. Of those classed as yeoman, 26 percent living in Norfolk from 1720 to 1729 were illiterate, and, of the husbandmen in Norfolk during this period, 87 percent could not read. For women the illiteracy rates were 44 percent for those in London and 74 percent for those in Norfolk; in 1750 64 percent of all brides in England could not sign their names.[49] Cressy's comparisons indicate that, even though the lower classes in London were more often able to sign their names than their counterparts in the country, a high percentage could not read. Of those who could, we cannot be sure how many would have read classics, or Fielding's novels, even if available. In *Pamela* Richardson suggests that classical learning is unusual for members of the servant classes since Mr. B. singles out Pamela's comment about Lucretia for special note.[50] Few, if any, of these people read novels; none, the classics.

Such were the educational alternatives to the public school available in the eighteenth century, which show that the classical learning of Fielding's readers was more diverse than scholars have generally assumed. The most educated readers were gentlemen and others who had received a thorough grounding in Latin and Greek at an early age and had continued reading the ancient authors throughout their lives; such readers knew many classical authors and could recognize even recondite allusions. Another group of readers, composed of some from the public schools and many from the dissenting academies, knew only a little Latin; they could certainly identify tags from school texts but would probably not remember much about the authors covered in school. The largest body of readers undoubtedly included women and those who attended the nonclassical private academies; because such an audience knew classical literature only through translations, they would be familiar with general allusions but would not be able to translate any of the Latin and Greek quotations. The lowest classes, who had no classical learning apart from Aesop's *Fables*, did not read well enough to be a significant part of Fielding's audience.

Although these groups were not equally conversant in Latin and Greek, the curricula and handbooks indicate that they read the same small group of classical authors, among whom Horace, Virgil, Terence, Ovid, and Cicero were the most popular Romans and Homer and Aesop, the best-known Greeks. But these sources are primarily a guide to those authors read at school; they do not necessarily indicate the reading tastes of people who had completed their education. To get a better idea of the ancient authors read by Fielding's "classical" and "English" readers, we must consider which Latin and Greek works were available from booksellers and libraries.

The Classical Canon in the Eighteenth Century

Because booksellers in the eighteenth century did not gauge the popularity of books and writers by assembling statistics about their sales, we can only ascertain which classical authors were most popular by determining how often they appeared in separate editions. Assuming that a bookseller would not want to bring out a new version of an ancient work if he did not think it would sell, we can use such numbers to get a fair estimate of the classical authors book customers most often requested and, presumably, read. *The Eighteenth-Century Short Title Catalogue (ESTC)* provides the best raw material for this type of assessment; it is more comprehensive and more accurate than any of the bibliographies published in the eighteenth century and, therefore, offers the largest sample of books available to readers from 1701 to 1750. From it we can assemble a list of Latin and Greek authors with whom Fielding's readers would probably be familiar.[51]

Although the discussion of classical editions that follows covers books published in England during the first half of the eighteenth century, we must remember that British booksellers were not the only ones bringing out classical texts. From library catalogs and printed bibliographies, we know that foreign editions of the classics were still very popular in England at this time; for example, John Clarke's *Essay on Study* (1731) includes a bibliography in which the proportion of foreign to English editions is nearly three to one.[52] Another indication that book imports were high appears in eighteenth-century copyright law; exempting learned works in the classical languages, Parliament added clauses to both the 1710 copyright act and a 1739 act to prohibit the importation of books reprinted abroad.[53] However, we cannot assess the impact of foreign editions because figures for book imports are sketchy.[54] Because the most popular continental texts—the Delphin classics, for example—were in the eighteenth century available in cheaper English editions, we can assume that the *ESTC* listings give us a fairly representative idea of what authors were most widely available to the general reading public.

The *ESTC* lists forty-two Latin authors in 540 separate editions; of these slightly fewer than half (266) contain only the Latin text, suggesting that many readers did not need any help in this language. Just over 44 percent (123 out of 274) of editions with an English translation also contain the original Latin, often facing the English on the opposite page. Such a format was useful for two groups of readers: those who were trained in classical languages could compare the English version easily with the original, and those attempting to learn Latin could use the translation as a crutch. Therefore, Latin works were published in a wide variety of formats for both English and classical readers.

Although many Latin authors were available to interested readers, only a few seem to have been very popular. As table 1.3 demonstrates, a small number of authors are mentioned frequently in the *ESTC*.

Table 1.3. Latin Authors with the Highest
Number of Editions in the *ESTC*

Author	Latin Editions	Engl./Lat. Editions	Transl.	Total
Horace	25	57	32	114
Ovid	26	13	19	58
Cicero	38	2	12	52
Virgil	18	12	16	46
Sallust	15	4	4	23
Terence	15	4	1	20
Phaedrus	12	6	1	19
Persius	11	2	3	16
Nepos	8	2	3	13
Pliny the Younger	4	0	9	13
Juvenal	10	1	1	12
Justin	7	2	2	11
Cato	2	4	4	10
Tibullus	6	0	4	0
Totals	197	109	111	417

These authors represent a disproportionately high share of the total editions: while the list contains 33 percent of the Latin authors, they comprise 77 percent of all editions printed from 1701 to 1750. As this table shows, the authors most often studied in the schools were also the most frequently edited: Horace, Phaedrus, Cicero, Ovid, Virgil, and Terence. Certainly the demand for such writers came from the schools, but the figures also suggest that readers wanted to own those writers whom they had read at an early age or about whom they had heard from brothers and friends who had studied them at school. Ten of the authors were not equally available in Latin and English; Latin versions of Cicero, Sallust, Terence, Phaedrus, Persius, Nepos, Juvenal, and Justin were far more common than English ones, indicating that few people read them who had not been introduced to them at school. Because Pliny the Younger and Cato were most often printed in English, they probably appealed to an audience without classical training. While many booksellers brought out individual editions of many Latin authors, then, they did not think the majority were sufficiently popular to warrant multiple versions.

Editions of single works and multiple issues of the same edition provide further information about the authors and works that were popular. For many writers, the Delphin editions were those issued most often; thirteen of the thirty-three editions issued three or more times were Delphin classics, the most popular of which were Phaedrus (nine issues), Virgil (nine issues), the select orations of Cicero (seven issues), Horace (seven issues), Ovid's *Heroides* (seven issues) and *Metamorphoses* (seven issues), and Persius-Juvenal (seven issues). Forty-five translations, both with and without the original Latin, appear in three or more issues, suggesting that a large market existed for certain authors in English. The list of translators indicates that their reputations probably played as great a role in the success of the editions as the Latin author: for example, Dryden (seven translations), Pope (four), Rowe (two), Swift, Addison, Tate, and Congreve all did popular translations of classical works. Also popular were literal translations of historians, useful for educators employing new methods of instruction: such an interest accounts for the number of reprintings of John Clarke's versions of Nepos (six issues), Florus (four issues), and Justin (four issues). Finally, the list of commonly issued editions once again illustrates the continuing demand for Latin authors studied in school since the authors reprinted most often are Horace (fifteen editions), Ovid (nine), Cicero (seven), Virgil (six), Justin (five), and Terence (four). (For a complete list of multiple editions and issues, see appendix A, tables A-2 and A-4.)

Editions and issues also indicate which specific works of certain authors were most often sold. For example, the list reveals that Horace's *Odes*, *Epistles*, and *Satires* were edited far more often than the *Epodes*. The single most important poem of Horace appears to have been the *Ars Poetica*, which appeared by itself six times. Virgil's *Eclogues* and *Aeneid* far surpass the *Georgics* in separate editions, suggesting the popularity of pastorals and epic. Both Cicero's philosophical works and orations appear in many separate versions, and individual philosophical works were printed alone many times. Although the poets were important, these lists reveal that readers were also very interested in Roman moralists, critics, and historians.

Although the number of Greek authors in the *ESTC* is nearly double the Latin (seventy to forty-two), they appear in fewer editions overall (368 to 540 for the Latin). During this period editions entirely in Greek were uncommon; only fifteen Greek authors have even a single Greek edition, and only five appear in more than one: Homer, Xenophon, Plutarch, Isocrates, and Lucian. The most popular formats combined both Greek and Latin texts (151 editions are in this form) or contained only an English translation (170 editions). The relative rarity of Greek-only texts confirms the evidence from the school curricula, which suggests that students learned Greek far less thoroughly than Latin.

The information on the Greek authors who were most frequently edited supports this conclusion about readers' knowledge of Greek. Table 1.4 consists of names of those Greek authors represented by ten or more editions in the *ESTC*. (For the complete list, see appendix A, table A-3.)

Table 1.4. Greek Authors Represented by the Largest Number of Editions in the *ESTC*

Author	Gr.	Gr./E.	E./L.	Lat.	Gr./E.	E.	Total
Homer	4	6	0	0	0	16	26
Aesop	0	4	4	1	0	16	25
Xenophon	4	11	0	0	0	9	24
Euclid	0	1	0	3	0	9	13
Anacreon	0	6	0	0	1	5	12
Plutarch	2	4	0	0	1	5	12
Cebes	1	7	0	0	0	3	11
Epictetus	0	5	0	1	0	5	11
Hippocrates	0	5	0	2	0	4	11
Plato	1	6	0	0	0	4	11
Sophocles	1	4	0	0	0	6	11
Theophrastus	0	5	0	0	1	5	11
Totals	13	64	4	7	3	87	178

When we compare these statistics with those for Latin authors published in similar amounts, we find that the Greek authors represent a smaller percentage of the total number both of writers (17 percent versus 33 percent for the Latin) and of editions (48 percent versus 77 percent for the Latin). These figures also reveal that a very small group of writers were widely read, among whom only Homer, Aesop, and Xenophon appear in large numbers. Surprisingly, many authors whom we would expect in this list do not appear; Lucian and Aristotle were printed in under ten separate editions, Longinus in only four, and Aeschylus in only two.[55] The sixteen translations of Aesop and nine of Euclid show that readers knew them far better in English than in the original. Finally, the tables indicate that, except for Homer, Anacreon, and Sophocles, Greek prose writers predominate, perhaps indicating that the public read Greek authors more for their content than for their literary value.

The information provided by editions of individual works and multiple issues of separate editions is also revealing. By far the most popular work of Homer is the *Iliad*; it appeared in twelve separate editions, several of which were reissued often: the Greek/Latin editions of Thomas Wood (five issues) and Samuel Clarke (three), and Pope's and Ozell's translations (ten and four issues, respectively) figure prominently. Among those editions issued frequently, a small group of other authors predominates: Euclid (six English), Longinus (two Greek/Latin, three English), Lucian (two Greek/Latin, two English), Xenophon (two Greek/Latin, two English), Cebes (three Greek/Latin), and Epictetus (one Greek/Latin, two English). This list is striking because it demonstrates the importance of Greek authors like Euclid, Cebes, and Epictetus, who were read more for their content than their literary style. Except for Pope's edition of Homer and the English versions of Homer, Plutarch, and Lucian by Dryden, the translators of Greek works were not distinguished authors but classical scholars, indicating that Greek authors were read in English for reasons other than the translator's reputation. This evidence shows that knowledge of Greek was primarily the province of classical scholars and that audiences were more interested in Greek writers for their moral, critical, or historical value than for their literary merit. (For a list of separate works and issues, see appendix A, tables A-3 and A-5.)

Even though a broad spectrum of Latin and Greek authors was available in English editions, how accessible were these books to less affluent readers? Books were printed in relatively small runs of five hundred to one thousand copies at a time; because of their limited interest, classical works probably appear at the lower end of this scale. Usually booksellers would reprint a book several times in small numbers rather than risk having one large run that they could not sell out. Consequently, even authors printed in several "editions" might not be as available as one might imagine. Another difficulty for those at the lower end of the economic scale was the cost of such books. Until 1780, folios and quartos usually sold for 10 to 12s., octavos for 5 or 6s., and duodecimos for 2s. to 3s. Both Richard Altick and Marjorie Plant point out that even when the price of books dropped, they were still too expensive for the common workingman; when we consider that before 1790 the average weekly salary in London for shop men was 8s., for clerks one pound, for ushers in schools 4s. to 8s. and for journeymen 15 to 20s., we can see that many people did not earn enough to buy books even in duodecimo.[56]

Some outlets were available for those who could read but lacked the funds to buy books, particularly in coffeehouses and circulating libraries, which provided a means for the limited number of books that were available to reach many people. Even though a book might be printed in a limited edition, it could be read by a great number of people if it were passed around in this way.[57] However, in Fielding's time few circulating libraries existed. The first reference to a lending library appears in 1728, when James Leake advertised his business at Bath, and about 1740 Samuel Fancourt opened the first subscription library in London. A catalog of this library (1746–48) shows that his stock consisted mainly of learned and technical works, including classics, rather than novels and other light literature. Only after the 1740s did the number of libraries in London grow rapidly.[58]

Very few library catalogs or guides remain from the first half of the eighteenth century to indicate how large each library's collection of classical literature might have been; however, we can glean some information from those that exist. For example, a catalog of the Norwich Public Library around 1732 shows that 114 of the 1474 total listings (or 8 percent) were editions of Latin and Greek authors or works about the ancient world or its literature.[59] The catalog of William Bathoe's circulating library in London (c. 1757) contains fewer classical entries; it offers 4735 items, of which 173, or 4 percent, are classical texts.[60] In John Noble's 1767 catalog, 231 of the 5535 items (or 4 percent) were related to the classics.[61] The sketchy evidence from these three libraries suggests that, even though they did not represent a significant portion of the total holdings, the classics were available to those who could afford to borrow from such sources.

Although we know relatively little about circulating libraries, we have a great deal of information about the loans made from those connected to cathedrals. Paul Kaufman has surveyed the circulation records of eight eighteenth-century cathedral libraries of this period, six of which were operating in the first half of the eighteenth century: Canterbury, Carlisle, Durham, Gloucester, Winchester, York, Exeter, and St. Paul's. He notes that nearly 10 percent of the works represented were classical texts or translations and that, of the five authors with the largest number of separate works or editions, four are classical: Homer (twenty-two), Cicero (seventeen), Virgil (ten), and Horace (nine). Like other readers we have examined, then, the patrons of cathedral libraries were primarily interested in those classical authors covered in the traditional classical curriculum.[62]

The borrowing records also tell us something about how often these and other classical authors were consulted.[63] Forty-nine Greek and forty-one Latin authors are represented in Kaufman's listings. Table 1.5 ranks the top ten authors in Greek and Latin by number of loans.

The figures confirm our information from other sources, since loans of Latin works outnumber the Greek and most of the Latin and Greek authors are ones that have appeared in school curricula, handbooks, and in many editions of the *ESTC* list. The only surprises are Tacitus and Thucydides, both historians and among the most difficult writers in their respective languages. Their relative popularity says something about the borrowers that cathedral libraries attracted.[64]

According to Kaufman, the cathedral libraries were open primarily to the deans and members of the chapter—canons and prebendaries—as well as a smattering of other diocesan clergy. With the approval of the dean and

Table 1.5. Total Loans for Individual Latin
and Greek Authors at Cathedral Libraries

Latin Author	Loans	Greek Author	Loans
Cicero	96	Homer	58
Virgil	63	Josephus	42
Horace	59	Plutarch	41
Tacitus	41	Herodotus	27
Livy	39	Plato	27
Ovid	21	Thucydides	27
Terence	19	Demosthenes	26
Caesar	17	Xenophon	26
Juvenal	17	Euripides	15
Seneca	16	Lucian	15
		Aristotle	14

chapter, a few laypeople also could borrow books, but probably only 10 to 15 percent of the borrowers were from outside the chapter. Interestingly, 20 of the 825 borrowers Kaufman identified were women.[65] Therefore, we can conclude that this type of library was mainly used by those educated at the universities; many probably had some scholarly interest in the classics, exceeding that of the average reader.

Unlike the users of cathedral libraries, the patrons of circulating libraries were usually laypeople from both the upper and middle classes. Fancourt's library catered to members of the learned and technical professions, but it did not survive long. Although Altick argues that tradesmen and artisans formed the dividing line in the reading public, we have no clear way of knowing the lowest class that used libraries. Undoubtedly the cost of belonging to a library was enough to deter many from using them; Bathoe and Noble charged 10s. 6d. and 12s. per year, respectively. Certainly such fees would be prohibitive for the poor, but perhaps they would allow tradesmen with modest incomes access to books they could not afford to buy themselves.

From this survey of education, editions, and library records, we can see that Fielding's potential readers were a diverse group, who fall roughly into three categories delineated by their classical education. As unequal as their training in the classics was, however, they were all familiar with the same classical authors, among whom Horace, Virgil, Cicero, and Homer are the most prominent. From these sources, we also learn which authors were outside the canon in this period, the most notable omissions being Aristotle, Aeschylus, Plato, and Lucretius. Given this information about Fielding's audience, we should reassess his classical learning and the commonplaces about those classical writers whose influence is most prominent in his work.

2
Fielding, the Classical Scholar

> If the good Genius of the Nation
> Should call me to Negotiation;
> *Tuscan* and *French* are in my Head;
> *Latin* I write, and *Greek* I—read.
> —Fielding, "To the Right Honourable
> Sir Robert Walpole"

> The master of the GREEK and ROMAN page,
> —Christopher Smart, *Poems on Several Occasions*

The traditional accounts of Fielding's skill in Greek and Latin demonstrate the assumptions and methods that have dominated all discussions of Fielding and the classics. Relying almost exclusively on our somewhat sketchy information about his education and on the sale catalog of his library, scholars have supposed that Fielding was equally fluent in Latin and Greek, a significant generalization because it has led to another commonplace about Fielding and ancient literature—that the Greek satirist Lucian had a greater effect on him than any other classical writer.[1] Because scholars have cited Lucian's "influence" on Fielding to buttress arguments about his sense of genre, his use of quotation, and his narrative technique, we must reexamine the validity of such commonplaces and the evidence used to support them. In fact, scholars have not taken full advantage of the biographical information and have virtually ignored Fielding's journalism and translations, which can offer valuable clues to his knowledge of and use of classical authors. What do we learn from these sources about Fielding's skill in Latin and Greek? What classical authors figure most prominently in his writing? What does this information suggest about the most significant ancient influences on Fielding?

A review of the evidence demonstrates that Fielding had read widely in both Latin and Greek literature but that he was unable to read Greek without Latin translations and other aids. The references in his nonfiction prose demonstrate his command of Latin and suggest that Lucian did not influence Fielding as profoundly as some critics have argued; his work reveals that he was more interested in Latin authors, of whom the most prominent was Horace.

The Biographical Facts: Eton, Leyden, and the Baker Sale Catalog

Sketchy as it is, the biographical information can provide hints about Fielding's relative skill in classical languages and about the classical authors in whom he was most interested.

Wilbur Cross's account of Fielding's education has been generally accepted by all subsequent Fielding scholars but offers little conclusive evidence about the extent of Fielding's classical learning. After studying with a private tutor for a few years, Fielding attended Eton from October 1719 until 1724 or 1725, where, as we have seen, the classical curriculum emphasized Latin over Greek, poets over prose writers. Alone among Fielding scholars, Cross argues that Fielding's limited knowledge of Greek shows that he left before he reached the sixth form, where students did a set of Greek verses once or twice a week. This conjecture is suspect because Cross does not document Fielding's competence in Greek; even if Fielding's Greek were not very strong, that would hardly make him different from most of his contemporaries who *had* completed the entire Eton curriculum.[2]

Fielding must have developed a taste for classical literature in public school, because on 16 March 1728, he was enrolled at Leyden University in the classical curriculum, where Pieter Burmann (1668–1741) was professor of History and Eloquence (i.e., Latin) and Siegbert Havercamp (1684–1742) was professor of Greek.[3] Although Havercamp was known for editions of Lucretius and Orosius, Burmann was the better known classical scholar, having been responsible for texts of Phaedrus, Horace, Claudian, Ovid, Lucan, Valerius Flaccus, Petronius, Velleius Paterculus, Justin, Quintilian, and Suetonius. As the stronger figure, Burmann undoubtedly dominated Leyden at that time and significantly influenced Fielding; in fact, Fielding may have developed his aversion to textual scholars after his exposure to Burmann.[4] Because his pedantic method and style later became the specific butt of Fielding's satire in his plays and periodical writings, we cannot assume that the effect of such a scholar was entirely positive.[5]

Another source of information is the sale catalog of his library printed by Samuel Baker in 1755.[6] As Hugh Amory has rightly noted, we must accept the evidence of the catalog with caution. First, it is probably not a complete list of all the books Fielding owned, since Abraham Langford had already disposed of Fielding's lease on Fordhook Farm and his household effects there at an earlier sale; presumably some of those goods were books. The Baker catalog also suggests that the list does not represent Fielding's complete holdings because it indicates that certain volumes are missing from many of the sets.[7] Finally, the catalog provides few clues about when Fielding actually purchased books or whether he actually read them. Even though the catalog gives the dates of publication, it indicates that few of the volumes contain any inscriptions in Fielding's hand. Because only two of the classical volumes bear his annotations—Benjamin Hederich's *Greek Lexicon* (1732, no. 258) and Ainsworth's *Latin Dictionary* (1746, no. 419)—we cannot know with any certainty which books in his library Fielding had read.

Despite these constraints, the catalog offers some indications about Fielding's literary interests. Although most scholars have noted that the list shows Fielding owned many classical texts, they have not examined the distribution of the volumes among different authors or the types of editions Fielding characteristically purchased. A closer look at the catalog discloses forty Greek and forty-one Latin authors; those most often mentioned are listed in table 2.1. One striking feature of these lists is the high representation of prose authors: among the Greek writers in the catalog, seventeen are historians and only nine poets, while of the Latin, prose writers outnumber poets twenty-six to fifteen. Perhaps these figures are tied to the interest in classical historians Fielding exhibits in *The Journal of a Voyage to Lisbon*, where he says that he would have valued Homer more if he had written history instead of epic.[8] Another possible explanation for the number of prose works is that Fielding may have felt less need to own copies of the writers he had studied at Eton, since he had memorized them at school.

Table 2.1. Greek and Latin Authors Named Most Frequently in the Baker Catalog

Greek Authors	Editions	Translations	Commentaries	Total
Aristotle	3	0	11	14
Lucian	5	4	0	9
Homer	4	2	0	6
Plutarch	2	1	0	3
Polybius	1	2	0	3
Plato	2	0	0	2
Sophocles	2	0	0	2
Aristophanes	1	1	0	2

Latin Authors	Editions	Translations	Lives	Total
Horace	3	2	0	5
Cicero	1	2	1	4
Virgil	3	1	0	4
Lucretius	2	1	0	3
Persius	2	1	0	3
Justin	2	0	0	2
Juvenal	1	1	0	2
Plautus	2	0	0	2
Pliny the Elder	2	0	0	2
Seneca	2	0	0	2
Varro	2	0	0	2

The contents of the library also give us further information about Fielding's command of both Latin and Greek. Because nearly all the editions of Latin authors in the library were in Latin only, we can safely conclude that Fielding was fluent in that language. The editions of Greek authors, however, present a more mixed picture since all but three—Hesiod, Homer, and Theocritus—appear only in versions that had both a Greek and a Latin text. The largest group of all-Greek material is Fielding's collection of eleven Greek commentaries on a variety of Aristotle's works, suggesting that his interest in Aristotle surpassed that of his contemporaries, who knew him primarily by reputation and did not actually read his works. His possession of four Greek dictionaries (as opposed to one Latin dictionary), however, indicates that he probably had a harder time with Greek texts than with those printed in Latin.

Other volumes in the library reinforce this picture of Fielding's active interest in classical literature. He has a number of miscellaneous works on classical antiquity, including a Latin and a Greek grammar, Potter's *Antiquities of Greece* (1697), a copy of Bayle's *Dictionnaire Historique et Critique* (1734), Banier's *Mythology and Fables of the Ancients Explained* (1739), and commentaries by Vossius, Fabricius, and Lipsius. Also significant for his interest in the classics is the number of imported books; of the 152 items related to Greek and Latin literature in the catalog, 102 have foreign imprints. Like many of his learned contemporaries, Fielding had sufficient enthusiasm for the classics to purchase books from abroad that might not be readily available in England.

A close examination of the biographical facts and the contents of Fielding's only known library suggests that Fielding was among those whose interest in the classics extended beyond those authors commonly studied at Eton and the university. He was unusual in his effort to read the Greek commentaries on Aristotle, for example, even if he needed the help of Greek dictionaries and Latin translations to do so. Because ownership of these texts does not reveal how well, if at all, Fielding knew them, we need independent evidence that he did, in fact, read some of the books in his possession. One source of corroboration is provided by Fielding's translations, done both on his own and with his collaborator, William Young.

Translations from the Latin and the Greek

Fielding's translations of Latin and Greek authors have been largely ignored by scholars who have assessed the extent of his classical learning. However, his choice of works and practice as a translator can enhance our understanding of his classical learning.

His translations cover a variety of genres and classical authors. Many of his early efforts appear in volume 1 of the *Miscellanies* (1743): "A Parody, from the First Aeneid," "A Simile, from Silius Italicus," "Part of *Juvenal's* Sixth Satire, Modernized in Burlesque Verse," and "The First Olynthiac of *Demosthenes.*"[9] The previous year Fielding and William Young published their translation of Aristophanes' *Plutus* with critical and explanatory notes.[10] He also produced a prose version of book 1 of Ovid's *Ars Amatoria* (1747) and, towards the end of his career, probably translated Tibullus 1.1 in the *Covent-Garden Journal*, no. 58 (8 August 1752).[11] In the *Covent-Garden Journal* he also gave English renditions of virtually all the mottoes and frequently translated the lengthy anecdotes from historians that he used in his periodicals. Merely by their number, these translations suggest that Fielding was actively involved in making classical authors available to English audiences, thus demonstrating his skill in ancient languages, his reading in classics, and his efforts to be numbered among the more learned of his fellow authors. His method of translation can also reveal much about his skill in the ancient languages.

In the preface to Ovid's *Epistles* (1680), Dryden distinguishes three types of translation: metaphrase, which is a literal rendition of the foreign text; paraphrase, which he calls "Translation with Latitude"; and imitation, an independent work in which the "translator" takes only some hints from the original author.[12] Fielding's translations of Latin works are usually paraphrases, for he freely adapts the material to suit his eighteenth-century readers. Repeatedly, he uses the term "paraphrase" to describe his English versions of Latin texts, and he variously classifies his English translations of the mottoes in the *Covent-Garden Journal* as "paraphrases" or "modernizations."[13] For example, Tom Telltruth quotes a passage from Horace, which, he tells Drawncansir, he will render in English "after your paraphrastical Manner."[14] These "paraphrases" reveal how well Fielding understood his originals, because they require a more thorough understanding of the author's essential meaning than is necessitated by a more literal translation.

Fielding's paraphrases demonstrate that he was comfortable enough with Latin texts to take the liberties necessary to make them more palatable to his readers. For example, in his "modernized" version of the first 300 lines of Juvenal's sixth satire, he expands on Juvenal's brief allusion to the theater and offers his readers contemporary references to figures they recognized. Juvenal's Latin reads

> Ast aliae, quoties aulaea recondita cessant,
> Et vacuo clausoque sonant fora sola theatro,
> Atque a plebeijs longe Megalesia; tristes
> Personam, thyrsumque tenent, et subligar Acci.
> Urbicus exodio risum movet Attellanae
> Gestibus Autonoes; hunc diligit Aelia pauper.
>
> (Lines 67–72)

[But other women, when the curtains lie concealed and when the theater is empty and closed and only the law courts are active, and festival of Megalesia is far from the Plebeian holiday; sadly they seize on the character, and the stalk, and the kilt of Accus. Urbicus causes laughter in a comic afterpiece with the garment of Atellan Autonoe; poor Aelia falls in love with this man.] (My translation)

Because the classical references had little meaning for his classically illiterate readers, Fielding modernizes the text in this way:

> But others, when the House is shut up,
> Nor Play-Bills, *by Desire*, are put up;
> When Players cease, and Lawyer rises
> To harangue Jury at Assizes;
> When Drolls at *Barthol'mew* begin,
> A Feast Day after that of *Trin'*.
> Others, I say, themselves turn Players,
> With *Clive* and *Woffington's* gay Airs;
> Paint their fair Faces out like Witches,
> And cram their Thighs in *Fle—w—d's* Breeches.
>
> (Lines 101–10)[15]

Fielding's topical allusions capture the spirit of the original but in a form intelligible to his eighteenth-century audience. Because the Latin text accompanied his translation on a facing page, his classical readers could appreciate Fielding's own innovations on Juvenal's Latin. His contemporary references, moreover, allow him to pay offhand compliments to two of his favorite actresses—Kitty Clive and Peg Woffington—and make the application of the satire to modern society all the more pointed.[16]

Fielding's facility with Latin was also such that he was able to slant a translation in order to apply it to a given context. This practice is most obvious in his different versions of Horace's *Odi profanum vulgus* (I hate the uninitiated crowd) (*Odes* 3.1.1). In Horace the phrase is part of a ritualistic command to those who have never worshipped at the shrine of the Muses; it orders them to depart so as not to profane his "rites" with evil words. Fielding exploits the implications of these words as he applies them to a variety of situations. While discussing the origins of slander, he says, "This is that *malignant Temper* which Horace attributes to the Vulgar, when he says *he despises them*" (*Covent-Garden Journal*, no. 14 [18 February 1752]: 101). In no. 33 he renders the phrase "I hate profane Rascals," in introducing a description of a young tradesman in the country who acts like a buffoon. Finally, in no. 49 the phrase, now become "I hate the Mob," leads off an essay on the power of crowds in London. In each instance Fielding has changed the emphasis to suit his purpose but has remained partly faithful to the Latin original, thereby demonstrating that he knew his Latin well enough to exploit it skillfully.[17]

Fielding's translations of Greek authors indicate that he had less fluency in that language. First, the number is decidedly small: the only complete works he translated were Demosthenes' first *Olynthiac* and Aristophanes' *Plutus*. The evidence suggests, however, that he did neither of these translations alone. Although he published the Demosthenes as the sole author, we know from his correspondence with James Harris that he submitted it to his friend for corrections before including it in the *Miscellanies*.[18] The translation also differs from his work in Latin because it is a literal version that relies heavily on a Latin translation by Wolfius that Fielding owned.[19] Therefore, Fielding may have used the Greek as his basis, but he was uncomfortable enough with the original that he turned to the Latin text in difficult passages and consulted with a more learned friend before publication. Such was also the case with the *Plutus*; in fact, most scholars have plausibly assumed that William Young was responsible for the greater part of the translation and that Fielding probably wrote the introduction and some of the notes.[20] Because we have no way of knowing absolutely how they divided their responsibilities, the play offers us little indication of Fielding's skill in Greek.

This examination of Fielding's translations thus reinforces our initial impressions about his relative fluency in Greek and Latin. His paraphrases of Latin works show him able to preserve the spirit of the original and modernize the text freely, while his few literal translations from the Greek indicate that his ability in that language was far more limited. But his translations were not the only area in which he revealed his knowledge of Greek and Latin, for Fielding's periodicals are peppered with Latin and Greek quotations and allusions that bespeak the wide range of his reading and the ancient authors who may have influenced him most extensively.

Mock Learning, Authority, and Classical Parodies

Fielding's use of classical quotations and allusions in his essays indicates that he had read widely and knew many classical authors well and that he could exploit his knowledge skillfully to satirize others; they also suggest that he did not know many Greek works in the original.

Fielding especially demonstrates his own knowledge of the classics with his skillful use of Greek and Latin authors to ridicule the absurd learning of such pedants as Pieter Burmann and the members of the Royal Society. Imitating his targets, Fielding includes countless citations of ancient authorities that have been ripped from their original contexts. In the *Jacobite's Journal*, for example, John Trott-Plaid presents a lengthy disquisition on the premise that the ass is a more noble animal than it has lately been considered. To lend authority to his argument, Trott-Plaid offers several loci classici that, in his opinion, portray the ass in a positive manner; a close examination of his sources, however, shows how much he distorts their original meaning to buttress his own argument. In his first reference to classical literature, Trott-Plaid asserts that Homer "is well known to have liken'd one of his principal Heroes to this noble Animal."[21] In fact, in the lines in the *Iliad* (11.558ff.) from which this is taken, Homer compares Ajax to a lazy ass being driven out of a cornfield by small boys. Trott-Plaid also supports his position with misplaced citations of other classical authors: Ovid's *Metamorphoses* (11.157–93) and *Fasti* (1.415–40), Apuleius's *Golden Ass*, and Horace's *Satires* (1.1.90–91) and *Epistles* (1.20.14–16, 2.1.199–200). Although these references are part of Fielding's satire on the Jacobite's superficial learning, his ability to produce these misdirected references from a number of sources indicates that he knew a variety of classical authors well enough to use them freely.

While he frequently assumed another character when using mock learning in this manner, Fielding also employed classical authorities dexterously when he wrote satires in his own persona. He sharpens his criticism of factionalism in the *Jacobite's Journal*, no. 38 (20 August 1748) by translating the concept into an attack on the custom of supporting various colors at horse races. Fielding adds to the fun—and further trivializes this practice—by tracing its origins in classical literature. He quotes in the original Latin Pliny's *Epistulae* (9.6), Juvenal's *Satires* (11.197–201), Suetonius's *Life of Caligula* (4.55.2–3), Cicero's *De oratore* (2.61), and Virgil's *Aeneid* (1.282), and he gives an English paraphrase of Plutarch's life of Caesar (4.4) and alludes to Livy's *Ab urbe condita* (34.1.3). He demonstrates that he also knows their modern translators and commentators: he mentions the names of Melmoth, Dryden, Casaubon, Graevius, and Ferrarius. Fielding even presents his own derivation for the term "Prasina Factio" (green faction) that shows his skill in manipulating both Latin and Greek.

In short, the Word *Prasina* is ill rendered. It is not here derived from Πράσον, a Leek; but from Πρᾶσις and ὄνος; *i.e.* of the same Value with an Ass; or perhaps the true Reading is *Prasona, a Faction that behave themselves like Asses.*²²

In his own voice and those of his characters, Fielding mocks pedants, who, with only superficial classical learning, rip Latin and Greek quotations from their contexts and misapply them to justify their own prejudices. At the same time, the accumulation of classical references impresses the reader with the extent of Fielding's knowledge of the classics, thus adding to his authority.²³

Fielding often used classical authorities in a more serious vein. For example, in the *Covent-Garden Journal*, no. 67 (21 October 1752): 351–57, he traces the severity of punishments for adultery by citing a series of ancient precedents. Fielding begins the essay with a brief translation of a passage in M. Dacier's commentary on Horace (1691), a copy of which appears in the Baker catalog (no. 559). Although his essay has only a single Latin quotation (Horace *Odes* 3.6.17–20), Fielding offers the reader translations of passages from Horace, Diodorus Siculus, Plutarch's life of Lycurgus, and Tacitus's *Germania*. The essay also refers briefly to punishments for adultery mentioned by Homer, Valerius Maximus, Plutarch, Aristophanes, Juvenal, Livy, Suetonius, Stobaeus, and Pausanias. The length of some of these citations reveals that, though Fielding may have initially turned to handbooks to find his references, he was also familiar with the original works from which they were taken. This accumulation of classical authorities provides Fielding with a starting point for his own reflections on the serious nature of adultery; it also helps Fielding establish a learned persona that lends credibility to his arguments in the remainder of the essay.²⁴

While scholars have noted that Fielding cites many classical authors, they have not considered a significant piece of indirect evidence about Fielding's classical learning: the mistakes that appear in his citations. Some of the errors are probably the fault of the printer, but this explanation does not fit in a number of cases. For example, in the motto of the *Covent-Garden Journal*, no. 25 (28 March 1752): 161, Fielding cites Virgil as the author when he actually quotes lines from Ovid's *Metamorphoses*. The *Jacobite's Journal*, no. 29 (18 June 1748): 310, has an incorrect reference for a Greek quotation from Aristotle. He offers this quotation from Livy in the *True Patriot*, no. 2 (12 November 1745): 118: "Factiones fuere eruntque plurimis civitatibus exitium," when, as W. B. Coley notes, the actual text reads, "ex certamine factionum, quae fuerunt eruntque pluribus populis exitio" (118–19). Clearly, this version and the original are sufficiently different that we cannot blame the compositor. These errors suggest that Fielding probably knew certain classical authors well enough to quote (or misquote) them from memory.²⁵ Because of his training at Eton, this explanation is certainly plausible in respect to certain

Latin authors like Horace, Juvenal, Virgil, and Ovid, but his misquotations of Livy, Sallust, and Aristotle suggest that he had read these authors often enough on his own to attempt to cite them from memory.

Fielding's knowledge of Latin texts and his skill in that language are also evident from his parodies of the *Aeneid* in *The Vernon-iad* (1741) and *A Journey from this World to the Next* (1743). Although the mock scholarly footnotes in *The Vernon-iad* assert that the poem is a translation of a lost work by Homer, a puff of it in *The History of Our Own Times* (1741), which Thomas Lockwood attributes to Fielding, mentions Virgil: "A Poem which the Author humourously supposes to have been originally written by *Homer*, tho' it is indeed a Parody on the first Part of *Virgil's* Aeneid, where *Juno* bribes *Aeolus* to disperse the *Trojan* Fleet."[26] In fact, *The Vernon-iad* closely parallels *Aeneid* 1.1-89, as the respective openings of the two works demonstrate:

> Arms and the Man I sing, who greatly bore
> *Augusta's* Flag to *Porto Bello's* Shore,
> On Sea and Land much suffering, e're he won,
> *With Six Ships only*, the predestin'd Town;
> Whence a long Train of Victories shall flow,
> And future Laurels for *Augusta* grow.[27]

> Arma virumque cano, Troiae qui primus ab oris
> Italiam fato profugus Laviniaque venit
> litora, multum ille et terris iactatus et alto
> vi superum, saevae memorem Iunonis ob iram,
> multa quoque et bello passus, dum conderet urbem
> inferretque deos Latio; genus unde Latinum
> Albanique patres atque altae moenia Romae.
>
> (1.1–6)

[Of arms and the man I sing, who first came from the shores of Troy, exiled by fate, to Italy and the Lavinian shores, he much buffeted both on land and sea by the force of the gods above, on account of the mindful wrath of cruel Juno; having endured many things also in war, until he should found a city and bring the gods to Latium; from which source come the Latin race, the Alban fathers and the walls of high Rome.] (My translation)

Here *The Vernon-iad* follows the *Aeneid's* wording in almost every line, demonstrating Fielding's own intimate acquaintance with Virgil. Fielding's parody is not just striking for its verbal reminiscences of Virgil; he also adopts Virgil's word order and choppy phrasing, which is appropriate in Latin but sounds odd in English. His "learned" commentary cites a host of other authors who add to his display of classical learning in the main text: Horace, Homer,

Pope, Ovid, Pausanias, Dryden, Claudian, Plutarch, Bentley, Burmann, Aristophanes, Aulus Gellius, Cato, Euripides, Lucan, Hesiod, Lucian, Aristotle, Eustathius, Apuleius, Martial, Trapp, and Plautus. While Fielding is clearly mocking the pedantic footnotes of antiquarians, too preoccupied with trivialities to comprehend broader issues, these citations impress the reader with Fielding's ability to draw from a wide range of classical authors.

More striking for its technical virtuosity is the parody of the *Aeneid* in Julian the Apostate's narrative in *A Journey from this World to the Next*. Instead of relying on a specific section of Virgil's epic, Fielding composes a Latin imitation that combines lines from books 1 and 2 and recreates the tone of his Latin original.

> Mundanos scandit fatalis Machina Muros,
> Farta Sacerdotum Turmis: exinde per Alvum
> Visi exire omnes, magno cum Murmure olentes.
> Non aliter quam cum Humanis furibundus ab Antris
> It Sonus, & Nares simul Aura invadit hiantes
> Mille scatent et mille alii; trepidare Timore
> Ethnica Gens coepit: falsi per inane volantes
> Effugere Dei—Desertaque Templa relinquunt.
> Jam magnum crepitavit Equus, mox Orbis & alti
> Ingemuere Poli: tunc tu Pater, ultimus Omnium
> Maxime *Alexander*, ventrem maturus Equinum
> Deseris, heu Proles meliori digne Parente.[28]

[The deadly machine climbs the walls of the world, stuffed full with throngs of priests: then all seemed to go out through the belly, giving off an odor with a great rumbling. Not otherwise than when from human caves a raging sound goes and at the same time the smell invades the open nostrils. A thousand and a thousand others spout up; the pagan people begin to tremble with fear; flying through the void false gods escape—and they leave the temples abandoned. Now the horse rattled greatly, soon the earth and the high heavens groaned: then you, father, greatest Alexander, highest of all, will leave the womb of the horse full grown, oh progeny worthy of a better parent.] (My translation)

In the first line Fielding signals to the reader that this Latin passage is close to Virgil with a direct quotation of *Aeneid* 2.237-38 ("scandit fatalis machina muros") and two other close parallels to Virgil's epic: 1.55 ("magno cum murmure montis") and 1.90 ("intonuere poli"). To reinforce the Virgilian tags, Fielding adopts Virgil's phrasing and vocabulary throughout. While the Latin fragment graphically demonstrates the derivative work produced by Julian's incarnation as a poet, it also offers Fielding the opportunity to show off his Latin learning.

This survey of Fielding's use of learning in his quotations, allusions, and parodies leads us to several conclusions about the extent of his classical knowledge. (1) After an early exposure to Latin and Greek literature at Eton, he maintained an interest in the classics and read more widely in many other classical authors than those he studied at school. (2) His ability in Latin is indisputable; he felt comfortable doing paraphrases and parodies of Latin texts, and at times he quoted Latin authors from memory. (3) The scarcity of translations, parodies, and imitations from Greek indicates that Fielding was not fluent in this language. Although his citations of Greek authors show that he had read them at least in translations, Fielding's reliance on English and Latin versions of Greek texts suggests that he did not have a very thorough knowledge of the originals.

CLASSICAL CITATIONS IN FIELDING'S JOURNALISM

Scholars have speculated about the classical authors who exerted the greatest influence on Fielding's writing, but their studies have focused primarily on authors read at Eton and the evidence from the Baker Catalog. One important but ignored indicator of Fielding's reading is his journalism. Fielding's four principal periodicals—the *Champion* (1739–40), the *True Patriot* (1745–46), the *Jacobite's Journal* (1747–48), and the *Covent-Garden Journal* (1752)—contain 613 quotations and specific allusions to twenty-nine Latin and thirty Greek authors, a range of writers that far exceeds the list of those he read at school. A tabulation of these citations from each of the journals offers some indications of his reading habits over the fourteen-year period they cover; it also suggests the authors to whom Fielding probably felt the greatest affinity.[29]

In the *Champion* Fielding cites twice as many Latin as Greek authors (nineteen Latin, ten Greek), but he refers to Latin sources four times as often as he does to the Greek ones (139 to 32). The Latin authors are almost evenly divided between prose writers and poets—of the Latin, eight are historians or philosophers, ten are poets—whereas among the Greeks only Homer, Aeschylus, and Sophocles wrote poetry. If we compare this list of authors with those that Fielding read at Eton, we find that those most often studied there figure prominently: Horace, Virgil, Cicero, Ovid, Juvenal, and Homer represent 123 (or 72 percent) of the 171 total citations. Fielding most often cites Horace, who accounts for 5 direct allusions (where he is mentioned by name) and 48 quotations, of which 39 are mottoes. Another significant fact is that Fielding quotes Latin authors far more often than the Greek (109 times as compared to 6 times for Greek). Because the Greek quotations include one in English translation and two-word fragments from Longinus and Aristotle, both with translations, they support our earlier observations about the limits of his Greek learning (see appendix B, tables B-1 and B-2).

Because of its topical-political focus, the *True Patriot* has only 60 quotations and direct references to classical authors. However, the practice established in the *Champion* remains the same: Fielding cites eleven Latin and eight Greek authors, but the ratio of Latin to Greek references is still four to one. Of the Latin authors, most are poets (eight poets to three prose writers), although the number of Greek poets is also slightly greater than before (three poets, five prose writers). Of the 5 Greek quotations, those by Aristotle and Pythagoras are given in both Greek and English; only the 2 from Euripides appear in Greek without a translation. The most popular Eton authors—Horace, Cicero, Juvenal, Ovid, and Homer—account for little more than half the references, indicating that Fielding was including a wider range of classical authors. Perhaps this movement reflected his own reading at the time or was an attempt to counter attacks on his learning made by his critics (see appendix B, tables B-3 and B-4).

By the time Fielding composed the *Jacobite's Journal*, the range of authors to whom he referred broadened even further, since he mentions twenty Latin and thirteen Greek authors in 145 direct allusions and quotations. Latin prose writers now outnumber poets eleven to nine, and the ratio of Greek prose writers to poets, especially historians, remains high (ten prose writers to three poets). Despite these figures, a disproportionate number of allusions and quotations still come from the poets (80 of the 111 Latin citations, or 72 percent). Among the Latin authors, Horace, Ovid, Cicero, Virgil, and Juvenal still head the list, accounting for 80 of the references. Of the Greek authors, however, Aristotle is the most frequently mentioned and quoted, appearing three times more often than Homer. Although the references to Greek authors are more frequent than before—the Latin citations outnumber them by only three to one—Fielding's quotations of Greek writers are almost always in English translations rather than in Greek; only in a quotation from Euripides does he fail to provide an English text to accompany the Greek (see appendix B, tables B-5 and B-6).

The *Covent-Garden Journal* is the only one of the four periodicals in which Fielding translated nearly every quotation of a Latin or a Greek author. Probably Fielding began to translate all quotations in this journal because the reading public in the 1750s comprised a more diverse group than it previously had and, consequently, he could no longer assume that his audience could read or recognize citations from classical authors.[30] Because he had to translate all of his quotations, however, Fielding was now free to include more references to authors with whom his readers were less familiar. The number of Greek authors almost equals the Latin (twenty-two to twenty-four), and the ratio of Latin to Greek references is only two to one. Of the 237 citations, little more than half are of the standard authors; altogether he cites Horace, Ovid, Virgil, Cicero, Juvenal, and Homer only 124 times. Fourteen Latin and seven Greek writers are poets; prose writers account for ten Latin and fifteen Greek names. Once again Aristotle is high on the list of Greek authors, with only Homer's name appearing more often. The number of classical authors to whom he refers fosters the learned image that Fielding attempted to create, while the frequency of his classical allusions shapes his own image of the "learned" reader and projects his vision of the educational level to which his audience should aspire (see appendix B, tables B-7 and B-8).

When we compile the statistics from all four periodicals, we obtain a clear picture of the authors Fielding cited most frequently. Tables 2.2, 2.3, and 2.4 present the results of this compilation.

Table 2.2. Latin Authors Cited Most Frequently in Fielding's Periodicals

Author	Champion	T.P.	J.J.	C.-G.J.	Total
Horace	53 (31%)	11 (18%)	36 (25%)	56 (24%)	156 (25%)
Virgil	23 (13%)	5 (8%)	6 (4%)	16 (7%)	50 (8%)
Ovid	13 (8%)	5 (8%)	18 (12%)	12 (5%)	48 (8%)
Cicero	12 (7%)	7 (12%)	12 (8%)	12 (5%)	43 (7%)
Juvenal	10 (6%)	7 (12%)	8 (6%)	12 (5%)	37 (6%)
Tacitus	3 (2%)	0	3 (2%)	7 (3%)	13 (2%)
Livy	1 (.6%)	3 (5%)	5 (3%)	3 (1%)	12 (2%)
Seneca	2 (1%)	2 (3%)	1 (.7%)	6 (3%)	11 (2%)
Quintilian	3 (2%)	0	4 (3%)	4 (2%)	11 (2%)
Martial	2 (1%)	2 (3%)	3 (2%)	3 (1%)	10 (2%)
Totals	122 (71%)	42 (69%)	96 (66%)	131 (56%)	391 (64%)

Note: Percentages in the first four columns come from the total number of allusions and quotations for each periodical. The totals at the bottom of these columns show the percentage these authors represent of all the references for that periodical. Because not all authors are listed, the totals do not equal 100 percent. The final column gives the percentage each author represents of the total 613 references. Most decimals have been rounded off. This information also applies to table 2.3. *T.P.* = *True Patriot*; *J.J.* = *Jacobite's Journal*; *C.-G.J.* = *Covent-Garden Journal*.

Table 2.3. Greek Authors Cited Most
Frequently in Fielding's Periodicals

Author	Champion	T.P.	J.J.	C.-G.J.	Total
Homer	12 (7%)	2 (3%)	4 (3%)	16 (7%)	34 (6%)
Aristotle	3 (2%)	2 (3%)	12 (8%)	10 (4%)	27 (4%)
Plato	7 (4%)	1 (2%)	2 (1%)	8 (3%)	18 (3%)
Plutarch	4 (2%)	1 (2%)	5 (3%)	6 (3%)	16 (3%)
Longinus	1 (.6%)	0	1 (.6%)	7 (3%)	9 (1%)
Lucian	1 (.6%)	1 (2%)	0	5 (2%)	7 (1%)
Diodorus Siculus	0	0	1 (.7%)	4 (2%)	5 (1%)
Thucydides	0	0	2 (1%)	3 (1%)	5 (1%)
Totals	28 (16%)	7 (12%)	27 (17%)	59 (25%)	121 (20%)

Table 2.4. Latin and Greek Authors Cited
Most Frequently in the Periodicals

Author	Number of References
Horace	156 (25%)
Virgil	50 (8%)
Ovid	48 (8%)
Cicero	43 (7%)
Juvenal	37 (6%)
Homer	34 (6%)
Aristotle	27 (4%)
Plato	18 (3%)
Plutarch	16 (3%)
Tacitus	13 (2%)
Livy	12 (2%)
Seneca	11 (2%)
Totals	465 (76%)

These rankings lead us to several important conclusions about Fielding's use of classical literature. As we would expect, references to Latin authors far outnumber those to Greek writers, and, of authors cited most frequently, the first six are writers with whom his learned readers were familiar from school. Among both the Latin and Greek authors, however, historians, moralists, and educational writers figure far more prominently than we would expect from school curricula and records of book publications: four of the ten Romans wrote prose, while, of the Greeks, only Homer was a poet. Finally, these lists suggest that we must reconsider the question of the authors who influenced Fielding: in particular, the numbers indicate that we should reconsider the importance of the Greek satirist Lucian.

Lucian as a Classical Model

Most scholars have assumed, plausibly enough, that Lucian greatly influenced Fielding because of Fielding's statement in the *Covent-Garden Journal* that he had formed his style on the Greek satirist.[31] Consequently, critics have argued that Lucian is a source for Fielding's rhetorical technique, his narrative persona, and his dominant themes. Fielding's limited ability in Greek and the relative scarcity of references to Lucian suggest that we should take another look at Fielding's statement and the conclusions that have been drawn from it.

The two strongest proponents for Lucian's influence, Henry Knight Miller and Christopher Robinson, base much of their argument on evidence from the Baker catalog, which has nine items by Lucian: five Greek and Latin texts of his works, two French translations, one Latin translation, and one English translation.[32] As we have seen, Lucian is second only to Aristotle in the number of volumes listed by Baker. Impressive as these figures are, we must interpret them cautiously, since the catalog offers little indication of when Fielding acquired these books and none of them contain annotations in his hand. Only one (no. 417) has an imprint that provides us with a date from which we can establish the earliest year for its acquisition (1743). The presence of these books in the library hardly proves that Lucian was more influential than other authors; another very plausible explanation for the proliferation of Lucian editions and translations is that Fielding and Young were assembling texts for the English edition of Lucian they projected in 1752. As the better known and more solvent of the two, Fielding probably assumed the responsibility for collecting the necessary books. The references to the Dryden and Ablancourt translations in his puff for the proposed project support this conclusion (*Covent-Garden Journal*, no. 52 [30 June 1752]: 285–88).

Aware of this difficulty with the Baker list, Robinson supports his theory by claiming that Fielding made "many references" to Lucian in his journalism.[33] As my survey of the allusions and quotations in the periodical literature has demonstrated, this assertion is completely inaccurate. Fielding mentions Lucian seven times in his periodicals, and he never quotes him or uses him as an authority to support any position. If Fielding were so heavily influenced by Lucian, why does he not refer to him as often as he does to Horace (156 times), Homer (34 times) or Aristotle (27 times)? Fielding definitely knew that his audiences had limited ability in Greek and were probably unfamiliar with such writers as Lucian, Aristotle, Longinus, and Thucydides in the original; however, he cites Aristotle, whose works were as available in English as Lucian's, about four times more often than the satirist, directly quoting him seven times. Even if we consider that audiences recognized Aristotle's name without knowing his work, we cannot dismiss that Fielding also directly quotes Thucydides and Quintilian three times each; since Thucydides only appeared in five editions during Fielding's lifetime and Quintilian in one, his readers were less likely to be as familiar with these authors as they were with Lucian. Consequently, we can reasonably conclude that Lucian did not figure prominently in Fielding's thinking.

Although Fielding's references to Lucian are complimentary, most tell us little about the characteristics of that author that prompt his admiration. He alludes in passing to Lucian's wit, associating him with Rabelais, Cervantes, and Swift in two brief references, and he claims elsewhere that he reads Plutarch and Lucian with equal delight.[34] When marshaling his forces for the paper war in the *Covent-Garden Journal*, Fielding lists Lucian after Homer, Aristotle, Thucydides, and Demosthenes among the Greek forces.[35] Laudatory as they are, these passing comments reveal little about the features that separate Lucian from other writers or about the traits that influenced Fielding.

The lengthiest discussion of Lucian is Fielding's "puff" for the translation he proposed with William Young in 1752.[36] While the essay calls Lucian "the Father of true Humour" and compares him favorably to both Aristophanes (whom Fielding had translated with Young in 1742) and Swift, we must regard Fielding's remarks with caution. As we have seen in chapter 1, Lucian was not widely read in the eighteenth century; in fact, Fielding himself admits that no good English translations of this author had been done. Because most of his readers could barely read Greek, if at all, Fielding certainly realized that he had to convince them of the value of Lucian if he and Young were to be commercially successful. Not surprisingly, then, Fielding asserts that Lucian surpasses Swift, even though earlier in the *True Patriot* he stated the reverse in eulogizing his famous contemporary.[37] The translation proposed here was never done, quite plausibly because the public lacked interest in this Greek writer. Therefore, this essay may have been motivated more by Fielding's commercial aspirations than by his admiration for this ancient satirist.

Fielding's specific remarks about Lucian also suggest that we should not take his claims about the satirist's influence literally. In the essay he does compare Lucian favorably to Aristophanes, and he does discuss some of the features that he finds most praiseworthy: he notes Lucian's pleasant humor, neat wit, and poignant satire. While he attributes Lucian's success to the state of ancient philosophy and theology, which were especially suitable objects for satire, Fielding never implies that the situation in imperial Rome bears any resemblance to his own time. Nor does he indicate that he sees similarities between the subjects he treats and those addressed by Lucian. If Fielding felt a great affinity to this writer, he could have strengthened his claims about Lucian's effect by drawing such analogies; consequently, their absence undermines claims for Lucian's influence.

The most famous statement about his own relationship to Lucian appears at the end of the essay, where, to establish his own credentials as a translator, he says, "I will only venture to say, that no Man seems so likely to translate an Author well, as he who hath formed his Stile upon that very Author." He then praises the abilities of his partner, whose skill in Greek is universally admired by learned men.[38] The strengths of each man are suggestive, implying that Young would be primarily responsible for doing the initial translation from the Greek and Fielding would polish the translation and perhaps write a preface, as they probably did with the *Plutus* translation. Fielding's failure to mention his own ability in Greek also reminds us that he was not completely comfortable with that language. Since he was probably not able to read Lucian in Greek without some assistance (Latin translations and Greek dictionaries), how closely could he actually pattern his own style on the Greek author? Furthermore, when we consider the fundamental structural differences between Greek and English, we cannot take such an assertion about Lucian's influence on him literally.

To lend further support to their theory, both Miller and Robinson list several pieces that they assert Fielding patterned after Lucian. Admittedly, some are Lucianic imitations: for example, the underworld scene in *The Author's Farce* may have been influenced by similar episodes in *The Dialogues of the Dead*, and one of the *Champion* essays includes a summary of a Lucian dialogue and a dream vision closely paralleling it.[39] Even more pointed are the imitations in the *Miscellanies*, including "A Dialogue Between Alexander the Great and Diogenes the Cynic," "An Interlude Between Jupiter, Juno, Apollo, and Mercury," and possibly the first third of *A Journey from This World to the Next*.[40] Beyond these works, however, the influence of Lucian is more difficult to establish definitively. Fielding may not even have drawn on Lucian directly for inspiration, since the dialogue of the dead was a common form in the eighteenth century and he could just as easily have imitated Fontanelle or William King as Lucian.[41] Without specific references, we cannot assume he directly influenced any other works of Fielding.

Finally, to support their contention that Lucian had an important effect on Fielding, scholars have tried to identify thematic and rhetorical similarities between the two authors. For example, Miller notes that both Fielding and Lucian attack hypocrisy, malice, envy, slander, vanity, and greed, and both he and Robinson suggest that Fielding's use of mock pedantry and his concern for the proper use of language may have come from Lucian.[42] Such assertions are questionable. As even these scholars admit, many of Fielding's contemporaries—like Pope and Swift—were concerned with the same themes and used mock learning effectively to satirize their enemies.[43] Certain affinities may exist between the work of Lucian and Fielding, but the satirist's direct influence on Fielding is by no means clear.

Although Fielding speaks of Lucian in laudatory terms, the scarcity of direct references to this Greek author and the brevity of Fielding's remarks about him suggest that Lucian was not continually in Fielding's mind as he wrote. Fielding unquestionably did model some of his works—particularly in the *Miscellanies*—on the dialogue form of Lucian, but we have no way of knowing which themes and techniques shared by the two authors could have come directly from the Greek writer. Far more plausibly Fielding was heavily influenced by Horace, the Roman satirist, critic, and moralist.

HORACE AS CRITIC, MORALIST, AND MODEL

Even if we discount the mottoes in his periodical essays, Fielding quotes and alludes to Horace more than any other classical writer.[44] Clearly, Fielding admired the Roman poet greatly, and his comments about him give us a fairly detailed picture of his reasons for doing so.

In the periodical essays Fielding praises Horace as one of the most important figures in the history of criticism, advising the critics of his own time to use him as a model. For example, in the *Covent-Garden Journal* he says, "No Author is to [be] admitted into the Order of Critics until he hath read over, and understood, Aristotle, Horace, and Longinus, in their original Language."[45] The Court of Censorial Enquiry in the *Jacobite's Journal* even acknowledges that the precepts of Horace are held in great esteem, giving them the force of laws.[46] In matters of taste, then, Fielding refers to Horace and his "edicts" frequently.

While they underscore Fielding's general admiration for Horace, these allusions also reveal the characteristics of the Roman author's criticism that especially appeal to him. One of his favorite Horatian tags is the passage in the *Ars Poetica* in which the poet asserts that no one can be a great writer unless he combines genius with learning (lines 408–10).[47] He also cites Horace to demonstrate that custom primarily determines how words should be used and that few men can be good listeners.[48] The one critical issue that Fielding discusses most often is slander, and he usually uses citations from Horace to lend authority to his arguments. For example, in the *Champion* he asserts that

Horace was right in reminding those who listen to slander that they do not know when it will come back upon them.[49] When he attacks the current critical fashion of finding only fault with literary works, he states that this practice is contrary to the amiable spirit of the Roman poet.[50] Fielding also reminds his contemporaries of the harsh punishments in ancient Rome for slander, quoting Horace as an authority.[51] Although Lucian speaks frequently on this subject, Fielding relies exclusively on Horace, never mentioning the Greek satirist in this connection.

The characteristic of Horace's writing that most attracted Fielding was his moderation. In a lengthy *Champion* essay, Fielding criticizes many classical authors—among them Homer and Ovid—for their overindulgence in words, but he praises Horace highly for both his precepts on this subject and his own practice in his poetry.

> *Horace*, in his Art of Poetry, particularly recommends an exact and severe Defalcation of all superfluous Members in Poetry. He himself practices this Rule every where with the greatest exactness; so much dreading the contrary, that in one of his Epistles, when he apprehends himself in Danger of running into too great a Length, he stops short, and ends in almost an abrupt Manner,
> —*Ne me verbosi scrinia Lippi*
> *Compilasse putes—Verbum non amplius addam.*[52]

Fielding acknowledges his own affinity with Horace by using this same quotation from Horace to end his final number of the *Covent-Garden Journal*.[53]

Although he revered his critical views, Fielding was also attracted to Horace the moralist. He buttresses his own attacks on greed, adultery, and vice with quotations from Horace.[54] What especially appealed to Fielding was probably Horace's emphasis on the "golden mean," which he cites directly when he argues that happiness is not to be found in power or affairs of state but in some middle ground.[55] Since Fielding mentions him by name, Horace is a much more likely source of Fielding's opinions in these areas than Lucian.

Not only did Fielding express his admiration for the Roman poet by citing him as an authority; he also suggests that he has patterned himself after the Roman poet. In addition to the closing in the *Covent-Garden Journal*, Fielding acknowledges elsewhere the kinship he feels with him and his position in Rome. He says that, like Horace, he disdains the rabble and prefers only a few readers, and he warns those who attack him that, just as Horace did to his opponents, he will deride those who continue to criticize him.[56] While these allusions alone do not prove that Fielding identified with the critical and moral positions of Horace, they do offer us more visible indication of the influences on Fielding's thinking than a single essay devoted to Lucian.

In addition to the obvious similarities in thought and critical approach between the two authors, Fielding had a number of good reasons for relying so heavily on the Roman poet as a critical and moral authority. Because Horace was studied at the public schools and was read widely both in the original and in translation, Fielding's readers certainly knew his works well and respected his opinions; consequently, Fielding's citations of the Roman poet undoubtedly added weight to his positions in the eyes of the majority of his readers. But more important, Fielding's use of Horace connected him with other writers of the period, most notably Addison, Pope, and Swift, who wrote imitations of the Roman satirist and quoted him in poems and essays.[57] In his periodical writing Fielding consciously imitated Addison, even stating that he put mottoes at the beginning of each number so that his periodical would look more like the *Spectator* and reprinting an entire essay from the *Freeholder* in the *Jacobite's Journal*.[58] Fielding frequently aligned himself with the Scriblerians; naturally he would allude to a classical writer closely related to that circle. Because Fielding often showed his admiration of these writers in other ways, such a motive for his use of Horace is certainly plausible.

When we compare Fielding's use of Horace and Lucian, we must conclude that the Greek satirist played a far less important role in Fielding's writing than the Roman poet. Although Fielding may have been indebted to Lucian for the dialogue form, the Greek satirist did not have the all-pervasive influence on Fielding that some scholars have claimed.

Fielding clearly knew classical literature well and used it in a variety of ways in his essays and poetry; his practice suggests that the classical quotations and allusions serve more than a merely ornamental function. In his essays Latin and Greek references establish his credibility with the reader and provide a foundation on which he can build his own critical and moral theories. Fielding's display of classical expertise is an important component of the "learned" perspective from which he writes many of his essays on moral and critical issues, since this persona encourages the reader to believe what he has to say. Fielding often sets himself apart from those he wishes to attack—like Colley Cibber and his critics—by focusing on their inability to read and understand classical literature.[59] His critics often dismissed his writings as hack work; by using frequent references to classical authors, Fielding associated himself with respected figures like Addison and set his work in a broader tradition of classical criticism and moral philosophy stretching back to Aristotle, Longinus, Horace, Cicero, and Quintilian.

At the same time that he constructs a learned persona with his references to ancient authors, Fielding shapes the audience for his periodical essays. Often when he discusses education, Fielding argues that the decay of learning was responsible for many of the problems English society faced.[60] His use of classical references encourages his readers to become "learned"; as they read his essays, they begin to adopt his attitudes towards classical learning, and they discover indirectly the moral and critical truth of the ancients. His readers, in turn, affect his choice of authors and, in the *Covent-Garden Journal*, his decision to translate his quotations of Latin and Greek authors.

Fielding definitely varied his use of classics to suit his audience, his message, and his persona. He also drew on critical discussions of classical models—particularly epic—to define his "new species of writing" for his readers. Next, we will explore how he uses eighteenth-century discussions of epic to define his new genre and reexamine the relevance of the epic hero in the modern world.

3
Classical Epic and the "New Species of Writing"

> Now a comic Romance is a comic Epic-Poem in Prose;
> —Preface to *Joseph Andrews*

> when any kind of Writing contains all its other Parts, such as Fable, Action, Characters, Sentiments, and Diction, and is deficient in Metre only; it seems, I think, reasonable to refer it to the Epic,
> —Preface to *Joseph Andrews*

> I have attempted in my Preface to *Joseph Andrews* to prove, that every Work of this kind is in its Nature a comic Epic Poem, of which *Homer* left us a Precedent, tho' it be unhappily lost.
> —Preface to *The Adventures of David Simple*

The generic sources of Fielding's "new species of writing" have generated a lively critical debate over the last seventy years because they affect our understanding of his originality, his use of and place in literary tradition, and his affinities with other eighteenth-century authors. Like his contemporaries, Fielding could have drawn from several different literary models, among them classical epic, satire, romance, history, and spiritual autobiography. What he chose to imitate and which genres he invoked in his critical prefaces reveal both his purpose in writing fiction and the authors with whom he wanted his audience to identify him.

Although some scholars have argued that Fielding drew primarily on satire, the essay, and history, most of the discussion has centered on the importance of the epic and the romance in his concept of the novel. Critics who argue that Fielding wrote firmly in the epic tradition of Homer and Virgil emphasize Fielding's classical background and his ties to Dryden, Addison,

Swift, and Pope, who championed the classics in the debate between the ancients and the moderns.[1] But by asserting that Fielding relied heavily on romance—a genre used by such novelists as Richardson and Defoe—other scholars have maintained that Fielding is more "modern" than his classical references suggest and that his concept of fiction is similar to that of many eighteenth-century romance and novel writers.[2] Both of these positions have substantial limitations, however. Because they take Fielding's epic pretensions seriously, epic theorists cannot satisfactorily explain his use of the mock-heroic in *Jonathan Wild*, *Joseph Andrews*, and *Tom Jones* or the distinction between Fielding's use of the epic in his earlier novels and in *Amelia*. Romance theorists weaken their position by measuring Fielding's work against modern definitions of the epic rather than those familiar to Fielding and his readers; consequently, they have not considered the relationship of the critical essays in both *Joseph Andrews* and *Tom Jones* to eighteenth-century epic theory and have often claimed falsely that Fielding's plot devices, inflated language, and characters are signs of the influence of romance, not epic.

The problems raised by these theories demonstrate that several questions about Fielding's use of other genres remain to be answered. How frequently does Fielding allude to the epic, and how close are his statements to eighteenth-century epic theory? If he does consider his novels part of the epic tradition, why does he use mock-heroics? What connection exists between his use of epic in his earlier novels and in *Amelia*? Because Fielding's classical allusions and quotations indicate the importance of epic—and such genres as satire, romance, and history—to his conception of the novel, they are useful in addressing these issues.

A review of Fielding's references to classical literature reveals that the classical epic more profoundly shaped his theory of fiction than many recent critics have been willing to allow. Albeit at times ironically, he deliberately defines his new genre in terms that would relate it to eighteenth-century discussions of epic familiar to both him and his audience, and, in his introductory chapters, he distances his work from the romance by his repeated attacks on the form. At the same time that Fielding identifies his work with epic in his prefaces, his mock-heroics betray his ambivalence about the epic hero and his concern that the moral values inherent in these ancient poems were not compatible with Christianity. He introduces this theme in *Jonathan Wild*, *Joseph Andrews*, and *Tom Jones* but develops it most fully in *Amelia*, where he treats the epic analogy seriously in order to dramatize the difference between the heroic and Christian codes. Consequently, the use of epic shows a greater continuity between the early and late works than has been previously recognized.

References to Classical Epic Poets in Fielding's Novels

Two generalizations have long played an important role in discussions of the classical influence on Fielding's "new species." (1) Noting that Fielding seldom uses the term "epic" in his fiction, some critics have argued that his references to epic are too occasional and local to be taken seriously.[3] (2) Because of the reputed influence of Lucian, others have stressed the impact of classical satire on Fielding's theory of the novel.[4] As widespread as such views are, we must reconsider them in the light of Fielding's references to classical writers, which show that both these commonplaces about his use of ancient sources are questionable.

Although Fielding uses the term "epic" very few times, a tabulation of the classical allusions and quotations in the novels reveals that he refers to epic poets and theorists more often than scholars have generally assumed.[5] Tables 3.1, 3.2, and 3.3 list the Latin and Greek authors mentioned most frequently.[6]

Table 3.1. Number of References to Latin Authors Mentioned Most Frequently in Fielding's Novels

Author	JW	JA	TJ	Amelia	Total
Horace	3 (9%)	5 (9%)	35 (21%)	8 (11%)	51 (16%)
Virgil	9 (27%)	6 (11%)	24 (14%)	12 (17%)	51 (16%)
Ovid	2 (6%)	3 (5%)	12 (7%)	8 (11%)	25 (8%)
Cicero	1 (3%)	4 (7%)	14 (8%)	3 (4%)	22 (7%)
Juvenal	0	1 (2%)	9 (5%)	3 (4%)	13 (4%)
Terence	0	0	8 (5%)	1 (1%)	9 (3%)
Seneca	0	2 (4%)	3 (2%)	0	5 (2%)
Lucan	1 (3%)	0	1 (.6%)	2 (3%)	4 (1%)
Persius	1 (3%)	1 (2%)	2 (1%)	0	4 (1%)
Pliny the Elder	1 (3%)	1 (2%)	2 (1%)	0	4 (1%)
Totals	18 (54%)	23 (42%)	110 (65%)	37 (51%)	188 (59%)

Note: In tables 3.1 and 3.2, the percentages in the first four columns come from the representation of each author in the total references for each novel (n = the number of references in the novel). The totals for these authors do not equal 100 percent because these lists only give those writers listed most often. The percentage in column five comes from the total number of Latin and Greek references for all the novels (n = 330).

Table 3.2. Number of References to Greek Authors
Mentioned Most Frequently in Fielding's Novels

Author	JW	JA	TJ	Amelia	Total
Homer	3 (9%)	9 (16%)	22 (13%)	13 (18%)	47 (14%)
Aristotle	3 (9%)	6 (11%)	10 (6%)	4 (6%)	23 (7%)
Plato	2 (6%)	3 (5%)	6 (4%)	2 (3%)	13 (4%)
Aeschylus	0	7 (12%)	0	0	7 (2%)
Plutarch	1 (3%)	1 (2%)	2 (1%)	0	4 (1%)
Aristophanes	0	2 (4%)	1 (.6%)	0	3 (1%)
Thucydides	0	0	1 (.6%)	2 (3%)	3 (1%)
Herodotus	1 (3%)	0	1 (.6%)	0	2 (1%)
Totals	10 (30%)	28 (50%)	43 (26%)	21 (30%)	102 (31%)

Table 3.3. Latin and Greek Authors Most
Frequently Mentioned in Fielding's Novels

Author	Total
Horace	51 (16%)
Virgil	51 (16%)
Homer	47 (14%)
Ovid	25 (8%)
Aristotle	23 (7%)
Cicero	23 (7%)
Juvenal	13 (4%)
Plato	13 (4%)
Total	246 (76%)

As these tables show, two of the three authors Fielding refers to most often in the novels are Homer and Virgil, who account for 98 (or 30 percent) of his 330 allusions and quotations, whereas in the periodicals the two epic poets represent only 84 (or 14 percent) of the 613 references. The numbers suggest that Fielding deliberately added references to these poets to associate his work with the epic genre. These direct references to Virgil are reinforced by the structural parallels between *Amelia* and Virgil's *Aeneid*, which Fielding designated as the model for this novel in the *Covent-Garden Journal*, no. 8 (28 January 1752): 65.[7] Such evidence implies that Fielding conceived of his novels—and wanted his readers to think of his novels—in relation to the epic tradition.

The number of references to Horace and Aristotle, who account for 74 allusions and quotations, or 22 percent of the total, is also important, because both were associated with eighteenth-century epic theory and many of Fielding's quotations and allusions come from their critical works. In *Tom Jones*, where Fielding writes extensively about his theory of fiction, the narrator quotes or alludes to Aristotle 8 times: half of these are to his criticism or the *Poetics*; the other half, to his *Politics*. Of the narrator's 24 references to Horace—many of which appear in the prefatory chapters treating Fielding's theory of the novel—20 are specifically related to the *Ars Poetica* and his other critical works. For example, when he discusses the question of probability in the opening chapter of book 8 of *Tom Jones*, Fielding alludes to Horace's *Ars Poetica* (lines 188, 191) and Aristotle's *Poetics* (24.19, 9.1-3) (*Tom Jones*, bk. 8, chap. 1, 1:397-402).[8] Such allusions and quotations indicate that Fielding wanted his readers to relate his concept of the novel to classical criticism and acknowledge that the rules for his "new species" grew out of those set down by Horace and Aristotle for the epic. His reliance on classical critics also heightens the authority of his pronouncements and encourages his readers to compare his narratives to the ancient epics.

The scarcity of references to Horace's *Satires* and other ancient satires suggests that this classical genre did not play a large role in Fielding's fiction. In the course of all four novels, Fielding mentions Horace's *Satires* only 6 times; when we compare this number to the abundance of references to the Roman writer's critical works, we see that Horace was more important to Fielding as a critical and moral standard than as a satirist. The references to other prominent satiric poets support this conclusion: Fielding quotes or alludes to Lucian, Persius, and Juvenal only 19 times (or 6 percent of the total). As in the journalism, Lucian is unimportant; he is mentioned only twice: once in *Tom Jones* and once in *Amelia*, where Fielding puffs his proposed translation of the Greek writer.[9] This evidence suggests that, while Fielding may have drawn on modern satirists like Cervantes and Scarron, ancient satiric poets had little effect on his fiction.

Clearly, Fielding was thinking of the classical epic poets as he wrote his novels, and he alludes frequently to epic theorists to give his fiction the weight of ancient authority. His use of epic theory as a background for the critical essays in *Joseph Andrews* and *Tom Jones* also shows his ties to eighteenth-century epic theorists and indicates why he wanted his readers to identify his works with epics rather than romances.

Epic Theory and the Critical Discussions of the New Species

While Fielding alluded frequently to Virgil, Homer, and epic theorists, he also derived many of the guidelines for his new genre from eighteenth-century discussions of the epic, which would have been familiar both to him and his audience. Ethel M. Thornbury and James L. Lynch have noted that Fielding drew on eighteenth-century theories of the epic in his preface to *Joseph Andrews*, but they have not discussed the extent to which the prefatory essays at the beginning of each book of *Joseph Andrews* and *Tom Jones* address issues that concerned eighteenth-century epic theorists.[10] These references to contemporary issues align Fielding with such writers as Dryden, Pope, and Addison, who wrote about and translated epics, and they suggest how Fielding conceived of the purpose of his novels and their place in the literary hierarchy.

Nearly all the eighteenth-century critics who wrote about epic used the formal definition taken from René Le Bossu, whose *Treatise of the Epick Poem* (1695) was one of the most influential works on this ancient genre. Le Bossu's description of the epic, derived from Aristotle and Horace, emphasized its didactic purpose rather than its formal elements.

> The *EPOPEA* is a Discourse invented by Art, to form the Manners by such Instructions as are disguis'd under the Allegories of some one important Action, which is related in Verse, after a probable, diverting, and surprizing Manner.[11]

This definition provided a framework for discussions of the epic in the eighteenth century, since epic theorists followed Le Bossu in discussing the fable, action, moral, characters, machines, and language of the epic poem.[12] Fielding and his readers were clearly aware of this definition and the topics usually covered in treatments of epic because many of the critics and writers with whom they were familiar also used it. For example, Dryden structured his entire discussion of the *Aeneid* around Le Bossu's topics, and, in his translation of the *Odyssey*, Pope includes an abbreviated version of Le Bossu, entitled "A General View of the Epic Poem and of the *Iliad* and *Odyssey*. Extracted from *Bossu*."[13] Addison's famous series of essays on *Paradise Lost* in the *Spectator* also follows Le Bossu topic by topic. In chapter 1, I demonstrated the popularity of Dryden's and Pope's translations of the epic poets; consequently, even if Fielding and his readers had not read Le Bossu's entire treatise in French or in an English translation, they could easily learn indirectly about this author and his critical pronouncements from such well-known sources. Because of their familiarity with Dryden, Pope, and Addison, ling's readers also would associate Fielding's critical remarks with this description of the epic, and they would relate the topics discussed by Fielding to the epic genre.

Fielding's critical essays in *Joseph Andrews* and *Tom Jones* reflect the extent of his awareness of epic theory and the key issues that concerned epic theorists. In addition to Aristotle and Horace, the two most important ancient critics related to discussions of the epic, Fielding also refers to seventeenth- and eighteenth-century scholars who wrote treatises on this genre. For example, in *Tom Jones* he lists Le Bossu and Dacier along with Aristotle and Horace as examples of the great critics the world has produced (bk. 11, chap. 1, 2:569–70). Although he does not mention them by name, Fielding comments on the theories of Richard Bentley and René Rapin about the divisions in Homer's epics (*Joseph Andrews*, bk. 2, chap. 1, pp. 90–91).[14] While his use of their names does not guarantee that Fielding had actually read these critics, his detailed comments about their positions indicate more than a passing knowledge of their theories.

Fielding's knowledge of epic theory is important because, in his introductory essays, he applies Le Bossu's definition and his list of topics to his new genre. The statements most closely related to Le Bossu appear in the preface to *Joseph Andrews*, where he initially describes his new form of writing. Although he realizes that some may object to his use of the term epic because he writes prose, not poetry, Fielding says, "[W]hen any kind of Writing contains all its other Parts, such as Fable, Action, Characters, Sentiments, and Diction, and is deficient in Metre only; it seems, I think, reasonable to refer it to the Epic" (preface, 4). Later in the preface, when he distinguishes between his comic work and serious epics or romances, he once again uses Le Bossu's categories (4–5). Because Fielding's narrator is often ironic, some scholars have dismissed the references to epic in this passage, suggesting that Fielding here means no more by the term "epic" than narrative. Fielding may well be parodying serious discussions of the ancient genre; nevertheless, his choice of terms would resonate with readers familiar with the discussion of the epic written by such critics as Le Bossu, Dryden, Pope, and Addison. Thus, the repetition of these criteria establishes a connection between Fielding's novels and this classical genre even as the humor implies a distance between these two forms.[15]

The essays that introduce individual books of *Joseph Andrews* and *Tom Jones* also show that Fielding was aware of epic theory and that he wanted to draw on his audience's understanding of epic to define his new form. For example, his introductory essays reveal his concern with unity, an important concern in treatments of the epic. Le Bossu had prescribed that the action of the epic be one, entire, and great; in other words, the episodes of the story must bear a close relation to the main action.[16] Fielding is clearly thinking of this matter in *Tom Jones* when he advises critics not to condemn any of the incidents in his story as "impertinent and foreign to our main Design" (bk. 10, chap. 1, 2:524–25). He also alludes to this issue when he justifies his right to make rules for this new genre and discusses his decision to select from Tom's early life only those events that are significant to the narrative (*Tom Jones*, bk. 2, chap. 1, 1:75–78; bk. 5, chap. 1, 1:209–10). He invokes this criterion for an epic to contrast his work with loosely organized romantic tales whose complex plots did not revolve around a single great theme.

Although Fielding's adoption of epic terminology ties his work to the best of the classical tradition, his discussions of epic show that he did not believe that his novels should slavishly follow epic conventions or even that such devices were desirable in modern works. His comments about probability are typical of his ambivalence about certain features of epic. Epic critics in the seventeenth and eighteenth centuries hotly debated the extent to which epics could violate the laws of probability by including supernatural beings and fantastic episodes; some theorists argued that fairies and magic did not violate probability, whereas others maintained that works using such devices were no more than romances. Fielding clearly agrees that a work should be probable and that supernatural events have no place in his new species. In *Jonathan Wild* his naïve narrator assures his audience that he would rather have Wild hanged than violate "the strictest Rules of Writing and Probability" (bk. 4, chap. 6, p. 205). In *Joseph Andrews* he relates the probable directly to his objections to the romance:

> for I would by no means be thought to comprehend those Persons of surprising Genius, the Authors of immense Romances, or the modern Novel and *Atalantis* Writers; who without any Assistance from Nature or History, record Persons who never were, or will be, and Facts which never did nor possibly can happen: Whose Heroes are of their own Creation, and their Brains the Chaos whence all their Materials are collected. (Bk. 3, chap. 1, p. 187)

In *Tom Jones* Fielding devotes an entire introductory essay to "the Marvellous," in which he discusses the distinction between the possible and the probable and considers which marvelous events and characters are suitable for novels; he argues that the fictions of romance are contrary to the demands of probability (bk. 8, chap. 1, 1:395–407).[17] Thus, Fielding uses this issue to associate his work with epic and distance it from romance.

At the same time, Fielding cannot take seriously critics' lengthy debates over the use of divine machinery in modern epics, in which some advised their contemporaries to substitute angels and saints for heathen gods and goddesses.[18] He alludes to this controversy both in *Jonathan Wild* and *Tom Jones*, where he asserts that he will not bring in supernatural agents to rescue heroes, as the ancient epic writers frequently did with heathen deities.[19] Fielding underscores his own disdain for the issue when he humorously concludes that the only supernatural agents fit for modern works are ghosts but advises that they be used sparingly, since the writer using them will most likely elicit a "horse-laugh" from his reader (*Tom Jones*, bk. 8, chap. 1, 1:399).

Fielding's remarks about character reveal that he is not slavish in his thinking about this issue either. He readily agrees with epic theorists that a key problem is whether characters should be perfectly good or have some bad characteristics.[20] In *Jonathan Wild* he refers to this issue when he defends the "weakness" that Wild shows towards Heartfree by observing that "Nature is seldom so kind as those Writers who draw Characters absolutely perfect" (bk. 4, chap. 4, p. 200). Later Fielding advises critics who read *Tom Jones* not to condemn characters with some blemishes, citing the authority of Horace (bk. 10, chap. 1, 2:526–27). Although he accepts that novels, like epics, should have consistent characters, he rejects the requirement that the only suitable heroes and heroines are nobles, choosing instead "low" characters, who have noble qualities but with whom his readers can identify more easily. Consequently, Fielding reveals that he shares many of the artistic concerns of epic poets but that he does not think that novelists can, or should, imitate epics in every respect.

Fielding does not simply use these criteria to show to what degree his works resemble epics; he also deliberately invokes epic topoi to distinguish his works from romances. Even though the writers of seventeenth-century heroic romances may have drawn their critical pronouncements from epic theory, many eighteenth-century critics held the form in contempt and used the term "romance" pejoratively. According to writers on epic, romances were written merely for entertainment and lacked the didactic purpose that Le Bossu considered essential to the epic poem. Fielding is thinking of this criticism in *Joseph Andrews* when he ranks his works with Fénelon's *Télémaque* and the *Odyssey* instead of romances, because the latter contain "very little Instruction or Entertainment" (preface, 3–4). Because epic theorists attacked romances for violating the rules of probability, Fielding repeatedly maintains that his works differ from romances, which abandon truth and are the products merely of the fertile imagination of the author. For example, in *Tom Jones* he says that the historian who ignores probability becomes a writer of romance (bk. 8, chap. 1, 1:402).[21] He also alludes to the loose, episodic structure that critics associated with romance when speaking of a brook in *Tom Jones* "which Brook did not come there, as such gentle Streams flow through vulgar Romances, with no other Purpose than to murmur" (bk. 5, chap. 12,

1:264). Although Fielding used romance plot devices and other features associated with this genre, such were the negative associations of this term that in his critical comments he carefully distanced his work from it.

In his prefaces and the critical essays in *Tom Jones* and *Joseph Andrews*, Fielding clearly tied his new species to the epic genre and demonstrated how the reader should distinguish his work from the romances written in both prose and verse. His use of epic terminology and categories demonstrates that the term "epic" meant more than "prose narrative," the definition used by many modern critics. Drawing on Le Bossu, Aristotle, and Horace, Fielding used the term to indicate to his readers that, unlike romance, his new genre had a didactic purpose, unified organization, realistic characters drawn from ordinary life, and an appropriate mixture of the probable and the surprising. By equating his new genre with the ancient form, Fielding aligned his work with a type of narrative at the top of the literary hierarchy, giving it an aura of respectability the romance lacked. At the same time, Fielding's comments about various issues of interest to epic theorists reveal that he did not think that novelists should adopt epic conventions entirely. While he considered his novels part of the classical tradition, he recognized that the novel was a more appropriate vehicle for eighteenth-century readers than the epic. The allusions to epic criticism also heighten the reader's awareness of the verbal epic devices he used in his novels, which are frequently mock-heroic.

Mock-Heroics and Classical Epic

Although Fielding's mock-heroics have been widely noted, few critics have given them more than a passing comment because of the difficulties they raise both for those who dismiss the influence of epic and for those who regard seriously his allusions to this ancient genre.[22] The number of times Fielding imitates epic conventions in his novels belies the claim that he rarely draws an analogy between his new species and the epic form; at the same time that it reinforces the connections established in the prefaces, the parody of epic convention may undermine its authority.[23] Claude Rawson demonstrates the dual nature of the epic parodies when he asserts that the mock-heroic elements of *Jonathan Wild* demonstrate the interplay between the world of the novel and the past, but he maintains that the epic parallels in Fielding's later novels do not share this quality.[24] When we examine Fielding's mock-heroic diction, however, we find the same attitudes toward epic revealed in the prefaces and critical essays; furthermore, the mock-heroics address some of the liveliest critical debates of his time.

One of the primary functions of the mock-heroics in Fielding's novels is to distance the reader from the story. In addition to mock-heroic battle descriptions, Fielding uses rhetorical devices associated with classical epic, which are striking because he carefully calls the reader's attention to their artificiality: invocations to the Muses, formulae for dawn and sunset, and epic similes.[25] Sometimes he signals the epic convention with a chapter title, such as "A Battle sung by the Muse in the *Homerican* Stile, and which none but the classical Reader can taste" (*Tom Jones*, bk. 4, chap. 8) or "An Invocation" (*Tom Jones*, bk. 13, chap. 1). He often completes an epic simile with a translation "in vulgar Language" or with a lengthy interpretation that forces the reader to note what has preceded it.[26] He also heightens our awareness of his artificial diction with direct parodies of scenes in Homer and Virgil.[27] For example, the description of Joseph's cudgel in the "battle" involving Joseph, Adams, and the dogs recalls the shield of Achilles in book 18 of the *Iliad* and the armor of Aeneas in *Aeneid* 8.608–731 (*Joseph Andrews*, bk. 3, chap. 6, pp. 238–42).[28] With these allusions and figures, he reminds us that this book is a work of art and not a factual history, thus keeping us from getting too involved with the characters he has created.

Fielding probably chose to rely on epic rather than romance conventions because these devices were probably more effective at distancing readers from the narrative than the romance diction used by so many of his contemporaries. Sheridan Baker has noted that few readers would be especially conscious of the romance elements in novels, for, by the eighteenth century, the real world had adopted romance diction, the ideal of conduct, and the romance success story. Consequently, such elements would strike the reader not as artificial but as realistic.[29] Since it is more consciously contrived, epic diction remains distinct from the real world and keeps the reader continually attuned to the literary form. When Fielding introduces epic invocations before his description of Sophia and the scenes in London, he prevents readers from becoming too involved in the world of the novel. Thus, they will be more likely to question the values of the characters and the world in which they live.

Fielding's calculated use of these rhetorical techniques is also closely related to his attack on romance in both *Joseph Andrews* and *Tom Jones*. As Ronald Paulson and other critics have noted, Fielding was writing an antiromance in the tradition of Cervantes and Scarron.[30] Like Quixote's delusion, Adams's preoccupation with the heroic world makes him a ridiculous figure in contemporary society. Adams interprets his surroundings through the mirror of the heroic past, and his battles with ravishers, dogs, and squires for the honor of Fanny Goodwill are to him akin to the deeds of Achilles, Odysseus, and Aeneas. The juxtaposition of the real and epic worlds reveals how unworkable Adams's values are in modern society, and it suggests that the classical heroic ideal may be unsuitable in the Christian world.

While they demonstrate that Adams's view of the world is unrealistic, the mock-heroics also indicate the shortcomings of Adams's opponents, whose behavior is guided by self-interest and ignorance. By engrafting the epic world on the real one, Fielding calls attention to the disparity between ancient and modern values. The epic rhetoric encourages the reader to see that modern society—and such writers as Richardson and Cibber, who glorified it—does not measure up to the standards set by the ancients. The technique is similar to that of *The Tragedy of Tragedies* (1731), in which Fielding elevates a midget to gigantic proportions to underline the limited aspirations of those in his own world.

As in *Joseph Andrews*, the use of epic motifs in *Tom Jones* underscores Tom's unrealistic view of the world and his imprudent actions early in the novel. Unlike Adams, who fights battles for a virtuous young girl, Tom selects inappropriate objects for his chivalry. Neither Jenny Jones nor Molly Seagrim lives up to Tom's idealistic image, and both cause him to abandon his true love, Sophia. Similarly, Tom reveals his heroic code when he chooses to become a soldier after Allworthy sends him away. When Tom abandons his military aspirations and pursues Sophia to London, the epic battle descriptions cease. Although Fielding ennobles Tom by identifying him with epic heroes, therefore, he calls into question the morality of the ancient heroic ideal.

Epic diction in *Tom Jones* also reveals the unsavory features of minor characters. When Fielding describes Mrs. Partridge as an Amazon, he suggests her ability to fight with and dominate her husband (*Tom Jones*, bk. 2, chap. 4, 1:89). The predatory natures of Mrs. Deborah Wilkins and Miss Bridget appear in the epic similes that Fielding uses to describe them (*Tom Jones*, bk. 1, chap. 6, 1:47-48; bk. 1, chap. 8, 1:56). Overall, the use of epic, reinforced by the attention Fielding calls to it, makes the reader more aware of the pretenses that lie behind the behavior of such characters.

Although the epic devices enhance the reader's awareness of the limitations of the modern world with which the heroic world is compared, then, they indicate a certain ambivalence toward heroic morality that Fielding shared with his contemporaries. Ian Watt has noted that both Defoe and Richardson objected to the vicious behavior inherent in the Homeric ideal.[31] While valuing the epic form above all others and imitating the epics of Homer and Virgil, even Pope and Dryden were uncomfortable with the heroic code of honor, which is distinctly non-Christian. For example, among Homer's defects Pope lists "the vicious and *imperfect Manners* of his *Heroes*."[32] Thus, Fielding's approach to epic associates him with others in the eighteenth century who were uncomfortable with the epic hero.

The epic devices in *Jonathan Wild*, *Joseph Andrews*, and *Tom Jones* indirectly reflect this ambivalence toward the heroic world. In all three novels nearly all the epic similes disclose the vicious nature of the characters. Although

Adams's picture of the heroic world offers an alternative to the sordid values of modern society, Fielding indicates that it hardly enables Adams to deal effectively with the people he encounters on the road. Fielding enunciates the problem with the heroic world more clearly in *Tom Jones*, where Tom's heroic pretensions are associated with imprudent choices. Consider the women of questionable virtue or the military life, whose brutality and ignorance is represented by Northerton: only when he abandons the heroic ideal does Tom develop the restraint that helps him win Sophia. Such uses of heroism are tied to the phenomenon Rawson has noted in *Jonathan Wild*. Fielding's allusions to Virgil and Homer underscore the sordidness of the moral world that Wild inhabits, but the analogy between Wild and Aeneas suggests that epic heroism itself is unacceptable.[33]

Fielding identifies his use of inflated language with epic rather than romance by allusions to and parodies of Homer and Virgil. These devices distance the readers from the characters and story and encourage them to contrast the values of the modern and epic worlds. Each comments on the other: the idealism of the epic heightens the readers' awareness of the selfish motivations lying behind the pretensions of many characters, and the limitations of the heroic code become apparent when characters who adopt it prove ineffectual in the modern world.

AMELIA AND THE *AENEID*

In *Amelia* Fielding abandons the epic devices he relies on in his earlier fiction and draws a deliberate parallel between *Amelia's* structure and that of the *Aeneid*. Although many scholars have detailed the similarities between these two works, none has been able to explain satisfactorily why Fielding used Virgil's epic. Maurice Johnson claims that the Virgilian framework exalts the modern domestic characters of the novel, implying that epic heroism may show itself in human nature.[34] Lyall Powers suggests that Booth's victory over Bath represents a victory over a passé code of honor, which parallels Aeneas's victory over Turnus, the victory of *pietas* over *violentia*, and that, like Aeneas, who triumphed by submitting to the will of the gods, Booth succeeds by yielding to providence.[35] While each theory is partially true, neither considers eighteenth-century objections to the heroic code and concern with its applicability in a Christian world.

To account for the differences in the endings of *Amelia* and the *Aeneid*, scholars imply that the heroic code is a positive ideal, thus ignoring the ambiguity of the *Aeneid's* closing scene, which is implicit both in the original and in Dryden's version of the epic. As I have already shown, many eighteenth-century critics and writers questioned the validity of the Homeric concept of heroism, and Virgil's epic shares this ambivalence. Aeneas's murder of Turnus at the end of the *Aeneid* is not simply the victory of a pious man over a violent one; when Aeneas refuses to grant his opponent mercy, he violates the injunction laid upon him by his father Anchises in book 6: "tu regere imperio populos, Romane, memento / (hae tibi erunt artes), pacique imponere morem, / parcere subiectis et debellare superbos" (6.851–53) [Remember to rule the people in your empire, Roman (this will be your skill), and to impose law in peace, to spare those who have been subjugated, and to make war on the proud] (my translation). In his final confrontation with Turnus, he does not show him mercy, killing him violently. Thus, Virgil suggests that Aeneas has succumbed to his own rage and is little better than the man he defeated.

Although Dryden asserts in his dedication that Aeneas's defeat of Turnus is a victory for *pietas*, the ambivalence of the heroic ideal is apparent in his translation of the final lines of book 12.

> In deep Suspence the *Trojan* seem'd to stand;
> And just prepar'd to strike repress'd his Hand.
> He rowl'd his Eyes, and ev'ry Moment felt
> His manly Soul with more Compassion melt:
> When, casting down a casual Glance, he spy'd
> The Golden Belt that glitter'd on his side:
> The fatal Spoils which haughty *Turnus* tore
> From dying *Pallas*, and in Triumph wore.
> Then rowz'd anew to Wrath, he loudly cries,
> (Flames, while he spoke, came flashing from his Eyes:)
> Traytor, dost thou, dost thou to Grace pretend,
> Clad, as thou art, in Trophees of my Friend?
> To his sad Soul a grateful Off'ring go;
> 'Tis *Pallas, Pallas* gives this deadly Blow.
> He rais'd his Arm aloft; and at the Word,
> Deep in his Bosom drove the shining Sword.
> The streaming Blood distain'd his Arms around:
> And the disdainful Soul came rushing thro' the Wound.
>   (Lines 1360–77)[36]

Dryden's emphasis on Aeneas's wrath and the blood of Turnus links the gory death of Aeneas's opponent to the violent behavior of Achilles when he slaughters Hector in the *Iliad*. Aeneas's violation of Anchises' injunction enhances the reader's sense of discomfort with the ending.[37] Thus, Dryden's version demonstrates that Fielding and his readers undoubtedly knew this interpretation of the final scene of Virgil's epic.

Fielding shares Dryden's concern about the epic hero. The connection between greatness and the violence of war is apparent in the poem "Of True Greatness," where he derives the image of the plain drenched with gore from the battle scenes in Dryden's *Aeneis* and Pope's *Iliad*.[38] In *Jonathan Wild* he draws the parallel between Homer's heroes and the behavior of Alexander when Wild expresses his admiration for both at the same time (bk. 1, chap. 3, pp. 12–13). Clearly Fielding associated the heroic ideal with greatness, which he repeatedly condemns for its violence and cruelty. In *Tom Jones* he acknowledges that women love men because they are glorious, citing Penelope in the *Odyssey* as an example (bk. 4, chap. 13, 1:202). When Lady Bellaston tries to persuade Lord Fellamar to rape Sophia, she uses the example of Paris's behavior towards Helen and the Romans to the Sabine women (bk. 15, chap. 4, 2:794–95). Again, Fielding associates the heroic code with violence and cruelty.

In *Amelia* Fielding underscores the relationship between the soldier's concept of honor and the heroic code in his allusions to the *Aeneid* and Homer's epics. When Dr. Harrison and Colonel Bath discuss the conflict between honor and Christianity, Harrison denies that the Greeks and Romans dueled. But Bath cites examples from both Homer and Virgil that implicitly establish a connection between the code of honor that he follows and that of the Greeks and the Trojans (bk. 9, chap. 3, pp. 365–66). Fielding reinforces the connection between Bath and the Homeric hero at the masquerade when Bath pulls off his mask before the bucks, who flee "as the *Trojans* heretofore from the Face of *Achilles*" (bk. 10, chap. 2, p. 416). Clearly, Fielding associates the military code of honor followed by Booth, Bath, and Colonel James with the heroic code of classical epic.

Dr. Harrison returns to the conflict between the Christian and the heroic ideal after Amelia reveals that Colonel James has challenged Booth to a duel. He argues with Amelia that her concern for her husband's military honor is wrong. He relates this concept to classical heroism by observing that in Homer Helen criticizes Paris for unheroic behavior after he fights Menelaus (bk. 12, chap. 3, p. 504). When she again mentions the importance of Booth's "reputation," Harrison replies, "*Virgil* knew it a great While ago. The next Time you see your Friend Mrs. *Atkinson*, ask her what it was made *Dido* fall in Love with *Aeneas*" (bk. 12, chap. 3, p. 505). Even in his discussions with Mrs. Atkinson, he remarks that Homer's *"Pollemy"* is "the true Characteristic of a Devil" (bk. 10, chap. 4, p. 427). While Harrison consistently maintains that his favorite classical writers were critical of the heroic ideal, he and other characters establish a connection between the epic heroes and the soldier's code of honor that is unmistakable.

Within the context of this conflict between Christianity and Homeric morality, Fielding's use of the *Aeneid* and his departure from Virgil's ending are understandable. As a soldier, Booth is bound to the traditional military code of honor. Early in his marriage to Amelia, his honor dictates that he abandon his wife and follow his regiment to Gibraltar, undermining the domestic happiness that Fielding designates as the main subject of the novel. Later Booth threatens his marriage again when he must fight a duel with Colonel Bath. His preoccupation with obtaining a military position distracts him from the threats to his wife's virtue offered by the Peer and Colonel James, which nearly destroy his marriage. Finally, after Booth recognizes the value of Christianity, Amelia is able to avert the duel between him and Colonel James, providing the novel with a Christian rather than a heroic ending. Significantly, at the end of *Amelia*, Booth abandons the military life in order to live happily, surrounded by his family.

Although it uses epic structure and avoids the burlesque diction of mock epic, Fielding's *Amelia* offers his final comment on the heroic code of behavior. In *Joseph Andrews* Fielding views the Homeric hero as an ideal against which to measure the sordid values of the modern world, but he suggests that such a hero cannot be an effective guide to modern life. The perception of the epic world reflected in both *Jonathan Wild* and *Tom Jones* is more ambivalent: while the heroic world represents an ideal that offsets the sordidness of reality, its connection with that reality throws its values into question. Finally, in *Amelia* Fielding seriously considers the viability of the heroic ethic in the domestic and Christian world and finds it completely lacking.

Although Fielding probably did not consider his novels "epics" in the traditional sense, he drew plentifully on his audience's familiarity with epic theory and the translations of Pope and Dryden to define his new form and heighten the reader's awareness of the conflict between the ancient and modern worlds, between the world of romance and reality, and between the heroic and Christian ideals. He also used epic effectively as a thread that unites his novels from *Jonathan Wild* through *Amelia*. He exploits the associations aroused by epic as part of a strategy to make his readers more discerning about the story; the ways in which Fielding uses quotations and allusions to educate his readers will be the subject of the next chapter.

4
Classical Allusion and the Judgment of Character

> But however cunning the Disguise be which a Masquerader wears: however foreign to his Age, Degree, or Circumstance, yet if closely attended to, he very rarely escapes the Discovery of an accurate Observer; for Nature, which unwillingly submits to the Imposture, is ever endeavouring to peep forth and shew herself; nor can the Cardinal, the Friar, or the Judge, long conceal the Sot, the Gamester, or the Rake.
> —Fielding, "An Essay on Knowledge of Characters of Men"

> How absurd then must appear the Conduct of *Cenodoxus*, who having had the Advantage of a liberal Education, and having made a pretty good Progress in Literature, is constantly advancing learned Subjects in common Conversation? He talks of the Classics before the Ladies; and of *Greek* Criticisms among fine Gentlemen. What is this less than an Insult on the Company, over whom he thus affects a Superiority, and whose Time he sacrifices to his Vanity?
> —Fielding, "An Essay on Conversation"

Although reader-oriented studies of Fielding's novels have drawn our attention to the ways in which he challenges his readers to reconsider their preconceptions about literature, morality, and language, they have ignored the role played in this process by the classical allusions and quotations used by both the characters and narrator.[1] Steeped in classical literature, Fielding was as concerned about the debasement of Latin and Greek authors as about the corruption of his own language, and he recognized that his readers were often unable to distinguish true from false learning because they were blinded by their own prejudices or because they lacked sufficient knowledge. Therefore, he manipulated classical allusions and quotations to encourage his readers to reassess these ways of judging character.

Two factors have hindered a thorough analysis of the importance of the classics in Fielding's presentation of his characters and narrator. First, Lucian's reputed influence has encouraged scholars to regard the classical allusions and quotations as purely ornamental. Assuming that Fielding imitated Lucian when he quoted other authors, Christopher Robinson has argued that, like the Greek satirist, Fielding used quotations and allusions merely for display or entertainment.[2] As we have seen, Lucian did *not* influence Fielding as strongly as scholars have assumed and the quotations and allusions occur far too often to be ornamental. Such a theory also does not account for the obvious differences in the way that the characters and narrators use classics, suggesting that the quotations and allusions deserve closer scrutiny.

The standard view of Fielding's method of characterization has also discouraged serious consideration of his characters' quotations and allusions. Scholars have generally adopted John Coolidge's approach to Fielding's characters: he argues that in *Joseph Andrews* and *Tom Jones* Fielding presents characters fully when he first describes them and that they remain consistent throughout the rest of the novel. Only in *Amelia* does Fielding attempt to mislead his readers by providing false or incomplete information.[3] Although some critics have questioned the applicability of this view to individual characters, none has challenged the validity of its basic assumptions.[4] Because Fielding's readers did not share the same background in classics, they undoubtedly responded to his references to ancient literature differently, and they would not all similarly judge characters who use the classics. Consequently, we must ask if Coolidge's argument about conservation of character in Fielding needs some revision.

Fielding's allusions and quotations raise some tantalizing questions about his characters and narrators. What do the classical references reveal about his implied readers and the way in which they view those who use classics? How does his characters' and narrators' use of ancient literature alter the audience's perception of the role the classical tradition plays in their society? How do quotations and allusions shape his readers' interpretation of the narrator and the characters who employ them?

A review of his classical citations suggests that Fielding anticipated different responses from his readers. Through the allusions and quotations, he depicted the abuse of classical tradition in eighteenth-century society and explored its limitations as a means of communicating truth among those who did not thoroughly appreciate ancient literature. Furthermore, Fielding exploited classics in order to undermine the credibility of his most influential characters and to teach his readers to be discerning about "exemplary" figures they encounter in fiction and real life. He offered the narrator as a model for using classics appropriately in the eighteenth century, thus enhancing his authority and reinforcing his bond with his audience.

Classical References and Fielding's Readers

Fielding knew that his readers varied radically in their knowledge of the classics, and he shows his sensitivity to these different audiences when he depicts his characters' reactions to others who use ancient allusions and quotations. While their responses provide some key to the differences that Fielding anticipated among his readers, they offer his audiences a mirror in which they can view their own way of judging those who use the classics, enabling them to assess their reactions more objectively.

Because many of the characters in the novels have no classical training, their responses often have little to do with the quality of what they hear and depend more on their opinion of the person addressing them. Very often illiterate or semiliterate audiences accept classical allusions and Latin quotations as evidence of the speaker's authority and learning if the speaker is one whom they consider their superior. For example, Shamela praises Williams's learning after he uses a few mangled Latin phrases, and Mrs. Tow-wouse is greatly impressed when the doctor rattles off a Latin and a Greek quotation, firmly convinced from Adams's silence that he has been put in his place.[5] Murphy the lawyer gains the respect of inmates at the prison in *Amelia* because his speech bristles with legal Latin; in fact, Miss Mathews claims that he is too learned for her (bk. 1, chap. 10, pp. 60–61). These audiences, incapable of judging the validity of the references they hear, consider them authoritative when they come from an individual whom they respect or whose ideas they approve.

Regardless of class, characters without classical learning respond negatively when others of whom they disapprove use Latin phrases and other classical references. Such reactions often reflect a low opinion of the speaker or ignorance about what has been said. When Adams argues that ancient literature is superior to actual travel, the innkeeper dismisses his classical references as unimportant, in part because they contradict his own prejudices (*Joseph Andrews*, bk. 2, chap. 17, pp. 180–84). Mrs. Slipslop reveals her hostility to classical learning among classes she considers inferior when Adams suggests that Joseph learn Latin; she argues that footmen do not need education, especially when their masters have none (bk. 1, chap. 3, p. 26). Lady Booby also expresses her impatience with Adams's attempts to show off his son's Latin learning, demonstrating her own ignorance of the classics and her disdain for the parson and his family (bk. 4, chap. 9, pp. 314–15). In *Tom Jones* Squire Western belittles the lawyer's use of Latin phrases to assess the legality of Blifil's theft of Sophia's bird (bk. 4, chap. 4, 1:164). Since most characters think he is little better than a servant, Partridge evokes some of the most violent responses. For example, both the serjeant and the landlady at Upton become furious with him after he uses Latin phrases that, in their ignorance, they assume are insults (*Tom Jones*, bk. 9, chap. 6, 1:517; bk. 10, chap. 4, 2:540–41). Displays of feminine learning arouse great suspicion in both *Tom Jones* and *Amelia*; to the characters in Fielding's novels, no respectable woman would use Latin, and those who do cannot possibly do so correctly.[6]

Characters with a smattering of classical education respond in very similar ways to the use of classical quotation. Like the illiterate, they are frequently guided by their perceptions of the speaker, not by the quality of his or her learning. For example, "wits," whose total knowledge of Latin consists of a few mangled citations out of Lily's Latin grammar, receive high praise from those who share their limited command of the classics.[7] This audience frequently greets superior learning with suspicion and aggression. When Adams appears before the judge, the parson and the rest of the gentlemen assembled distrust his references to Aeschylus and assume incorrectly that he has stolen the Greek text in his possession (*Joseph Andrews*, bk. 2, chap. 11, pp. 148–49). Northerton rails against Homer and other classical authors because they remind him of his mistreatment at school, reflecting his own ignorance and his aversion to Tom (*Tom Jones*, bk. 7, chap. 4, 1:372–73). The only character who reacts positively to a show of superior learning is Mr. Wilson, who believes that Adams is a bishop because he can discuss Homer at length and recite a hundred lines of the *Iliad* in Greek (*Joseph Andrews*, bk. 3, chap. 2, pp. 196–99).[8]

The most reliable responses come from those characters who have the greatest knowledge of Latin and Greek. Often the reaction of the learned listener reveals the faultiness of the quotation or allusion another has used. For example, Tom's criticism of Partridge's inappropriate quotations provides the reader with evidence that his companion is not the master of Latin that he claims to be, and Tom also reveals the faulty learning of the Man of the Hill when he smiles at a misapplied reference to Horace (*Tom Jones*, bk. 12, chap. 3, 2:628, 676–77; bk. 8, chap. 13, 1:471–72). Harrison's incisive comments about the classical quotations and allusions used by the young clergyman and Mrs. Atkinson provide some indication of the deficiencies in the learning of each.[9] Because of their superior learning, classically literate characters reveal that ancient allusions vary widely in their validity.[10]

But even characters with genuine knowledge of ancient literature have trouble consistently assessing what they hear because very often they are blinded by their prejudices toward the speaker. Dr. Harrison and the young clergyman with whom he converses each distrust the other's learning. Harrison's reactions to characters who use classics in *Amelia* are also colored by the conviction that he is preeminent in classical learning; his hostility to the views of both Colonel Bath and Mrs. Atkinson arises partially because they do not pay due homage to his extensive knowledge.[11] These characters demonstrate that learning does not insulate an individual from mistaken judgments; even Fielding's learned readers need to attend objectively to the classical references used by others.

Occasionally a learned audience responds with complete ignorance to a classical reference or quotation. For example, although Adams is very conscious of incorrect form in classical quotations, he is easily taken in by someone who seems to have classical authority. He reacts enthusiastically to the gentleman at the squire's house who relates the story of Socrates and the king, in part because it flatters him, and, when Wilson mentions classical subjects, Adams also responds spiritedly (*Joseph Andrews*, bk. 3, chap. 8, pp. 249–51; bk. 3, chap. 2, pp. 196–99). Although he demonstrates a certain amount of classical learning himself, he is incapable of discernment about the learning of those towards whom he is well disposed.

By portraying so many different reactions, Fielding suggests that the differences among audience responses are determined not by class but by the level of classical learning, the type of utterance, and the predispositions of the hearer. The similarities between the responses of those with different levels of learning indicate that readers must be wary of determining the validity of a classical reference from audiences in the novels, since even the well-educated can be blinded by their preconceptions. Thus, Fielding uses classical quotations as a means to train his readers to abandon stock responses to those who use classics and judge each person individually by his or her actions.

Through his characters and some of his narrators, Fielding also demonstrates how professionals, writers, and others in his society have perverted the classical tradition by exploiting it for selfish reasons.

Professionals, Wits, and the Misuse of Classics

Once Fielding's readers become aware of their own responses to classics in the novels, they become more attentive to characters who allude to ancient literature. Glenn Hatfield has analyzed Fielding's concern with the corruption of language in various segments of eighteenth-century society.[12] Fielding also demonstrates how those who exploit ancient literature have robbed ancient languages of their original meaning by wrenching quotations from their original contexts in order to impress those around them with the appearance of learning.

Since Fielding's readers certainly expected the clergy to be the most learned of all those who use the classics, other characters often refer matters requiring classical training to the local cleric. When a question arises about the book in Adams's possession, for example, the judge and his companions logically turn to the parson, because they think that he is the only one among them with the requisite learning (*Joseph Andrews*, bk. 2, chap. 11, pp. 148–49). For the clerics, Latin is as much a mark of their authority as their cassocks: both Williams and Supple believe that their ability to cite Latin demonstrates their superiority over others, and Supple particularly betrays his condescending attitude when he carefully explains to Sophia that he is quoting a "classical line" and gives her the name of its author (*Tom Jones*, bk. 4, chap. 10, 1:188, 189–90). Although Supple is convinced that his learning sets him above his audience and adds to the weight of his opinion, such gratuitous information can mean little to the young woman. The respect that these citations usually evoke from listeners (and possibly from some of Fielding's uneducated readers) demonstrates the power of the classics to lend automatic credibility to any argument.

Despite the aura of learning generated by such allusions, readers with a minimal amount of classical training—that is, who had studied such works as Lily's Latin grammar and the *Epigrammatum Delectus*—could easily see that the learning of Fielding's minor clergy is not very extensive. Many of their snippets of Latin are proverbial or come from standard sources that anyone with rudimentary knowledge of Latin had probably memorized in school. For example, Williams's entire store of classical learning consists of three short phrases and a misquotation of a line in the *Epigrammatum Delectus*; of Supple's three attempts at Latin, two are quotations of Juvenal found in Lily's grammar, and the other is a two-word phrase from Horace that he could have learned in school.[13] Both the parson who examines Adams's Aeschylus and the Ordinary of Newgate who counsels Jonathan Wild display their ignorance without using any Latin at all. Even though the parson recognizes that the writing in Adams's book is Greek, he mistakes it for the catechism. The Ordinary reveals the limits of his knowledge by stating that he could not describe the pains of Hell even if he had "the Eloquence of *Cicero*, or of *Tully*" (*Jonathan Wild*, bk. 4, chap. 13, p. 241). Although he maintains that both Plato and Aristotle spoke foolishness, the Ordinary refrains from quoting any specific passages because, he claims, they are too numerous to mention (bk. 4, chap. 13, p. 249); after his inaccurate comment about Cicero, Fielding's readers must wonder if he could cite any passages at all.

Although the quotations by Fielding's clerics are superficial because they largely come from school texts, readers with extensive classical training would realize that such citations also demonstrate ignorance of the *substance* of classical literature. The original contexts of many classical references reveal that the clergymen drastically misapply the classics they use. For example, Parson Williams in *Shamela* speaks of Booby's "ingenium versatile," suggesting that he has always been prone to vice (22–23); only Fielding's more learned readers would recognize that the phrase comes from a passage in Livy where it describes Cato the Elder, well known for his moral rectitude. Supple uses Juvenal's "rara avis in Terris, nigroque simillima Cygno" to describe the dress that Molly Seagrim wore to church, even though in its original context the line refers to the ideal maiden that a man would choose to marry (*Tom Jones*, chap. 4, bk. 10, 1:188). Their abuse of classical literature symbolizes the shallowness of all their learning. Their quotations are so inappropriate to the situations in which they have used them that learned readers can only assume that the clergy have gotten these passages from handbooks and have never read the works from which they were originally taken. Just as they misapply Latin and Greek literature, the clergy misdirect their religious learning to mask their own vices or vindicate individuals whose favor they desire. They demonstrate that preserving the outward appearance of religion and learning is more important to them than remaining faithful to their substance.

Professionals of various kinds show a similar tendency to capitalize on the ignorance of their audience and intimidate their listeners with an empty show of learning. Lawyers use legal jargon in Latin, which frequently silences their opposition, who cannot understand it. Because people trained in the classics have difficulty following their unique brand of Latin, however, readers must wonder whether even the lawyers themselves comprehend the meaning of their Latin phrases. For example, in *Amelia* Murphy rattles off a series of tags when he discusses the legal situation of Miss Mathews, but Booth, who has a fairly extensive background in ancient languages, is unable to understand him (bk. 1, chap. 10, pp. 60–64). Fielding confirms the reader's suspicion that the lawyer's learning is less than his legal jargon suggests when Murphy tells Miss Mathews that *Tace* (be silent) actually means "candle."[14]

Doctors in Fielding's novels also exploit the ignorance of those around them by using classical tags that their listeners do not understand so that they can impress their patients and prevent close scrutiny of their methods. At the same time, Fielding's educated readers can see that their misuse of the classics reveals the superficiality of their learning. After the doctor in *Joseph Andrews* tries to put off Adams's questions by showing off his superior knowledge of Galen and Hippocrates, he rattles off the Latin phrase *Veniente occurite Morbo* and the Greek *Ton dapomibominos poluflosboio Thalasses* to demonstrate his command of these two languages (bk. 1, chap. 14, pp. 62–63). In addition to the grammatical mistake (*veniente* should read *venienti*), readers with a minimal classical education could recognize the Latin citation as a tag out of Lily's Latin grammar, while those with some Greek would know that the second quotation is a jumble of two unrelated phrases from the *Iliad*. The surgeon who initially looks after Tom uses another hackneyed Latin phrase to speak of festering wounds: *Nemo repente fuit turpissimus* (No one was completely depraved suddenly) (*Tom Jones*, bk. 7, chap. 8, 1:380–81). Some of Fielding's readers would know that this phrase comes from the short quotations in the *Epigrammatum Delectus*; others, who recognized the original passage in Juvenal, would realize that the phrase applies to moral degeneracy, not wounds.

Clergymen, doctors, and lawyers are not the only ones in Fielding's novels whose use of classical learning reveals their ignorance; the novels are full of characters who have minimal classical training but abuse it to demonstrate their superiority over others. Often their incorrect citations backfire because their grammatical errors rob their Latin and Greek of meaning, betraying not their wisdom but their ignorance. The wits in both *Joseph Andrews* and *Amelia* think that they will intimidate Adams and Booth's party with a series of Latin quotations, but classically literate readers of Fielding's novels would realize that the phrases they use are mangled versions of Latin tags taken from Lily's grammar (*Joseph Andrews*, bk. 2, chap. 11, pp. 146–47; *Amelia*, bk. 9, chap. 9, p. 396). For example, one of the wits confronting Adams offers this line: "Molle meum levibus cord est vilebile Telis." By corrupting several words of the original—*levibusque*, *cor*, and *violabile*—the wit turns hackneyed but intelligible Latin into gibberish. His next quotation is even more meaningless, since it consists of a list of Latin nouns in the masculine gender. Such gibberish signals the logical result of the separation of learned forms from their content; the attempts of wits to pass these snippets off as learning demonstrate their own emptiness and that of the society around them.

Other characters with a smattering of classical learning use it to justify their own prejudices about the world. Jonathan Wild considers the characters in classical epics proof of the antiquity of priggism (bk. 1, chap. 3, p. 12). Square in *Tom Jones* cites classical philosophers to rationalize the pursuit of his own desires, adopting either Plato's or Aristotle's views as convenient (bk. 3, chap. 3, 1:124–25). Colonel Bath in *Amelia* cites the example of the epic heroes to defend his penchant for dueling (bk. 9, chap. 3, pp. 365–66). Such figures exploit ancient literature by using it to validate their own behavior, even when its morality is questionable.[15]

A few characters in *Amelia* render classical quotations even more meaningless by aping those they consider their "betters." One of the female inmates of the prison repeats Murphy's legal *se defendendo* in her own mangled version, indicating that she has no idea of the import of what she says (bk. 1, chap. 10, p. 62). The keeper of the prison warns Booth to be careful about his clothing and his company, repeating the words of the lawyer Murphy, *Noscitur a sosir;* from the keeper's statements, readers cannot tell if he thinks the quotation should be applied to Booth's dress or his companions (bk. 2, chap. 9, p. 98). The bailiff who tricks Booth into leaving his house also turns a citation from Virgil into a meaningless phrase (bk. 8, chap. 1, p. 309). While these sayings might impress those who understand no Latin whatsoever, such misquotations reveal both the ignorance of these characters and their social aspirations, since they unwittingly betray their own perception of the Latin phrases used by others; like the lawyers, doctors, and clergy they respect, they use ancient languages to give the appearance of learning. In other words, they use classics for ornamentation—and are judged for doing so. Their inferiority to their sources is demonstrated by their inability to preserve even the correct form of the original.

Female characters also attempt to show off what classical learning they have acquired in order to impress others and dominate their uneducated listeners. All readers could judge the quality of Aunt Western's classical learning from the books she owns, because the only one pertaining to the ancient world is Echard's *Roman History*, which Fielding criticizes in *A Journey from this World to the Next* (*Tom Jones*, bk. 6, chap. 2, 1:273; *Journey*, bk. 1, chap. 9, p. 44). Although her classical knowledge is clearly limited, she is fond of citing ancient authorities to silence Sophia and Squire Western. When the squire is reluctant to propose a match with Blifil, she cites King Alcinous in "*Pope's* Odyssey" as precedent, and she reminds Sophia about "what *Plato* says" about a child's obedience to a parent (*Tom Jones*, bk. 6, chap. 2, 1:277; bk. 7, chap. 3, 1:336). The shallowness of her knowledge is readily apparent when she tells Sophia that the philosophers Socrates and Alcibiades did not ask the opinions of their students (bk. 7, chap. 3, 1:332). Even readers with classical learning gained from translations would know that the cornerstone of Socrates' method was dialectic and would also recall that Alcibiades was not a philosopher.

Although she does not claim to have the classical scholarship of Aunt Western, Lady Bellaston also invokes ancient examples to dismiss Lord Fellamar's objections to raping Sophia. She reinterprets the stories of Helen and the Sabine women in order to prove that women respond well to such violent treatment and that he has history on his side (*Tom Jones*, bk. 15, chap. 4, 2:794-95). Clearly, Lady Bellaston will adopt any means of persuasion to achieve her goals, but her choice of such references suggests the cachet of ancient authorities. By resorting to these sources despite her limited knowledge, she also shows how little she thinks of her audience and of classical tradition itself.

Fielding's minor characters demonstrate how professionals, wits, women, and others have all robbed classical tradition of its meaning by separating its *form* from its *content*, thus reminding readers who could evaluate their flawed quotations that the classical tradition was often meaningless in the modern world. Fielding was also concerned that modern writers lacked sufficient grounding in the classics; he examines the effects of their poor training when he portrays the narrators of *Shamela* and *Jonathan Wild*.

Shamela, Jonathan Wild, and Fielding's Satire on Narrators

In both *Shamela* and *Jonathan Wild* Fielding presents a narrative persona similar to the one who appears in the *True Patriot* and the *Jacobite's Journal*—the bumbling author, whose abuse of classical learning betrays his prejudices and ignorance. Eric Rothstein and Leo Braudy have explored how the narrators of *Shamela* and *Jonathan Wild* satirize specific writers like Colley Cibber and Conyers Middleton and certain kinds of historians.[16] These narrative personae also demonstrate how writers and critics in the eighteenth century misused the classical tradition, and they imply the alternative that Fielding will offer in the narrators of his other novels.

Like the characters in Fielding's fiction, the narrators of *Shamela* and *Jonathan Wild* so mangle their classical allusions and quotations that they undermine their credibility rather than reinforce it. While Keyber's assertion in *Shamela* that he has modeled his style on Euclid is clearly a part of the topical satire on Cibber and Middleton that Rothstein has treated extensively, the reference also shows that he cannot distinguish between classical authors whose style should serve as a model and writers like Euclid, whose works were important only for nonliterary reasons (dedication, xi–xii). Such an obvious mistake in judgment undermines the validity of Keyber's narrative, encouraging readers to question whether he has chosen an appropriate subject for his biography. Parson Oliver reintroduces this issue when he compares Pamela's actual account with the "*Ciceronian* Eloquence" of her biographer (*Shamela*, 6). Although this statement is a topical allusion to Conyers Middleton's biography of Cicero, it also ironically implies the difference between Pamela's biographer and the ancient orator, who emphasized in his philosophical and rhetorical works that a writer or speaker must be sufficiently moral to know if he is employing rhetoric for moral ends.[17] According to Oliver, the author of Pamela's story has done just the opposite: he has made Pamela's life so appealing that his narrative encourages others to imitate her self-seeking lifestyle. The references to Euclid and Cicero reveal that the moderns have a limited understanding of the ancient world; in fact, Keyber knows so little that he conflates all classical writers. We cannot even tell from Oliver's remark if he realizes the incongruity of associating Pamela's narrative with Cicero. Both narrators demonstrate that modern writers cannot compare with the ancients because they lack the moral judgment to decide what material is suitable for a biography. Even readers with a knowledge of the classics gained through translations would recognize the faultiness of such distinctions.

Fielding's satire on the narrator of *Jonathan Wild* is even more extensive, since that narrator's pedantic misuse of classical learning and choice of Wild as a subject reinforce our condemnation of him. Braudy has shown that the narrator is a bad historian who tries to impose his own predetermined pattern on the life of his hero.[18] Through the narrator's misuse of classical citations, Fielding also suggests that his failure stems from his faulty understanding of ancient literature and history, from which he has drawn certain models without understanding their content or moral implications.

Because the narrator is the only source of quotations in *Jonathan Wild*, he seems to be the most credible authority in the novel, but a close examination of his quotations reveals his superficiality. Four of his sixteen quotations are two-word fragments that almost anyone could understand, and eight others appear in standard sources like Lily's Latin Grammar or the *Epigrammatum Delectus*, suggesting that his knowledge is secondhand.[19] The narrator even admits at one point that a quotation from Horace comes from Lily's grammar (bk. 2, chap. 12, p. 113). Readers with minimal Latin training, therefore, would realize that the narrator's show of learning is as unremarkable as it is pretentious.

But the narrator's limitations do not end there. When we compare his citations with their original contexts, we see that the narrator's application of these quotations is *always* faulty. He has so misused his references that those with classical training would recognize that the passages he quotes frequently achieve the opposite effect of what he intends. For example, after Wild's hanging, he cites a section from Lucan's *Pharsalia* to eulogize the great deeds of his hero (bk. 4, chap. 15, p. 260). In Lucan these lines describe Cato the Elder, known for his moral rectitude; therefore, the narrator has unwittingly used a classical reference that calls attention to Wild's moral depravity. His description of Laetitia backfires in a similar way when he quotes a line from Ovid's *Metamorphoses* to praise Laetitia's garments (bk. 1, chap. 9, p. 36). In Ovid the line refers to the raven, whose plumage changed from white to black because of its chattering tongue (*Metamorphoses* 2.541). Consequently, the quotation has a very different application to Laetitia than the one the narrator intends. Within the context of his description, he obviously means the classical citation as a compliment, but it actually highlights one of her most odious faults.[20]

The narrator's learning is not just superficial; it is also pedantic. The most obvious example of his pedantry occurs when he glosses Wild's comments about hats because his exposition does little to explicate the story; instead the narrator shows that he is so preoccupied with minor details that he ignores the larger perspective (bk. 2, chap. 6, p. 91). In fact, his citations from Latin and Greek authors demonstrate that he has no real understanding of his subject, Jonathan Wild, or of the classical authorities he cites. Yet another instance of his obsession with minutiae occurs when he derives the term *Honosty* from the Greek for "ass," a derivation that suggests he is willing to twist classical allusions to justify his own prejudices about his character and his thesis about greatness (bk. 4, chap. 15, p. 256). Even readers with no knowledge of Latin and Greek would see that such references undermine his credibility and show that his concern with detail blinds him to the real significance of historical events and characters.

With his references to classical historians, the narrator also implies that he is drawing an analogy between himself and the great historians and biographers of the ancient world—Lucan, Herodotus, Sallust, and Plutarch. In the beginning of his narrative, he cites Plutarch, Nepos, and Suetonius to demonstrate that historians should not bestow praise or blame on individuals too quickly, and twice he sees similarities between events in Wild's life and stories related by Herodotus (bk. 1, chap. 2, p. 2; bk. 1, chap. 3, pp. 9–10; bk. 3, chap. 1, pp. 120–21). To justify the discrepancy between Wild's speeches and his ungrammatical letter, he declares that he is using the precedent of Sallust, who wrote that the historian should embellish the actual speeches of the characters (bk. 3, chap. 7, p. 144). These references suggest that the narrator believes he is equal to the ancient historians whose techniques he has copied; they also imply that he considers his account of Wild's life equivalent to the work of these ancient writers. Readers who knew of such authors either in the original or translation would acknowledge the faultiness of this analogy. His misapplied citations and choice of subject undermine his claim by revealing he has assimilated the formal conventions of ancient histories and biographies without considering their ethical implications.

In his presentation of this narrative persona and that of *Shamela*, Fielding analyzes the limitations of both critics and writers of his time, whose superficial learning masks their inability to discriminate good literature from bad, good people from bad. Unlike the classical historians and epic writers they choose to imitate, the narrators of both *Shamela* and *Jonathan Wild* are not concerned with the moral issues involved in glamorizing the life of a villain. The narrators' faulty citations suggest a connection between their superficial understanding of classical history and their inability to judge successfully characters like Pamela and Wild. Instead of enhancing their credibility, their shallow learning encourages readers to doubt their assertions.

While the narrator's bungled classical allusions expose their limitations, they also impress the learned audience with Henry Fielding's cleverness. The ironic twist he gives to the narrator's classical references reveals that Fielding understands the substance of classical tradition well enough to exploit fully such opportunities. He implicitly draws a contrast between himself and the narrator, thus reinforcing his own authority as an author.

The misuse of classics by Fielding's minor characters and the narrators of *Shamela* and *Jonathan Wild* relates to his concern with the corruption of language in eighteenth-century society, since minor characters are more interested in the *form* than the *content* of classical quotations and allusions. When using any Latin tag, no matter how misapplied or unintelligible, they assume that such superior learning will impress their audience and will earn automatic credibility for their opinions. Thus, Fielding emphasizes that classical tags have been separated from their original meanings, if not reduced to gibberish. The misuse of the classical tradition also demonstrates how it has been exploited for selfish ends; because of the authority exerted by the ancient classics, characters twist what little learning they have to justify their own prejudices and manipulate those around them. From his portrayal of these characters and their misapplication of ancient wisdom, Fielding teaches his readers to be more discerning about those who use classics. Against this backdrop, where readers are taught to be wary of those who rely on classical authority, he encourages us to scrutinize more carefully a number of major characters whose hallmark is the use of classical literature.

Adams and the Relevance of the Classics in the Modern World

Through his major characters Fielding attempts to mislead his readers into making false assumptions in order to force them to reassess their way of judging people and viewing reality. One such character whom critics have sometimes misread is Abraham Adams, considered by many scholars as one of Fielding's most positive models for behavior.[21] But is Adams really an exemplary character? Some critics have questioned whether Fielding intends the reader to see him as a model; an examination of Adams's use of classical literature supports the skeptical interpretation of his character.[22]

In *Joseph Andrews* Fielding sets Adams apart from other characters because Adams alone has studied the classics in depth and uses his knowledge extensively in his speech. When Adams first appears, Fielding impresses the reader with his learning:

> Mr. *Abraham Adams* was an excellent Scholar. He was a perfect Master of the *Greek* and *Latin* Languages; to which he added a great Share of Knowledge in the Oriental Tongues, and could read and translate *French, Italian* and *Spanish*. He had applied many Years to the most severe Study, and had treasured up a Fund of Learning rarely to be met with in a University. (Bk. 1, chap. 3, pp. 22–23)

Fielding reinforces the initial impression created by this description by emphasizing the parson's fondness for Aeschylus; the choice of this author distinguishes Adams from others because few people in the eighteenth century could read Greek and, of the major Greek authors, Aeschylus was one of the least known.[23] Even if Fielding's readers were not familiar with the reputation of the Greek dramatist, they could divine it from the confused responses of the parson and Mr. Wilson to Adams's comments about this author, since neither recognizes Aeschylus. Adams's learning also probably impressed some readers of Fielding's novels (and many of his modern critics) in his two lengthy disquisitions on classical subjects and in his statement to Wilson that he has never read Homer in translation (*Joseph Andrews*, bk. 2, chap. 17, pp. 181-84; bk. 3, chap. 2, pp. 196-201; bk. 3, chap. 2, pp. 196–97).

Although Adams's classical learning surpasses that of the other characters, who use Latin and Greek references without understanding their original contexts, his application of that knowledge proves on close examination to be less original than it first appears. A surprising number of his Latin quotations are proverbial or come from standard sources: of nineteen quotations, eleven are short phrases of only two or three words that anyone with a minimal Latin education would be able to use, and three others appear in Lily or the *Epigrammatum Delectus*. Among the remaining five, at least one is a proverbial expression most schoolboys probably memorized.[24] Although all are aptly applied to the situations in which they are used, the unremarkable quality of Adams's quotations undermines our initial impression of his great learning and our unquestioning belief in his character.

Even the learning that he displays in his discussions with the innkeeper and Mr. Wilson is less impressive than it originally seems. To support his contention that he has learned far more about the world from books than the innkeeper has from travel, Adams rattles off a lengthy series of place-names and sites in the ancient world. But the unidentified quotation from Horace that he uses to lead off his discussion appears both in Lily and the *Epigrammatum Delectus*, and in his breathless catalog he also mistakes Daedalus for Icarus. Although Adams's recital may have impressed Fielding's less learned readers, those with classical training probably recognized that his list could have come as easily from secondary sources as from primary ones.

His treatment of Homer and the epic when he meets Wilson is quite similar. Even though Wilson is clearly impressed with Adams's show of learning, many of the sentiments Adams expresses appear in the standard discussions of the epic in the eighteenth century. In chapter 3 I pointed out that Adams covers the topics provided by Le Bossu in his treatise on the epic, and he also repeats the sentiments of the traditional authorities on Homer: Aristotle, Horace, and Cicero. Consequently, little of what Adams says would be new or unfamiliar to eighteenth-century audiences. Thus, while the parson's speech displays his knowledge of the *Iliad* and its critics, it also betrays his pedantic approach to the classical world.

Pedantry also marks his use of quotation throughout the novel. Adams seldom considers his audience when he uses Latin and Greek, and, because he almost always leaves his quotations unidentified and untranslated, he fails to communicate any message to his listeners, who are very often uneducated. Therefore, he cannot possibly expect that anyone will understand what he means by such references to ancient sources. His practice exemplifies his inability to translate the classical world and classical literature into a form that his eighteenth-century listeners can understand; quite literally, he speaks a foreign language. Thus, no one responds when he shouts "Eureka" (bk. 2, chap. 13, p. 161), the women are frightened when he raps out one hundred Greek verses (bk. 3, chap. 2, p. 199), and Lady Booby is impatient over his excitement with the *Quae Genus* (bk. 4, chap. 9, p. 314).

Adams's use of the classics enhances our awareness of his most prominent flaw—his conviction that he is the greatest schoolmaster in the world. This topic, which is introduced early in the novel when Adams expresses interest in teaching Joseph Latin (bk. 1, chap. 3, p. 26), is a prime example of Fielding's skill at misleading his readers. At first, Adams's belief seems a minor foible, which makes the character more realistic. As one would expect from a schoolmaster, many of his Latin phrases come from the standard Latin grammar, and his responses to others' use of classics are usually colored by a pedantic concern with technical correctness. For example, when the woman telling the story of Leonora mentions Croesus and Attalus, Adams automatically corrects her mispronunciation (bk. 2, chap. 4, p. 110). His sole reply to the wits who challenge him to cap verses is that his eight-year-old son knows the grammatical example better than they do (bk. 2, chap. 11, p. 147). In the amusement occasioned by such reactions, Fielding's readers could easily miss their significance; because Adams focuses rather on the form than the substance of what he hears, he risks missing the point of the classical references others use.

The faultiness of Adams's application of his classical knowledge becomes even more apparent when he and Joseph argue about the merits of public and private education (bk. 3, chap. 5, pp. 229–32). He punctuates his short speech on the superiority of a private education with a series of short Latin phrases, but because Joseph understands no Latin, Adams can hardly use the phrases to communicate to the young man. Fielding's readers can only conclude that Adams is taking advantage of his classical training and the ignorance of his audience to "prove" his superior wisdom and authority.[25] Like the pedants who fill Fielding's journalism and plays, then, Adams uses his classical learning not to teach but to intimidate others and show off his skill at accumulating a mass of detail.

Although he is vain about his teaching ability, Adams's standing as a pedagogue is completely undermined when he attempts to display the learning of his son Dick to Lady Booby (bk. 4, chap. 9, pp. 314–15). After he is told that his son has drowned, he reveals that the boy was an apt pupil and had progressed far for his years. But Dick's exhibition of his Latin for the company belies Adams's assertions, for he does not know the meaning of the verb *lego* and cannot even remember the imperative form. Because his best student needs extensive prompting, readers see that, though Adams may know his own Latin well, he has difficulty instructing others in what he has learned.

Through Adams's use of the classics, therefore, Fielding suggests that the character is less exemplary than critics have assumed. Although he has clearly read extensively in both the Latin and Greek classics, he does not communicate the substance of what he has read in a form that his audiences can understand. When he displays his learning, he also reveals his pedantry; he is more interested in repeating a string of secondhand opinions that will impress his audience than with communicating ancient wisdom to those around him. In his teaching, he is preoccupied with form, which frequently blinds him to abuses of substance. Consequently, Adams represents the limitations of relying too heavily on the ancient world for authority; he shows one risks devaluing experience totally, and he demonstrates that not all classical learning is necessarily good. Though he has read Latin and Greek literature, it has not given him any insight into those around him, so that his knowledge of the classical world does little to prepare him adequately to face his own.

While Adams shows the dangers of too much classical knowledge indiscriminately applied to modern situations, Partridge reveals the problems created by too little learning placed in the wrong hands.

Partridge, Tom, and Classics among the Lower Classes

In *Tom Jones* Fielding explores another type of classical learning through his portrait of Partridge, Tom's companion. Although, like Adams, Partridge prides himself on his skill as a schoolmaster and fills his speech with snippets of Latin and Greek, the shallowness of his learning brings him closer to minor characters than the parson. Thus, Partridge reveals the problems that occur when those with a superficial classical education attempt to use it extensively.

Early in the novel Fielding demonstrates that Partridge has limitations both as scholar and schoolmaster. As Fielding observes, Partridge offers no challenge to Eton or Westminster, and few of his students have much ability (bk. 2, chap. 3, 1:82); he later acquiesces when his wife dismisses Jenny Jones, in part because he is well aware that her Latin learning has begun to surpass his own (bk. 2, chap. 3, 1:85). Partridge's library also indicates the quality of his learning. Among his books are Echard's *Roman History*, Pope's Homer, and two works in Latin: *Ovid de Tristibus* and *Gradus ad Parnassum* (bk. 8, chap. 5, 1:421-42). Readers with classical training would know that the first was probably a schoolbook and that Ovid is one of the easiest Latin authors; the *Gradus* is a lexicon from which students memorized vocabulary and Latin *sententiae* used to illustrate specific meanings. Partridge's pride in this collection suggests that he does not appreciate how superficial his knowledge is.

Despite the obvious limitations of his Latin learning, Partridge frequently employs Latin tags in his speech, which would betray to Fielding's educated readers his scanty knowledge of ancient literature. Nearly half of his tags (twenty-two out of fifty-one) appear either in Lily or the *Epigrammatum Delectus*, and twelve of the other phrases are short enough that any schoolboy with a little Latin could produce them.[26] Like the narrator of *Jonathan Wild*, Partridge sometimes freely admits that he learned some of these sayings from textbooks (bk. 12, chap. 3, 2:630). He also unwittingly betrays his second-hand learning when he asks Tom to translate a quotation from Horace because he finds that Latin author too difficult (bk. 12, chap. 3, 2:629); Fielding's educated readers would find this comment ironic, since six of his tags come from that Latin author.

With his superficial training, Partridge exemplifies how classical tradition has been misused by the moderns. According to the standards of eighteenth-century society, his learning is remarkable for one of his class—even Tom acknowledges that his attainments are far superior to those of the average barber (bk. 7, chap. 5, 1:419)—but Partridge cannot apply his learning meaningfully. Because his range of *sententiae* is small, he repeats the same tags over and over again, regardless of context, and often his quotations are applied to situations at odds with their original significance.[27] Twice he uses the phrase *Tempus edax Rerum* (bk. 8, chap. 5, 1:421; bk. 8, chap. 13, 1:471); in both instances Partridge uses the phrase to imply that time heals all wounds, whereas in Ovid it suggests that time devours all things young and healthy. While readers with basic Latin education would recognize the phrase from Lily's Latin grammar, then, more learned readers, who knew the original passage in Ovid's *Metamorphoses*, would know that he has completely missed the sense of the Latin phrase.[28]

Partridge's knowledge of forms without content encourages him to assert himself in situations where he should not, especially when it prompts him to correct those whose education and social status is superior to his own. For example, during the story of the Man of the Hill, Partridge interjects his own corrections and comments whenever the Man uses classical references. After the Man identifies his mother as "Xantippe," Partridge comments, "'so was the Wife of *Socrates* called,'" clearly a gratuitous remark since only the Man and Tom are present (bk. 8, chap. 11, 1:451). Later he corrects the

Man's grammar when he cites a line from Ovid that happens to appear in Lily (bk. 8, chap. 12, 1:461–62). When Tom quotes a lengthy passage from Horace, Partridge attempts to match it with a short tag culled from his grammar (bk. 12, chap. 3, 2:629). Tom finally becomes impatient after Partridge tries to chastise him for using an incorrect form while they argue over using Sophia's money, observing that Partridge ignores the content of his master's argument and focuses only on his grammar (bk. 12, chap. 13, 2:676). Although Partridge believes his learning is equal to that of the educated people around him, his pedantic responses betray his limited command of the forms of ancient literature and his complete ignorance of its substance.

Another problem with Partridge's use of the classics is his choice of audience when he displays his learning. Often he employs Latin to address Tom, who has enough knowledge to understand him, but he also uses tags with those who cannot possibly know what he is saying: the people in the kitchen at Upton (bk. 9, chap. 6, 1:515-17), Mrs. Honour (bk. 10, chap. 4, 2:540-41), and a clerk (bk. 12, chap. 7, 2:646). When he meets with hostile responses from these audiences, he does not attempt to clarify his statements, revealing that he is not concerned with using the classics as a means of communication. Instead, he wants his classical tags to set him apart from the servants, innkeepers, soldiers, and barbers whom he and Tom encounter on their travels. Over and over he asserts that he is not a servant, and his classical quotations signal his pretensions to higher social status. With his Latin tags Partridge attempts to assert his equality with characters like Tom, the Man of the Hill, and even Allworthy; by matching their learning, Partridge believes that he can also share their social status. But his "learning" achieves the opposite effect since, far from impressing those he considers beneath him, his Latin phrases often offend others. Instead of earning Tom's respect, he is abused because of his faulty citations, signaling that he is much closer to the servants than to their masters.

In demonstrating the limitations of lower-class learning, Partridge also provides a contrast to Tom. While Fielding gives no lengthy account of Tom's tutelage under Thwackum, readers can infer his ability in the classics from his quotations; even when he uses short tags, Tom demonstrates a genuine knowledge of the original Latin authors, and in two instances he quotes fairly lengthy passages of Horace.[29] Unlike Partridge, who indiscriminately uses Latin without any consideration for his audience, Tom judiciously tailors his use to his listeners, disclosing a greater sensitivity to those around him, which evokes a more positive response from the novel's readers. With Partridge he uses fairly short Latin tags that his companion will understand and translates longer quotations.[30] In speaking to the Man of the Hill, he makes a passing reference to Cicero that shows deference to his listener's learning (bk. 8, chap. 15, 1:485). The only problem with Tom's use of the classics is that he frequently misjudges the expertise of his audience. Because he assumes that the officers share his knowledge of ancient epic, Tom compares their soldiers to the Greeks and the Trojans (bk. 7, chap. 12, 1:372–73), and he assumes that the lawyer Dowling knows enough Latin to recognize without a translation a lengthy quotation from Horace praising Lalage. The lawyer's response, however, indicates that he has no real understanding of the content and has probably never read any Latin (bk. 12, chap. 10, 2:659–60). Therefore, though Tom's use of Latin demonstrates greater restraint than that of his companion, his choice of audiences underscores his lack of judgment.

In *Joseph Andrews* and *Tom Jones* Fielding employs classical allusions and quotations to suggest that many characters are not as exemplary as they first appear, demonstrating that he reveals his characters more slowly than Coolidge has argued. The classical quotations and allusions also challenge the standard view about Fielding's method of characterization, because they indicate that Fielding's presentation of Harrison and the other major characters in *Amelia* does not differ substantially from his practice in the earlier novels.

AMELIA AND THE ABUSE OF AUTHORITY

Amelia has posed difficulties for Fielding scholars because, unlike his other novels, it lacks the guiding presence of the omniscient narrator. Repeatedly, they have sought a character who represents the "norm" in the novel against which the behavior of the others characters can be measured. As Battestin's notes to the Wesleyan edition imply, all too often scholars have considered Dr. Harrison, one of the most learned characters in all of Fielding's writing, to be that normative figure.[31] An examination of Harrison's use of the classics, however, suggests substantial flaws in this character that undermine his credibility as an authority figure and as the mouthpiece for Fielding's opinions; this indicates that the novel is more similar to his earlier work than scholars have generally assumed.

At first Harrison seems a plausible substitute for the authority of the narrative persona, since he is the only character in Fielding's novels who undeniably demonstrates his facility with both Latin and Greek. Very few of his quotations and allusions come from standard sources, and many are of sufficient length to preclude the possibility that he learned them out of manuals. Many of his discussions about the classics are fairly lengthy, including references to a number of different classical scholars, among whom are Dacier, Eustathius, and Barnes. He alludes to a wide range of authors in both languages; he shows a special fondness for Thucydides, whom he quotes in English twice (bk. 3, chap. 10, pp. 139–40; bk. 4, chap. 3, p. 166).[32] He even has sufficient knowledge of texts to argue very closely with the gentleman's son and to correct a fine point about Virgil when he speaks with Mrs. Atkinson (bk. 9, chap. 8, pp. 388–91; bk. 10, chap. 1, pp. 408–10). He is also clearly considered an authority by many other characters. Both Amelia and her sister repeat classical sayings they have heard him use, and Miss Mathews comments on his authority and learning (bk. 2, chap. 7, p. 121; bk. 10, chap. 9, p. 451; bk. 2, chap. 3, p. 77). Even Booth, whose classical learning is substantial, looks to the cleric for guidance and does not dispute his authority. Fielding seems to lead his readers to believe that they should trust the judgments of this character about other characters and the world in general.

While Harrison is undoubtedly learned, a more careful look at his use of the classics undermines our initial impression. Especially revealing is his letter to Booth and his wife, reporting that Amelia's mother has died and that Amelia has been disinherited (bk. 3, chap. 10, pp. 136-40). Although Harrison's two Latin quotations and translation of Thucydides initially impress readers with his learning, this string of ancient authorities is inappropriate in this situation. First, Harrison cannot resist the temptation to be pedantic; after quoting a line from Cicero in Latin (without a translation), he writes, "'Which Passage, with much more to the same Purpose, you will find in the Third Book of his *Tusculan Disputations*'" (p. 138). Such statements in a consolatory letter are at best gratuitous, especially because Amelia has no classical learning whatsoever. Consequently, such suggestions for further reading leave the reader with the impression that Harrison is more concerned with displaying his erudition than with comforting the Booths. Second, Harrison reveals that he worries more about the cold reception that his ideas receive in the outside world than with the suffering of his parishioners when he quite aptly compares himself with the Roman *Aretalogi*, philosophers who were treated as buffoons. Because he does not gloss this reference, neither Amelia or Booth may get his meaning. The notes appended by the narrator to translate the Latin phrases and explain other classical references serve as silent comments on Harrison's learning; like Amelia, many in Fielding's audience would need help to understand the doctor's message.

The failure of this letter is reinforced in the exchange between Booth and Miss Mathews after he finishes reading it. Miss Mathews completely misses its main point. Although Harrison advises the Booths not to make too much of the affairs of this world and to forget their loss of Mrs. Harris's fortune, Miss Mathews initially regrets that the Booth family has not come into the inheritance. After chiding her for missing the point of the doctor's letter, Booth shows that he too has not really gotten its message. While admiring the philosophy of this epistle, Booth calls attention to Dr. Harrison's loan of one hundred pounds, which, to him, is much more important than all the philosophy. Thus, Harrison's classical learning does not have the effect intended, because even Booth, who can read and understand all his quotations, does not obtain the message from this sermon that he should.

Harrison's credibility is also undermined when he employs his classical learning to dominate other characters, especially those who do not sufficiently respect his superior wisdom. After the young clergyman argues that benevolence is a heathen concept, citing the character of Axylus in Homer, Harrison quickly stresses that the young man has relied heavily on Joshua Barnes for his opinion and show of learning and counters his opponent by citing biblical and classical authorities to demonstrate that his own opinion is more correct (bk. 9, chap. 8, pp. 388–89). Although Harrison's corrections do prove that the young clergyman has gotten much of his learning from secondary sources, they also reveal the pedantic streak implicit in his letter to the Booths. Not surprisingly, Harrison's disquisition on benevolence has little effect on the young man, for later both the gentleman and his son demonstrate that any respect they have shown for the doctor is a sham and that they have humored him because both hope that he will use his influence to further the son's clerical career (bk. 9, chap. 10, pp. 404–5).

Harrison's most venomous attacks are reserved for Mrs. Atkinson, Fielding's most extended portrait of the learned lady. This type is especially repugnant to the doctor, for whom the ideal woman is Amelia. He is somewhat offended by the challenge to his learning from a university-trained scholar, but Mrs. Atkinson's pretenses to equality in learning are completely intolerable to him. In their conversation, he counters her assertion that women can master classical learning by domesticating a series of current debates about the importance of various classical authors (bk. 10, chap. 1, pp. 407–10). Reducing a scholarly dispute to a disagreement between a man and his wife, Harrison expresses his own contempt for the abilities of the woman, since his discussion implies that she is incapable of understanding the situation on any other level. When Mrs. Atkinson refuses to accept his "superior" argument, Harrison then attempts to show her that her understanding of Latin grammar is faulty. But his focus on minor grammatical points suggests that the debate is not progressing as he anticipated and underscores the preoccupation with minor points that is the hallmark of his interest in classics. As in other situations, his show of learning hardly achieves its intended effect, since both he and Mrs. Atkinson acquire a hatred for each other as a result of their debate and both are more confirmed in their opinions than before.[33]

Harrison often uses his knowledge to dominate other characters, and, like many of the figures in Fielding's novels, to stifle resistance to his opinions. Regardless of his audience, he seldom translates his Latin or Greek quotations, leaving the impression that he is not trying to use his classical expertise to educate his listeners but to dominate them by demonstrating his superior mastery of classical authorities. Although he wears his classical learning like his clerical attire to lend credibility to whatever he proposes, this abuse of classical learning suggests that Harrison is not much better than those who know only the forms of ancient literature and not the substance.

Harrison's learning does not help him guide others in the novel, and in many instances it does not enhance his ability to act. Despite his extensive reading, he readily believes the lies told by Booth's neighbors and imprisons Booth for debt. He is also blind to the moral problems inherent in the epics he loves. Rather than appreciating the classical knowledge of others, he frequently considers it a threat to his authority. Like Adams, whose reading in the Stoic writers does not ultimately prevent him from overreacting to his son's "drowning," Harrison's experience of classical literature has not enabled him to gain control of his own passions.

In *Amelia* Booth and Mrs. Atkinson offer the two major alternatives to Harrison's abuse of classical learning, but they prove to be as unsatisfactory as the doctor. In his command of Latin and Greek, Booth's learning seems to match that of his mentor. As the narrator tells us, his father had brought him up with a tolerable share of Greek and Latin, and, of all the characters, Harrison shows the greatest respect for his learning (bk. 3, chap. 5, p. 324). In discussions with both Mrs. Atkinson and the author at the sponging house, he displays knowledge of several different authors and works (bk. 6, chap. 7, pp. 257–59; bk. 8, chap. 5, pp. 324–30). His use of the classics seems more judicious than Harrison's, for, unlike the doctor, he refrains from gratuitous classical references and mentions the ancients only with audiences likely to understand them. When speaking to Miss Mathews and his wife, for example, he seldom resorts to Latin or Greek phrases.[34] Therefore, his use of learning seems more appropriate than the doctor's.

Although Booth shows more restraint than his mentor when using Latin and Greek, he does display a similar hostility to those who pretend to equal his learning. When he discusses the classics with both Mrs. Atkinson and the author, he first uses his learning to determine the quality of their knowledge of Latin. He leaves Mrs. Atkinson alone only after he prods her into displaying her knowledge of ancient authorities in a discussion of second marriages (bk. 6, chap. 7, pp. 257–58), and his treatment of the author is very similar to Harrison's behavior with the young clergyman and Mrs. Atkinson. After he has determined that the author knows little Latin and no Greek, Booth continues to press him about his views of Lucan, using the author's ignorance about the interpretation of a specific line in the *Pharsalia* to demonstrate his own command of the fine points of Latin grammar and his knowledge of the commentaries. Finally, he rattles off a list of Latin names when the author cannot assess the reputation of Lucan in respect to other classical writers (bk. 8, chap. 5, pp. 324–30). While he exposes the limited attainments of the author and Mrs. Atkinson, he unwittingly reveals a pedantic concern with grammatical form and a desire to show off his superior abilities. His reading in the classics has also not made him a more effective human being or a good judge of character, since his reversals throughout the novel attest to his failure to translate the lessons he has learned in reading Greek and Latin literature to his own life.

As Fielding's most detailed presentation of a learned woman, Mrs. Atkinson exemplifies another group in eighteenth-century society with incomplete knowledge of the classical tradition but pretensions to great learning. Although her knowledge of the classics is extensive for a woman, the range of authors she actually quotes is decidedly narrow. She shows a thorough acquaintance only with Virgil's *Aeneid*; otherwise she produces a few inaccurate snippets of Horace, Juvenal, and Homer. As Dr. Harrison quickly ascertains, Mrs. Atkinson knows no Greek, for she does not even realize that the Delphin series only covers Latin authors (bk. 12, chap. 7, p. 528). Because she knows some Latin, however, she obviously believes that she is the intellectual equal of her male companions; she is repeatedly offended when Dr. Harrison challenges her displays of learning, and she assumes that her quotations from Virgil will impress Booth (bk. 6, chap. 8, p. 258). Very often her efforts do not achieve their intended effect: Harrison reacts to her Latin quotations with hostility; Booth is amused; and Amelia is frightened.

Like many other characters, Mrs. Atkinson does not seem to have benefited from her classical training. Although she knows less than Booth and Harrison, she employs her Latin in similar ways. Even though her audience does not share her expertise, she rarely explains her allusions or translates quotations. For example, she uses several Latin sayings in her discussions with Amelia, but she does not try to make them intelligible to her companion (bk. 8, chap. 9, p. 346; bk. 10, chap. 8, p. 445). Readers must conclude that Mrs. Atkinson does not quote ancient literature to communicate with Amelia; instead, she expects that her citations will impress her listeners with her superior wisdom. She also demonstrates that the learning she has acquired has had no effect on her judgment. Despite her citations of classical authorities against second marriages, she marries Serjeant Atkinson, and her classical training does not help her avoid her aunt's anger or discern the peer's designs on her virtue. Consequently, any classical learning she has acquired proves completely ineffectual in helping her cope with life.

Fielding's characters and the narrators of *Shamela* and *Jonathan Wild* portray the full range of abuses of the classical tradition in eighteenth-century society. Despite their educational level, they are all preoccupied with the forms of classical literature and virtually ignore its substance. Characters usually use classical references to distinguish themselves from their peers and to embellish their opinions. Seldom do they tailor their learned displays to the knowledge of their audiences, thus revealing that their allusions and quotations are not designed to enhance communication. From their own behavior and from the responses of their listeners, those who use classics also reveal that their classical training is ineffectual. Although some may have mastered the content of several ancient authors, they do not act wisely, nor can they use their classical learning to guide others effectively. Thus, Fielding examines his readers' preconceived notions about ways of using and hearing classical references and exposes their deficiencies.

Because none of his characters benefit from their classical training, they raise the possibility that ancient tradition is completely irrelevant in the modern world. But Fielding does offer a model for the effective use of the classical tradition in the narrators of *Joseph Andrews*, *Tom Jones*, and *Amelia*.

THE CLASSICAL TRADITION AND THE INTRUSIVE NARRATOR

Within the plots of his three major novels—*Joseph Andrews*, *Tom Jones*, and *Amelia*—Fielding presents only characters who misuse the classics through ignorance or selfishness. Around his stories, however, he builds an external frame dominated by a narrator who explains the literary theory underlying his novels and provides a running commentary on the characters and the plot.[35] In this narrative persona Fielding offers his readers a model for the effective use of the classical tradition.

The narrator demonstrates that he has read widely in classical literature, because, unlike many of the characters who rely almost exclusively on tags from Lily and the *Epigrammatum Delectus*, he usually selects longer quotations that do not normally appear in the standard reference books. Of thirty-nine quotations of specific authors in the three novels, only four appear in Lily or the *Epigrammatum Delectus*. He also refers to a wider range of authors than the characters normally mention; overall he cites ten Greek and fifteen Latin authors. He suggests that he has derived his allusions and quotations from the original texts because he usually names his source, whereas most of the characters use Latin and Greek quotations without acknowledging the author.

Despite his learning, the narrator uses classical allusions and quotations so that they will be intelligible to a broad audience, thus distinguishing himself from characters who use their learning inappropriately. He relies more heavily on allusion than direct quotation and draws references from myth and history familiar even to readers who knew the classics only in translation. For example, he compares Joseph and Fanny to Oedipus (*Joseph Andrews*, bk. 4, chap. 15, p. 336), calls London "those terrestrial *Elysian* Fields" (*Tom Jones*, bk. 13, chap. 2, 2:689), and compares Amelia to Andromache (*Amelia*, bk. 9, chap. 4, p. 368).³⁶ All these allusions are so common that even readers without classical training would recognize them. When he occasionally uses more recondite allusions to appeal to his "classical" readers, he provides a gloss for those ignorant of ancient literature in the original. His description of Lady Booby's reaction to Joseph's rebuff includes references to the son of Croesus and the statues of Phidias and Praxiteles, but, for the classically illiterate, he offers examples from Hogarth (*Joseph Andrews*, bk. 1, chap. 8, pp. 40–41).³⁷

His quotations and allusions to specific Latin and Greek authors also display his efforts to make his use of the classics understandable to all his readers. He usually confines his Latin to short phrases of one or two words that had probably become common even among the minimally educated: for example, *verbatim et literatim* (*Joseph Andrews*, bk. 4, chap. 5, p. 289; *Tom Jones*, bk. 15, chap. 10, 2:824) or *una voce* (*Tom Jones*, bk. 2, chap. 4, 1:90).³⁸ He relies much more heavily on English paraphrases than on direct quotations in the original, and, for all longer quotations, the narrator provides translations—often from English versions familiar to his readers. Although occasionally the narrator does quote longer passages from the original without a translation, he provides the reader with contextual clues to the meaning. For example, in *Amelia* he cites Lucan's comment about Caesar and Pompey: *Nec quenquam jam ferre potest Caesarve priorem / Pompeiusve parem* (Neither was Caesar able any longer to endure anyone superior to him nor Pompey anyone equal to him). To demonstrate how this statement applies to the apparent jealousy between Mrs. Ellison and Mrs. Bennet, the narrator says, "Indeed, I believe, it may be laid down as a general Rule, that no Woman who hath any great Pretensions to Admiration, is ever well pleased in a Company, where she perceives herself to fill only the Second Place" (bk. 5, chap. 3, p. 204). Though the English is not a direct translation of the Latin, it shows how the passage relates to the situation of the two women.³⁹ Thus, the narrator demonstrates that, unlike his characters, he recognizes that not everyone in his audience is fluent in ancient languages.

While the narrative persona shows that he is interested in making the classical references accessible to his readers, he also reveals that his own knowledge of classical literature is extensive as he applies his learning in appropriate situations. His practice of relying on allusion requires a thorough understanding of the authors he cites, since he is not just repeating their words but is summarizing their ideas. His paraphrases also indicate his mastery of the classics because they do not stick closely to the original wording but maintain its spirit. For example, he translates the sentence *De non apparentibus, et non existentibus eadem est ratio* (That which is not seen must be treated as if it did not exist) as "When a Woman is not seen to blush, she doth not blush at all" (*Tom Jones*, bk. 1, chap. 8, 1:56). The quotation is a legal maxim, but the narrator has translated it in such a way that he makes it applicable to Bridget Allworthy, who "hides" her blushes from the public when she hears anything offensive. Bridget's deception has legal implications that the narrator has emphasized by choosing a phrase used in law.[40] His practice differs from that of characters like Partridge or the narrator of *Jonathan Wild*, who also attempt to adapt quotations to different contexts; their references are totally at odds with their intentions, whereas the narrator of *Tom Jones* exploits the original meaning and context of the quotation to supplement our understanding of a character or a situation.

Fielding's narrators offer his readers more than a model for their own use of the classics; the narrators also serve as a norm against which readers can measure the classical learning of his major characters. In *Joseph Andrews* Fielding encourages his readers to draw comparisons between the narrator's use of the classics and that of Abraham Adams by presenting occasions for them to treat similar subjects and cite identical sources. For example, the narrator defends Adams when he flees from the dogs by referring to heroes in Homer and Virgil who also leave the field of battle (bk. 3, chap. 6, p. 238), recalling a discussion between Adams and a man who has disinherited his nephew because of his cowardice (bk. 2, chap. 9, pp. 135-37). Both the narrator and Adams mention Hector's fear and cite further examples. While Adams confesses that he can give no modern instances of men who fled when the situation was hopeless, the narrator applies the ancient example to "some great Men living, who, tho' as brave as Lions, ay, as Tigers, have run away the Lord knows how far, and the Lord knows why, to the Surprize of their Friends, and the Entertainment of their Enemies" (bk. 3, chap. 6, p. 238). Adams uses the classical allusion less effectively because it may not be applicable to the young man's situation, demonstrating that he has missed the point of the uncle's objections, which probably have less to do with the nephew's lack of courage than with his defiance of his uncle's wishes. The narrator applies the reference aptly to Adams, who often imagines himself to be an epic hero.

What the narrator and Adams say about epic further reinforces this comparison. In the preface, the narrator invokes Le Bossu's topics of discussion to demonstrate how his efforts are connected with the classical tradition, and he refers to Aristotle and Horace to bolster his theory about his new genre. By contrast, Adams's disquisition on Homer has no clear purpose; he covers the material in a predictable manner and leaves the impression that he is a pedant more concerned with exhibiting his learning than communicating with his audience. Unlike the narrator, he fails to indicate how the information he has accumulated is relevant in the modern world.

In *Tom Jones* Fielding contrasts his narrative persona with Partridge, his complete opposite. Partridge shows no real understanding of the Latin authors he cites and draws most of his quotations from secondhand sources, whereas the narrator displays his thorough knowledge of the originals in his allusions and quotations. The narrator's fondness for Horace also demonstrates the superiority of his learning over the schoolmaster's, since Partridge confesses that he finds the writer too difficult. Consider how each uses the phrase, *Noscitur a socio* ("He is known by the company he keeps"): the narrator provides a paraphrase that shows his audience how he relates the *sententia* to the particular situation (bk. 3, chap. 2, 1:119), but Partridge uses the expression without translating it before a group of uneducated listeners at Upton who would certainly not know its meaning (bk. 10, chap. 5, 2:542). The difference between the narrator and this character suggests that Fielding may have given Partridge such a prominent place in *Tom Jones* as part of his rhetorical strategy to make his readers more aware of how effectively the narrator uses his classical learning.

Even though the narrator of *Amelia* is less obtrusive than in the two earlier novels, Fielding contrasts his learning with that of the other characters, particularly Doctor Harrison. He compares the narrator's classical learning with Dr. Harrison's most obviously when he glosses the doctor's classical references and quotations, which are almost always left in the original. For example, in his letter to the Booths, Harrison does not translate his quotations of Ovid and Cicero or explain the term *aretalogi*, but the narrator provides the necessary translations and explanations in the footnotes, suggesting that he is more sensitive to the needs of his audience than this character (bk. 3, chap. 10, pp. 133–34). These distinctions enhance the narrator's credibility while undermining that of the clergyman.

Such comparisons between the narrators and the major characters have important implications for criticism. In *Joseph Andrews* and *Amelia*, Fielding contrasts his narrator favorably with Adams and Harrison, both customarily interpreted as exemplary figures. Adams's moral values unmask the selfishness and moral depravity of other characters, and many characters—and modern critics—regard Dr. Harrison as the most positive role model in *Amelia*. Because the narrator proves that his classical learning surpasses these characters', he implies that he is, in fact, a more worthy authority than they, thus heightening his credibility.

The narrator's use of classics in all three novels also supports Eric Rothstein's theories about the narrator's authority over the readers of *Tom Jones*.[41] Because of the acknowledged power of ancient authors in the eighteenth century, the classical allusions and quotations used by the narrator enhance his standing with the audience. But the allusions do more than reinforce his authority; such references also distance the audience from the characters, for, in contrast to the narrator, the characters do not use classics effectively. As the classical quotations and allusions continually remind readers of the narrator's authority, which proves to be superior and preferable to any of the characters, they begin to judge the characters much as the narrator does, and they adopt his attitude toward the narrative and the characters. Thus, the classical references separate the audience sufficiently from the text to help them observe Fielding's narrative techniques more easily.

While Fielding clearly manipulated the narrative persona to guide his audience's response to the story, he also recognized that many of his readers would identify the narrator with Henry Fielding. By depicting a narrator who uses the classics effectively and authoritatively, he creates a learned portrait of himself that would align him with classically trained writers like Dryden, Pope, Swift, and Addison and would counter the attacks of those who considered him a hack writer. Even though his uneducated readers did not understand his clever use of allusion and quotation, his learned audience would, and such references would lend validity to his work among such readers. Because he worked in a genre so closely identified with romance as to be considered disreputable, the presence of the learned narrator providing commentary and showing how his novel grew from classical theory proved an effective means to anticipate and counter his critics.

Fielding deliberately used classical allusions and quotations in his novels as an important part of his strategy to force his readers to abandon their automatic responses to certain characters and to become more discerning judges. He also set up a contrast between the narrator and his main characters that enhances the narrator's authority and ensures that the readers will retain their objectivity toward the story. Finally, the prominence of the classical references indicates that they can help us determine how Fielding situated his work in the eighteenth-century debate between the ancients and the moderns.

5
The Ancients, the Moderns, and the English Novel

> The Ancients may be considered as a rich Common, where every Person who hath the smallest Tenement in *Parnassus* hath a free Right to fatten his Muse. Or, to place it in a clearer Light, we Moderns are to the Antients what the Poor are to the Rich.
> —Fielding, *Tom Jones*

Although scholars generally agree that Fielding repeatedly invokes the classical tradition and calls himself an ancient rather than a modern, they are divided about the effect of the classics on Fielding's outlook and his fiction. Ian Watt and Michael McKeon dismiss the classical references as mere ornament, while Martin C. Battestin and Henry Knight Miller maintain that ancient literature profoundly affected Fielding's perspective and philosophy.[1] The solution to this problem is not as straightforward as it first seems for two reasons. First, a paradox surrounds Fielding's novels: unlike other eighteenth-century ancients, who chose genres already established by classical writers, Fielding worked in what he himself called a "new species of writing," little known in antiquity. Recent reassessments of such labels for the eighteenth century as "Augustan" and "Neoclassical" also demonstrate the complexity of this issue, since some scholars have argued that many eighteenth-century writers who professed their admiration for the ancient world were ambivalent about some of classical civilization's most renowned figures—for example, Horace, Virgil, and Augustus.[2] Consequently, we cannot assume that Fielding's allegiance to the classics was unqualified merely because he quotes and alludes to ancient authors frequently.

New definitions of the terms "ancient" and "modern" further complicate the issue. Since Joseph Levine reconsidered the meanings of these ideas as defined by R. F. Jones, scholars have realized that many different types of ancients and moderns existed in the seventeenth and eighteenth centuries.[3] In the eighteenth century the debate was not only over science and progress, but also over literature, history, philosophy, and rhetoric. Ancients clearly felt an affinity to the classical past; few, however, accepted all of the ancient world uncritically—they selected those authors they found useful and rejected the rest. The ancients were also divided about the relative importance of philosophy and rhetoric, with some choosing one and some the other. Finally, not all believed that their contemporaries should slavishly imitate classical forms; such ancients argued that the classics were important as guides in ethics and literary taste, but were not necessarily superior as generic models.[4]

Our understanding of the moderns whom Fielding and others frequently attack in their writings needs to be equally complex. While some completely rejected the classical tradition, arguing that it had no application in the eighteenth century because it was the product of a primitive culture, others acknowledged the superiority of classical authors in certain fields—particularly literature and rhetoric—but attacked classical philosophy and science. Ironically, many of the moderns were classical scholars like Richard Bentley, whose studies in philology and antiquities buttressed attacks on the classical tradition. Their commentaries, dictionaries, and footnotes shifted attention from the wisdom of the ancients to factual questions about the nature of ancient civilization. Such detailed accounts of Greek and Roman society made people aware that ancient societies were distinct from their own; consequently, people increasingly considered the classics less useful as literary and philosophical authorities.[5]

Scholars agree that Fielding thought he was an ancient rather than a modern. But what type of ancient was he? Was his admiration for the ancients merely superficial, or did it affect the direction of his fiction, his essays, and his plays? Did he align himself with such writers of the Augustan age as Horace and Virgil, or, like the Scriblerians, did he feel ambivalent toward these authors? How does this information clarify his relationship to these authors and affect our understanding of his novels?

A review of his comments about the ancient-modern controversy and about the characters involved in the "Augustan" circle reveals that the classical tradition profoundly influenced Fielding's view of literature and his philosophy. It shows that he did not have the same reservations about Augustus and the Augustan writers found in the works of Pope and his contemporaries. Furthermore, his position as an ancient did affect the shape of his fiction and his choice of artistic models.

Fielding and the Moderns

Although Fielding says little directly about the ancients and the moderns, we can deduce his position from his comments about the authors of his time. He targets two groups in his attacks on the moderns: (1) authors and critics who write and judge without any classical training whatsoever, and (2) antiquarians, who have undermined the influence of the ancients by concentrating on philology and antiquity. His principal interests, then, align him with Temple and the Scriblerians. More important, they explain some of his artistic concerns when he develops his theory of fiction.

In Fielding's essays and novels, he repeatedly criticizes the writers and critics of his age for their lack of taste and their inability to distinguish art from hack work. When he measures their productions against those of the ancients, his contemporaries fall decidedly short in their lack of learning. For example, in *Tom Jones*, Fielding says, "For my own Part, I cannot conceive that *Homer* or *Virgil* would have writ with more Fire, if, instead of being Masters of all the Learning of their Times, they had been as ignorant as most of the Authors of the present Age" (bk. 14, chap. 1, 2:740).[6] As a result, Fielding argues, modern authors write only to entertain and, although they believe that their efforts equal those of the ancients, their works demonstrate the inferiority of contemporary letters. Critics, too, come under fire, since they have no standards by which to judge literature; consequently, they prefer the works of Tom Brown and Tom D'Urfey to the classics and indirectly encourage the productions of Grub Street hacks.[7]

Although Fielding considers most of his contemporaries inferior to the ancients because they have not bothered to acquire the learning he considers necessary for good writers or critics, he does acknowledge that writers and critics can acquire such training by studying the classics. In this area he also attacks most moderns for being deficient, relating their inability to understand Latin and Greek to their inept hack work. For example, in *Tom Jones* he discusses the critics of his time and points out their lack of discernment: "In reality, I apprehend every amorous Widow on the Stage would run the Hazard of being condemned as a servile Imitation of *Dido*, but that happily very few of our Play-house Critics understand enough of *Latin* to read *Virgil*" (bk. 10, chap. 1, 2:525-26).[8] Unintelligible or nonexistent classical learning is also a characteristic of Fielding's bumbling narrators in *Shamela* and *Jonathan Wild*. Fielding finds such individuals particularly offensive because they are unable to distinguish the good from the bad, both in literature and morals. Thus, they glorify bad literature and use literature to inculcate questionable values.

To Fielding the archetype of the modern without learning is Colley Cibber. Although Cibber had sufficient classical learning to write about Cicero in the 1740s, Fielding continually satirizes Cibber's ignorance of all things classical. For example, in the *Champion* Fielding writes a series of essays on Cibber that ridicules his *Apology*.[9] From the first Fielding treats Cibber as a child who writes without sense; he questions his use of *adept*, stating that it shows how little Latin Cibber actually knows. In the next essay he argues that Cibber is an example of the advantages of writing without learning because from his work, Fielding says, "I think it is plain that he must have learnt as far as the *pleasant Accusative Case*, and not quite so far as the *Participles*" (2:158). Thus, Fielding associates Cibber's inability to write comprehensible sentences directly with Cibber's ignorance of classical languages. Although Fielding may detest Cibber for other reasons, he concentrates on the detrimental effects of Cibber's willful neglect of the classics; his satires show that he connects Cibber's lack of learning with his faulty style and with his inability to judge plays and other literature accurately—especially Henry Fielding's. Thus, Cibber represents the worst result of the moderns' desire to abandon the classical tradition.[10]

Fielding's criticisms of the moderns for their ignorance may partially account for his frequent use of classical learning and his prefatory essays in *Jonathan Wild*, *Joseph Andrews*, and *Tom Jones*. As Fielding says in *Tom Jones*, Addison introduced mottoes into the *Spectator* to scare off imitators; he has written his prefaces because his contemporaries lack sufficient learning to imitate this part of his novels (*Tom Jones*, bk. 9, chap. 1, 1:487-89). By frequently quoting and alluding to the classics, Fielding exhibits the range of his learning, just as Homer and Virgil did in their epics, which are full of allusions to their predecessors. Furthermore, his lengthy prefaces demonstrate that, unlike the moderns, he writes according to classical rules; where necessary, he has created new rules that grow out of the classical tradition.[11] Therefore, his classical learning has given him taste and judgment that his "modern" contemporaries lack, making his work superior to theirs.

While Fielding frequently attacks moderns for their ignorance and neglect of the classical authors, he also often criticizes antiquarians and philologists, whose classical studies concentrate solely on minutiae. He rejects their preoccupation with trivia on several grounds. First, they have diminished the influence of the classics because they have shifted the focus from ancient literature as a standard of taste and morality to such trivia as the true country of Homer or whether Horace used *splendebat* or *fulgebat* in one of the Epodes.[12] Second, Fielding attacks antiquarians and philologists because they usually search for the blemishes in classical culture and in the great classical authors; he repeatedly calls such criticisms slander.[13] He also finds the work of these scholars annoying because it is deceptive: although they claim that they are objectively seeking truth, their researches usually reflect their own prejudices.[14] Finally, he complains that often their commentaries achieve exactly the opposite of what they originally intended; instead of clarifying what was obscure, the mass of evidence "tends to darken and embarass a Case which was plain enough before."[15] Therefore, he labels their work pointless and, in an extended essay on the subject in the *Covent-Garden Journal*, contrasts this folly with the "most erudite and consummate Works of Art or Wisdom" (*Covent-Garden Journal*, no. 24 [24 March 1752]: 154-58).

Among the antiquarians and commentators, Fielding most often criticizes and satirizes Richard Bentley, whose classical learning supported the moderns more often than the ancients. For example, Bentley deployed his learning to attack Sir William Temple, questioning the authenticity of the *Epistles of Phalaris* and arguing that Homer's epics were not unified poems but unrelated collections of ballads. His derogatory remarks about Pope's translation of Homer also earned the enmity of the Scriblerians and their admirers, among whom was Fielding. Fielding's assaults on Bentley parallel many of his remarks on commentators in general. For example, he mentions Bentley's obsessive concern with a particular reading of a passage from Horace; in *Amelia* Dr. Harrison even suggests that Bentley would not "have given up his *Ingentia Fata* to an Angel."[16] Fielding returns several times to Bentley's theories about Homer, in particular disparaging Bentley's theory about the composition of the Homeric poems.[17] When defending Pope, whose *Iliad* Bentley dismissed, Fielding belittles Bentley's knowledge of the Greek alphabet; he shows that he considers the scholar's theories about Homer's use of the digamma less significant than Pope's achievement in translating Homer for eighteenth-century readers (*Champion*, 12 June 1740, 2:328).

Obviously, Fielding cannot fault Bentley's understanding of Latin and Greek. In fact, the scholar was undoubtedly more learned than Fielding or any of those he defends. But Fielding maintains that Bentley misapplied his knowledge by focusing too much on minute details and petty debates. Bentley and those like him were undermining the classics by calling attention to the imperfect state of classical texts and the primitive condition of classical culture. Such "authorities" reinforced the arguments of moderns like Cibber—and Defoe and Richardson—who condemned classical civilization as morally corrupt and dismissed the literary, rhetorical, and philosophical significance of classical writers. By calling their method "scientific," these scholars implied that their approach to the classics was epistemologically sounder than that of writers and critics who appreciated ancient authors for their literary value. Such moderns are especially distasteful to Fielding because they have replaced taste and judgment with trivial detail and arguments that reflect their own prejudices. Thus, he considers the work of Bentley no better than slander and in the *Miscellanies* identifies him with the critics who write for the *Grub-Street Journal* ("Of Celia," in *Miscellanies* 1:64).

Fielding graphically depicts the absurdity of such commentaries by parodying the footnotes antiquarians used to display their ponderous learning. Such mock scholarship may derive from Swift and Pope, but it also illustrates many of Fielding's chief complaints against antiquarians and philologists. Bentley's name figures prominently in such performances.[18] Most of Fielding's mock footnotes are irrelevant to the passages they are supposed to gloss; although they begin with some tangential connection to the text, they stray from the topic as the commentator tries to display all the facts he knows. Furthermore, many of the comments contain obvious misinterpretations of the text and factual errors, which reinforce one of Fielding's prime criticisms of such commentaries: because they focus their attention on trivia, such scholars completely misread literature and miss its real significance. Their mistakes in interpretation also suggest that they have used classical authorities only to justify their own prejudices or the prejudices that have directed their classical research; thus, these footnotes undermine the claim of the antiquarian that his work is more scientific and somehow more objective than that of the ancients. Finally, Fielding's commentators often betray a blindness about character that parallels their narrow focus on facts. This feature of his mock footnotes reveals the true danger created by their obsession with minutiae: they diminish one's ability to make both literary and moral judgments.

Fielding associates antiquarians and philologists with another group of moderns who rejected the ancient world and claimed that their work was epistemologically sound because it was scientific: the Royal Society. He recognizes the link between the methodology used by members of the Society and that adopted by the classical scholars who were undermining the position of the ancients. For example, in a satire on the origins of a mythical group called the Robinhoodians, Fielding argues that his arcane show of classical learning entitles him to membership in the Royal Society (*Champion*, 7 June 1740, 2:307–13). He lists both antiquarians and the Society as examples of triflers in his essay on the subject in the *Covent-Garden Journal*, no. 24 (24 March 1752): 156–57. His parodies on the Society's scientific and travel narratives also contain many classical allusions and quotations that suggest the close relationship between the work of the antiquarians and these early scientists.[19] By identifying these two groups with each other, Fielding underscores some of his main reasons for disliking both of them: they have replaced wisdom with trivia, they accumulate knowledge for no practical end, and they often use their "evidence" merely to justify their own prejudices. Therefore, they can argue for any position, no matter how reprehensible.

His attacks on antiquarians, philologists, and the Royal Society bear directly on Fielding's artistic choices in his novels. Often Fielding calls his works "histories"; he carefully shows in his introductions, however, that his works are very different from the type of historical accounts produced by the moderns. For example, in *Tom Jones* he compares himself to historians who write down everything: "The Writer, indeed, seems to think himself obliged to keep even Pace with Time, whose Amanuensis he is; and, like his Master, travels as slowly through Centuries of monkish Dulness, when the World seems to have been asleep, as through that bright and busy Age so nobly distinguished by the excellent *Latin* Poet" (bk. 2, chap. 1, 1:76). Here he specifically contrasts the work of the moderns to the ancients; he implies that those who record facts indiscriminately cannot ferret out the most significant events and that they also prevent their readers from seeing the most important material. Thus, he argues that modern historians are little better than topographers or chorographers and that truth "is only to be found in the Works of those who celebrate the Lives of Great Men, and are commonly called Biographers."[20]

His opinions about antiquarians and annalistic writers also affect his attitudes toward contemporary fiction writers. For example, his response to the romance in the preface of *Joseph Andrews* sounds very much like his criticisms of the antiquarians, for he characterizes romances as "voluminous works," which he compares unfavorably to his novels and classical epics; he points out that, partially because of their length, they contain little to entertain or instruct (preface, 4–5). His attitudes about these modern scholars undoubtedly conditioned his response to the fiction of other novelists, especially Richardson and Defoe. In *Shamela* Fielding satirizes extensively Richardson's interest in recording each minute detail of Pamela's experience; he quite aptly demonstrates that it obscures the moral problems inherent in the story, even while such detail suggests that this type of narrative has more epistemological value than a story in which the author's hand is more evident. *Jonathan Wild*'s narrator also pays very close attention to minute detail; here the connection between the narrator's obsession with minutiae and his lack of judgment about Wild's true character is very clear. Because Fielding refers to Defoe's account in the preface to the *Miscellanies*, we can reasonably assume that *Wild* is, in part, a satire on Defoe's reportorial style and rogue biographies, which inadvertently glorify the lives of villains.

As we have seen, Fielding's attitudes about the moderns' ignorance and attention to petty detail did affect the shape of his fiction—especially in his prefatory essays, his use of literary allusion, and his careful choice of details to support his thesis. It also explains his response to many of the important writers and scholars of his time, such as Colley Cibber, Richard Bentley, Samuel Richardson, and Daniel Defoe. But ancient tradition was not just valuable to Fielding because it offered an alternative to the moderns. He also considered the classics important because of what ancient writers said about literature and philosophy.

Fielding and the Ancients

That Fielding admired ancient writers needs little demonstration.[21] But what qualities in them does he particularly praise, and of what use does he think they should be for his contemporaries? Although he seldom discusses these issues directly, Fielding suggests his opinions in many essays and prefaces.

From his comments about ancient literature in general and about particular authors, we find that Fielding valued various writers of antiquity for their great learning, their rhetoric, their literary taste, and their philosophy.

First, he praises the ancients, saying they had learning and good critical judgment. When he discusses the inadequacies of contemporary critics, he notes that he does not mean "any of those noble Critics, to whose Labours the learned World are so greatly indebted. Such were *Aristotle, Horace,* and *Longinus* among the Ancients, *Dacier* and *Bossu* among the *French,* and some perhaps among us; who have certainly been duly authorized to execute at least a judicial Authority in *Foro Literario*" (*Tom Jones,* bk. 11, chap. 1, 2:570–71).[22] Here Fielding shows that he considers the ancients important for their critical rules; mentioning such modern critics as Dacier and Bossu also suggests another important function of ancient literature, for works of the ancients can serve as yardsticks against which to measure contemporary productions. Dacier and Bossu used classical writers and critics as a standard for assessing the productions of their contemporaries, a practice that earns them a place in Fielding's pantheon of critics. Certainly Fielding came to appreciate Milton after judging his work against that of Homer and Virgil, for he frequently couples Milton's name with that of his ancient predecessors.[23] His comments about the moderns also indicate that, when he compares them with the ancients, the deficiencies of most modern writers become readily apparent. Therefore, ancient writers are important because of their critical strictures and the models of great literature they provide.

While Fielding appreciates the classics for what they can show about the function of criticism and the importance of good taste, he also regards ancient writers as a source of wisdom. Fielding not only praises the literary achievements of ancient writers; he maintains that moderns have a right to use ancient learning for their own benefit. For example, in *Tom Jones* he says, "The Antients may be considered as a rich Common, where every Person who hath the smallest Tenement in *Parnassus* hath a free Right to fatten his Muse."[24] Although he does not imitate classical genres, Fielding quotes and alludes to the classics because they add authority to other arguments he might use and they invariably express ideas tastefully and wisely. He also argues that the classics are not just useful to the writer seeking an appropriate aphorism; he asserts that those who are well read in ancient literature can find comfort in times of joy or sorrow.[25]

Like many other eighteenth-century ancients, Fielding does not equally embrace all classical authors or all of ancient civilization. I have already written extensively about his regard for Horace, who is by far the greatest influence on Fielding's persona and ideas. But other authors favored by the ancients also figure prominently in Fielding: particularly, Aristotle, Cicero, and Homer. Fielding's opinions on each of these authors provide important clues to those features of classical literature that he found most appealing and useful for his own age.

As R. F. Jones has demonstrated, hostility to the authority of Aristotle in the seventeenth century initiated the modern scientific methods that were so instrumental in diminishing the influence of antiquity. Fielding shows that he is aware of his countrymen's low regard for Aristotle. For example, Fielding defines "nonsense" in his "modern" glossary as "Philosophy, especially the Philosophical Writings of the Antients, and more especially of Aristotle."[26] He also recognizes that even Aristotle's criticism has fallen into disfavor, as he indicates at the beginning of the Paper War (*Covent-Garden Journal*, no. 1 [4 January 1752]: 18). Despite the contempt of the moderns, however, Fielding admires Aristotle for a variety of reasons.

First, Fielding regards Aristotle as one of the greatest critics of all time, and his authority and precepts are repeatedly invoked in his essays. He cites Aristotle when discussing probability and laments that we have no good definition of humor, noting, however, that Aristotle undoubtedly covered the subject amply in his lost treatise on comedy (*Tom Jones*, bk. 8, chap. 1, 1:400–401; *Covent-Garden Journal*, no. 55 [18 July 1752]: 298). Aristotle was valuable for his critical rules, but more important, he provided the model of what a great critic should be. Like Aristotle, Fielding argues, a great critic should not be too ready to find fault, and he should not attempt to appease slanderers (*Jacobite's Journal*, no. 8 [23 January 1748]: 136; no. 29 [8 June 1748]: 309). Because of his value, therefore, Fielding lists Aristotle among those critics that any modern aspiring to the job must read and understand thoroughly.[27]

Though he mentions Aristotle's philosophy less often, Fielding also considers the Greek writer important in this area. In the *Covent-Garden Journal*, for example, he indicates that Plato and Aristotle could help a man master prosperity or adversity if they were as readily available in English as other classical authors (no. 10 [4 February 1752]: 75). As Frederick Ribble has demonstrated, Fielding derives his ideas of prudence from Aristotle's *Nicomachean Ethics*.[28] Even some of Fielding's characters turn to Aristotle's philosophy: the philosopher in *Amelia* defines his subject by citing Aristotle, and Dr. Harrison refers to him several times when he tries to comfort his parishioners.[29] Fielding's only criticism of Aristotle appears in the *Jacobite's Journal*, when he comments that the portion of the *Politics* on education is the worst of the whole book (no. 22 [30 April 1748]: 257).

Fielding also praises Cicero, another classical author frequently maligned by the moderns. Although Fielding reveals his high esteem for Cicero by listing him only after Virgil and Horace in his account of the Paper War (*Covent-Garden Journal*, no. 1 [4 January 1752]: 17–19), his comments about Cicero's oratory and criticism are somewhat ambivalent. For example, Fielding notes,

"It requires the Genius of Cicero or Bolingbroke, to introduce their own Praises into every political Oration or Pamphlet" (*Covent-Garden Journal*, no. 60 [22 August 1752]: 323). Here he undermines his praise of Cicero's genius by calling attention to his egotism. In the *Champion* Fielding suggests that Cicero's oratory was not equal to Demosthenes'. He says that the Roman so thoroughly understood his own abilities that he did not borrow from Demosthenes those things he could not make his own; he undercuts Cicero even further by pointing out that the orator could not, however, resist writing poetry, for which he had no talent (20 November 1739, 1:15). Although Fielding does cite Cicero when discussing good taste and wit, his references to the Roman's criticism and oratory are infrequent and not uniformly complimentary.[30]

As Henry Knight Miller argues when discussing the *Miscellanies*, Fielding is much more interested in Cicero's philosophy and ethics than in his oratory, politics, or criticism.[31] Some of the references to Cicero's philosophical writings only suggest Fielding's esteem for him or mention his philosophy generally. For example, when he discusses the nature of fortune, Fielding remarks that Cicero was wiser than either Juvenal or Seneca (*Tom Jones*, bk. 14, chap. 8, 2:770–71); he also notes more than once Cicero's claim that the Sophists frequently considered any absurdity a philosophy (*Covent-Garden Journal*, no. 19 [7 March 1752]: 133–34; "An Essay on Conversation," in *Miscellanies*, 1:119). Many of his references to Cicero's philosophy relate to two issues that Fielding often discusses: good nature and the comfort derived from philosophy. His use of Cicero in these areas reveals his perspective on both questions. In the *Champion* Fielding writes, "NOTHING, says the great Cicero, in my Motto, *is more agreeable to the Nature of Man than Liberality*" (27 March 1740, 2:37, 39). When attacking slanderers, Fielding also cites Cicero, referring the reader to his definition of malevolence in the *Tusculan Disputations* (*Covent-Garden Journal*, no. 14 [18 February 1752]: 102). Citations from Cicero play a large part in "Of the Remedy of Affliction for the Loss of Friends" in the *Miscellanies*, where Fielding recommends philosophy, especially Cicero's, to calm the spirit and relates that Cicero, whose life was a fortunate one, would not choose to live his life over again if given the choice by the Gods (*Miscellanies* 1:212, 223, 225).

In his novels Fielding's characters also turn for comfort to Cicero's philosophy. In *Tom Jones*, for instance, Square encourages Tom to bear his illness stoically, citing arguments used by Cicero (bk. 5, chap. 2, 1:216–17). In *Amelia* Dr. Harrison quotes a passage from the *Tusculan Disputations* when he writes to console Amelia over the death of her mother (bk. 3, chap. 10, pp. 137–38); in the same novel Fielding refers to Cicero and Aristotle as the two great mental physicians for those who are suffering (bk. 4, chap. 10, pp. 174–75).

Fielding also uses a motto from Cicero to head an essay on the importance of knowing oneself and mentions Cicero's attitudes about the evil of excess (*Champion*, 20 November 1739, 1:13; 15 March 1739–40, 2:3). Therefore, although Fielding is clearly aware of Cicero's importance in oratory and rhetoric, he is far more interested and enthusiastic about Cicero the philosopher, to whose works he turns for his ideas of good nature and for comfort in loss.

Although both Aristotle and Cicero were important in the early phases of the ancient-modern debate, the controversy in the eighteenth century centered on the relative merits of Homer. As I have shown, Fielding did conceive of his novels in relation to classical epics. But did he regard Homer and Virgil as uncritically as do some of his characters—for example, Abraham Adams or Dr. Harrison? The evidence reveals that he did not share their unqualified adoration for the epic poets.

The controversy over the merits and translation of Homer raged primarily in France, but as Levine and Simonsuuri demonstrate, the English, including Fielding, were very much aware of the issues involved in this debate, and Pope's translation of Homer reignited the disagreement about the value of the Homeric epics. At various points, this debate included many of the seventeenth- and eighteenth-century critics whom Fielding mentions in his essays and novels: Dacier, La Motte, Bentley, and Pope, for example. Because she only looked for the beauties in the Homeric epics, for instance, Madame Dacier argued that the moderns unfairly attacked Homer; they lacked sufficient knowledge of Greek and read him only in translations, which by her standards were universally bad. She particularly attacked translations of Homer like La Motte's, because he took too many liberties with his classical original, thereby suggesting that Homer was imperfect and that modern writers could actually improve on what, to her, was a flawless standard of good taste. In her own translation of Homer, Dacier tried to present an accurate and literal version of the epics, which recreated the customs of the Homeric age as closely as possible; thus, she used her accumulated learning to demonstrate his value as one of the earliest and best examples of literature and a model that could curb the corruption of good taste she saw in her society.[32]

Not all her contemporaries admired Homer, however. Scholars like Charles Perrault completely rejected the epic poet because his work came out of a primitive culture that glorified brutality and lacked the refinement of modern civilization. Antoine Houdar de La Motte thought Homer worth translating, but he criticized the *Iliad* for being tedious and repetitious in places, for presenting gods and heroes with bad manners, and for including too many events that strained the reader's credibility. So, he rewrote Homer, selecting what he considered best and eliminating those passages that he thought objectionable. To Dacier such a "reworking" of Homer demonstrated how corrupt the taste of her age had become; to La Motte his efforts brought to Homer the refinement of the contemporary world.

When Pope translated the *Iliad* in the early eighteenth century, he read these French versions and knew the debate over Homer raging in France. Pope did not side with either Dacier or La Motte; he agreed with others who considered each party somewhat blind—Dacier to the defects, La Motte to the beauties of Homer. Although Pope relied heavily on Dacier in his notes, he admitted that Homer had faults, which he attempted to correct in his translation. To Pope what made Homer great was his poetic fire and his originality; he criticized Homer's heroes, however, and his presentation of the gods. Although his rendition of Homer diverged so much from the original that Bentley dismissed it as a lovely poem but no translation, Pope focused on Homer's strengths rather than his weaknesses and attempted to remain faithful to Homer's spirit, if not his words. Like Dacier, he dismissed Bentley and his other critics by identifying them with Zoilus, the ancient critic who established his reputation by searching for the trivial flaws in Homer.[33]

Like Pope, Fielding steers a middle course in his assessment of Homer but clearly identifies with Dacier and the other ancients who praised the epic poet. Homer leads the Greeks in the Paper War, and he is the first of those classical authors whom he considers the greats of Parnassus.[34] Among the best critics of the modern world, Fielding lists André Dacier, husband of Madame Dacier and himself a Homeric scholar (*Tom Jones*, bk. 11, chap. 1, 2:569); in *A Journey from this World to the Next*, Madame Dacier is sitting on Homer's lap (bk. 1, chap. 8, in *Miscellanies*, 2:37). Fielding also repeats Madame Dacier's criticism of La Motte: that it is easier to attack Homer than to understand him (*Champion*, 27 November 1739, 1:35; *Covent-Garden Journal*, no. 11 [8 February 1752]: 83). Such compliments place Fielding in the camp of the champions of Homer; they tell us little, however, about what in Homer's epics he finds particularly appealing. Fielding's more detailed remarks only tell us that he likes the epics primarily because of their learning and their originality. The most common compliment he pays Homer is that he was the master of all the learning of his time: his abundance of knowledge distinguishes his work from contemporary writers and enables him to write epics that instruct as well as entertain.[35] Fielding also recognizes that Homer was the original and provided a pattern for all later epics.[36] Besides these points, Fielding's praise of Homer remains quite general.

While he finds Homer greater than many of the moderns, however, Fielding also notes that Homer was sometimes napping (*Covent-Garden Journal*, no.1 [4 January 1752]: 16). As I have already shown, Fielding criticizes the concept of heroism in the *Iliad*; in the *Covent-Garden Journal* he mentions La Motte when he observes that Achilles made a silly choice when he preferred glory to life (no. 66 [14 October 1752]: 348). He also accuses Homer of excess. For example, he notes, "*Homer*, who hath been styled the Prince of Poets, is too often inclined to overdoing. He is too prolix in his Narrations, and much too frequent in his Repetitions; insomuch, that a very excellent Critic accuses him of an *Intemperance of Words*" (*Champion*, 15 March 1739–40, 2:3). In *Tom Jones* Fielding implies that he dislikes Homer's frequent use of supernatural agents because they make his story improbable (bk. 8, chap. 1, 1:397-98). Certainly, the marvelous elements in the *Odyssey* induced Fielding to claim in *The Journal of a Voyage to Lisbon* (1755) that he should have loved Homer more if he had written a true history instead of an epic poem (preface, vii–ix).

Although Fielding obviously admires the work of Homer and his achievement in creating the first epics, which served as models for all others, he questions whether some of Homer's values and artistic techniques are applicable in his own time. While he acknowledges the efforts of Madame Dacier to defend Homer, he recognizes that her uncritical admiration can also have a deleterious effect on literature. Like Horace, Fielding prefers the work of Virgil, whose epics are superior because they show judgment and are free of the excesses that mar Homer. This attitude toward Homer partially accounts for the mock heroics in his novels: his parodies of Homeric style and descriptions evoke the epic and relate his fiction to the epic tradition, but they also challenge the Homeric epics and allow Fielding to show his readers that his work in prose is more suited than Homer to the age in which he lives.

Fielding's attitude to Madame Dacier's uncritical admiration for Homer also suggests that he does not appraise all eighteenth-century ancients equally. Fielding identifies closely with those ancients who considered classical learning a necessary part of the training of a good author or critic. He agrees with them that the moderns who either rejected the past totally or who explored the classical world superficially by focusing only on trivia were completely lacking in judgment and encouraged the corruption in good taste. He also sides with those who turned to classical writers as a source of ethics and philosophy; he believes that such ancient authors as Horace, Aristotle, Cicero, and Plato provide a philosophical and ethical standard against which one can measure modern thinkers. At the same time, however, Fielding realizes that ancient authors or their values are not flawless; he rejects epic heroism, criticizes the prolixity of Homer and Ovid, and attacks the immorality of such writers as Aristophanes and Petronius. Furthermore, as he demonstrates in *Amelia*, he recognizes that fundamental problems exist when one tries to apply a pagan value system to a Christian society. Thus, unlike Dacier—and many English ancients—Fielding does not slavishly imitate classical values or literary models.

Fielding reveals his attitudes towards ancients who uncritically admire the classical world in some essays and in several of the characters he presents in his novels. In the *Covent-Garden Journal*, for example, Tom Telltruth argues that learning is much overrated. While Fielding is clearly satirizing the modern attitude toward scholarly learning, he does suggest that great learning alone does not make one a good judge of character or fit one for life. Telltruth observes that learned men often know nothing of the world; they frequently interpret their own society according to their reading in the classics, and, consequently, they make foolish errors (no. 42 [26 May 1752]: 239–40). Fielding's portrayals of Adams and Harrison provide graphic support for this assertion. Adams believes that knowledge from books is far superior to actual experience, as he observes to the innkeeper who saw the world as a sailor (*Joseph Andrews*, bk. 2, chap. 17, pp. 181-82). Because he interprets his experiences according to his reading in the classics, however, Adams makes some foolish mistakes: for example, he misjudges people because he trusts Socrates' statements on the reliability of physiognomy and tells Joseph that "Knowledge of Men is only to be learnt from Books" (bk. 2, chap. 16, p. 176). Harrison is also blind to the faults of the ancients; his great learning does not help him judge Booth and his family or solve their problems. Fielding demonstrates through these characters that, although one should know the classics well, one must measure the relevance of antiquity against one's own experience.

Fielding does not view the past with the clinical eye of a Bentley or with the uncritical adulation of Dennis or Dacier. He does, however, praise ancient critics, authors, and philosophers for providing a standard of good taste and good literature against which to measure the productions of his own time. The classical tradition, then, influences the direction of his fiction in its concern for the ethical implications of literature and in its rejection of the annalistic method of writing favored by some of Fielding's contemporaries. His interest in the classical tradition parallels the concerns of Pope and his fellow Scriblerians. But when we consider Fielding's use of ancient history, particularly that relating to the Roman Republic and the Augustan age, we find that he does not share their ambivalence toward the early empire and their reservations about the great writers of the Maecenean circle.

POPE, FIELDING, AND THE AUGUSTANS

For many years scholars have called the eighteenth century the "Augustan" or "Neoclassical" age, but such labels have become part of a vigorous debate over the eighteenth-century reputation of Augustus and the poets who surrounded him. Critics like Reuben Brower and Howard Erskine-Hill maintain that the term "Augustan" had positive connotations for eighteenth-century readers and that authors who imitated the Augustan poets Virgil and Horace did so primarily out of adulation. However, Howard Weinbrot and James William Johnson—among others—have argued that the Augustan label is inaccurate because many eighteenth-century writers rejected the classical past in general and Augustus in particular. Weinbrot notes that writers like Pope were distinctly ambivalent about the reign of Augustus in Rome; while he brought peace to the Roman Empire and encouraged the arts, he destroyed liberty. Although Pope and his friends clearly admired members of the Maecenean circle, particularly Virgil and Horace, they could not forget that their work was propaganda for the Augustan program. Thus, Weinbrot contends that Pope and others turn away from Horace and adopt a satirical stance heavily influenced by Juvenal; he concludes that such attitudes undermine the contention that they were "Augustans."[37]

Weinbrot observes that Fielding shares Pope's hostility to Augustus and the Augustan writers.[38] However, an examination of Fielding's comments about the late Republic and early Roman Empire does not support this conclusion. Like many of his contemporaries, Fielding is interested in ancient history and uses analogies drawn from ancient historians to interpret events in his own time. While he demonstrates that he is aware of others' reservations about Augustus, he also clearly shows that he rejects this ambivalent attitude. Consequently, Fielding's approach toward ancient history can help us understand his relationship with other eighteenth-century writers who also worked with the classical tradition.

What is particularly striking about Fielding's choice of historical exempla is that he is unusually reticent about Augustus or the politics of the Augustan age. Fielding's comments about Augustus's political behavior are sparse and decidedly vague. For example, he cites an incident in Suetonius, where Augustus criticized the attire of his fellow citizens and ordered the aediles to bar from the forum anyone not properly dressed; although this incident could reflect badly on Augustus, neither Suetonius nor Fielding suggests that Augustus's action was reprehensible or uses the anecdote negatively (*Jacobite's Journal*, no. 38 [20 August 1748]: 374). Fielding is somewhat more critical in the *Covent-Garden Journal* when he discusses Augustus's harsh treatment of adulterers, mentioning that both Tacitus and Juvenal considered Augustus's punishment too severe (no. 67 [21 October 1752]: 352, 356). The negative tone of this passage is mitigated, however, when we consider its context, for Fielding himself is attacking the practice of adultery rather sharply in these essays; in fact, he never actually says whether he himself considers the emperor's treatment of adulterers too extreme. Unlike Pope and some of his contemporaries, then, Fielding does not seem to be troubled by the political implications of Augustus's reign.

Fielding's comments about Augustus and his court usually concentrate instead on their effect on literature. For example, in the *Covent-Garden Journal* when Fielding discusses Horace's comments about adultery, he says, "We have before us the Words of a Man of the World, who lived in the Politest, and most splendid of Courts, and in the Intimacy of the greatest men of that Court" (no. 67 [21 October 1752]: 352). In "Of True Greatness" Fielding also stresses the refinement of the Augustan court, which he contrasts with his own age, in which poets are not valued for their true merit.[39] Fielding's only negative comment about Augustan patronage appears in the *Champion*, where he mentions that Virgil speaks of Augustus's descent from Venus to satisfy the emperor's vanity and reports that Ovid and Juvenal both criticize Virgil for acting in such a manner (17 November 1739, 1:8). Thus, Fielding stresses Augustus's role in encouraging literature and ignores the political problems raised by the early empire.

Such references to Augustus suggest that Fielding does not share the ambivalence of Pope and his other contemporaries. Weinbrot has demonstrated convincingly that Pope condemns Augustus as a tyrant, who had destroyed liberty, caused civil war, and degraded literature by forcing talented writers to produce propaganda for the *Pax Augusta*. But, although Weinbrot attempts to show that Fielding shared this attitude with Pope and the Scriblerians, Fielding's reluctance to discuss Augustus's political career indicates that he is more concerned about the great literature that resulted from Augustus's patronage than the tyranny fostered by the emperor and his propaganda machine. In the *True Patriot* Fielding even implies his approval of Augustus when he quotes Horace's *Odes* 1.6.9–11, which praises the emperor for defending the Roman people and bringing peace after years of civil war. Significantly, he chooses this reference to lead off an essay that lauds the king and his family after their victory at Culloden (no. 27 [29 April 1746]: 277). Not only does Fielding assume a role similar to that of Horace when he praises the royal family, but he demonstrates that he does not share Pope's doubts about the political career of the Roman Emperor.

The difference between Pope's and Fielding's treatment of Augustus is all the more marked when we contrast his treatment of Augustus with that of other political figures often discussed in the eighteenth century. While Fielding does not seem to judge Augustus's political career, he does consider the records of other Roman leaders known for their tyranny. When Fielding mentions such historical figures in his essays and novels, his approach to Roman history conforms closely to that of many of his contemporaries.[40] For example, Fielding repeatedly and unequivocally aligns himself with many other eighteenth-century writers by expressing his contempt for Julius Caesar. Fielding uses Caesar to symbolize a tyrant and Brutus to epitomize the patriot fighting for liberty. Unlike some eighteenth-century historians, Fielding cannot find any mitigating circumstances that could justify Caesar's rise and his destruction of liberty in Rome.⁴¹ In *Jonathan Wild* he expresses his sentiments clearly through his narrator: "[T]he mighty *Caesar*, with wonderful Greatness of Mind, had destroyed the Liberties of his Country, and with all the Means of Fraud and Force had placed himself at the Head of his Equals, had corrupted and enslaved the greatest People whom the Sun ever saw." He reinforces this interpretation of Caesar by coupling his name with other tyrants, often mentioning him together with Alexander the Great.⁴² Fielding uses Caesar as an example of greatness unmitigated by goodness; in the poem "Of True Greatness" he notes that Caesar will withdraw when John Churchill appears because Churchill has fought to defend his nation rather than promote himself (lines 105–6, in *Miscellanies*, 1:23). Although Fielding does not mention Caesar as often as he does other Roman politicians, he makes his attitude very clear by identifying him with other tyrants and discussing the "greatness" of his treatment of the Roman people in some detail.

Fielding also demonstrates his views on Caesar by contrasting him with other Romans of the period—particularly Brutus, Cicero, and Cato. His praise of the Bruti is frequent and completely unqualified; Fielding often uses both as exemplars of civic virtue. For example, in the *True Patriot* he claims that Brutus is the model of the true patriot and in *Jonathan Wild* contrasts him with Nero, his opposite in every respect.⁴³ In such comments Fielding shows that he appreciates Brutus's patriotism, his love of liberty, his incorruptibility, and his philosophy of Stoicism. Although in the *Jacobite's Journal* he mentions that both Brutus and Socrates had some faults, he never enumerates what they are. His treatment of Brutus is similar to that of Addison, Thomson, Young, and Lillo, who also considered Brutus the antithesis of Caesar and the model of the patriotic citizen.⁴⁴

While Brutus appears as an admirable figure in Fielding, his treatment of Cicero and Cato shows that he does not automatically accept the assessments of historians, either ancient or modern, about their careers. Although Fielding admires Cicero as a philosopher and critic, he rarely refers to his performance as a politician, and some of these references are ambiguous. For example, in the *Jacobite's Journal* when Fielding discusses the opposition, he refers to some men who "with *Cicero*, prefer the most unjust Peace to the justest War" (no. 9 [30 January 1748]: 141). Fielding also relates Cicero to Pompey by quoting and alluding to his speech on the Manilian Law, which gave Pompey an extraordinary command in order to combat the pirates effectively and eventually led to the first triumvirate.⁴⁵ Fielding refers to Cicero's prosecution of Catiline but only hints at his opinion of it; he implies his attitude toward Catiline when, in the *Champion*, he mentions that he forms no opinion of a man from his reputation alone, since some thought Catiline witty and brave.⁴⁶ He does not address Cicero's execution of the traitors, which created some controversy in the eighteenth century. Although Fielding never openly condemns Cicero, he also never openly praises him; when we compare these sparse comments with the frequency of his references to Cicero's philosophy and criticism, Fielding's silence about Cicero's political career implies that he does not value him highly as a patriot.

Fielding's reluctance to evaluate Cicero's career may stem from his interest in Cicero the philosopher and from his awareness of the controversy raging in the eighteenth century over the interpretation of the Roman's political activities. In both *Shamela* and *Joseph Andrews* Fielding attacks Conyers Middleton's adulatory account of Cicero's life; his repugnance for Middleton's biography stemmed in part from the offhand compliments to Walpole that many in the opposition found in the work.[47] George Lyttleton, who wrote *Observations on the Life of Cicero* (1733), a more balanced assessment of Cicero's political career, was Fielding's friend. Like Fielding, he does not consider Cicero as important in the history of the Roman Republic as Brutus. Weinbrot claims that Fielding praises Hooke's history in *A Journey from this World to the Next* because it questions the career of Augustus, but Fielding's compliment to Hooke might just as likely stem from the controversy over Middleton, since Hooke undertook his history to attack this version of Cicero's career.[48] Since Fielding very clearly attacks Middleton but does not express great reservations about Augustus, such an explanation for his praise of Hooke is very plausible.

Fielding's references to Cato the Elder are too brief to provide any clear picture of his thoughts about this figure. In the *Jacobite's Journal* essay on the opposition, Fielding alludes to Cato's famous *Carthago delenda est* when he claims that some Englishmen are so bent on destroying France that they do not consider which nation is more likely to win such a war (no. 9 [30 January 1746]: 141). Booth discusses a passage in Lucan's *Pharsalia* that praises Cato's devotion to his country, but his focus is more on a sticky textual problem than on Cato's behavior. Fielding's infrequent references to Cato underscore the prominence he gives to other figures—Brutus in particular—and it also relates his attitudes about the Roman Republic more closely with those of Lyttleton and many of his contemporaries who similarly interpreted events in the late Republic.

While Fielding often turns to Roman history when discussing liberty and patriotism, the classical figure that Fielding most commonly associates with tyranny and brutality is Alexander the Great. Even though some of his contemporaries admired Alexander for his refinement and his treatment of his men, Fielding unequivocally condemns the conqueror and invokes him repeatedly as an example of unrelieved evil. For example, in *Jonathan Wild* Fielding links Alexander with Caesar and measures Wild's crimes against those committed by these two figures.[49] In *A Dialogue Between the Devil, the Pope, and the Pretender* (1745), the Devil mentions his intimate acquaintance with

Alexander and the mischief that he allowed this disciple to do (*True Patriot*, p. 100). In "Of True Greatness" Fielding associates Alexander with the devastation and ruin created by war.[50] Unlike some of his contemporaries, Fielding condemns Alexander unconditionally; he repeatedly assures his readers that he does not consider the "merciful" acts Alexander performed sufficient to redeem his atrocities.

Fielding probably found Alexander a more acceptable archetype for a tyrant than Augustus or other members of the Julio-Claudian family for several reasons. As a Macedonian who lived hundreds of years before the Roman Empire, Alexander was sufficiently distant from the Augustan circle that Fielding's readers would not be reminded of the problematic politics of Augustus—or of Horace, prominent member of the Maecenean circle and court poet for the emperor. By focusing his attention primarily on Alexander, Fielding could avoid discussing the severity with which Augustus repressed freedom and could still express his admiration for the literature that Augustus encouraged. When Fielding does mention Roman tyrants, he always chooses Nero and Caligula, whose careers are somewhat removed from Augustus and whose cruelty was much more pronounced.[51] While he does discuss Julius Caesar, Fielding virtually ignores Caesar's relationship to Augustus and its implications. This selective use of Roman history suggests that he was aware that many of his contemporaries were uncomfortable with the politics of the Augustan age; it also reveals that he chose to ignore the political implications of Augustus's reign and to focus instead on the brilliant literature that resulted from the emperor's patronage.

While Fielding can and does address the political activities of various characters in ancient history, he differs from some of his contemporaries in that he acknowledges that what he presents as history—or what others present as history—is not objective truth but an interpretation of events, which have been selected to prove a point. Consequently, he can choose to ignore facts that do not support his message. Addison Ward observes that many writers applied Roman history selectively to contemporary events—few were concerned about the truth of what happened in Rome, and most did not acknowledge that their interpretation of events was not the only one. For Swift the history of the Republic represents what happens when the commons encroaches on the rights of the nobles; Steele uses the myth to attack the Oxford-Bolingbroke ministry.[52] Although Fielding does not deny that writers should employ history to teach lessons, he implies that they should use it ethically and that they should recognize that other possible interpretations exist. For example, in the *Jacobite's Journal* he shows that anyone can twist a story to show that a worthy man is infamous: "Thus we may say, that the elder *Brutus*, from Pride and Cruelty, put his own Sons to Death; that the younger *Brutus*, from Ambition, and a Desire of supplanting him in his Power, stabb'd his Friend."[53] Although Fielding ignores the political career of Augustus so that he can focus his readers' attention on the literary achievements made possible by the emperor, he acknowledges that other perspectives on these events exist.

Unlike some of his contemporaries, Fielding also recognizes that history is not necessarily more valid than novels or romance. In some respects, fiction is truer because the author acknowledges that what he writes is an interpretation—he does not try to deceive the reader into thinking that he is presenting the only version of events or, in fact, that such objective truth is possible (*Joseph Andrews*, bk. 3, chap. 1, pp. 185–91). Fielding's statements on this subject grow directly out of the disagreement between the ancients and moderns over history. Like Fielding, ancient historians considered histories literature; they were less concerned with factual accuracy than with exempla that could be derived from historical persons and events. The "moderns," however, tried to treat historiography as a science, whose object was to obtain the truth about historical events, even if it were morally objectionable. As Fielding demonstrates in discussing the antiquarians, however, such objective truth is unobtainable, because each person's research is colored by his or her prejudices.[54] Fielding's practice of treating historical figures as exempla is a direct outgrowth of these views on history.

Fielding often uses characters drawn from classical history to make points about his own society. In his early career Fielding identifies Caesar and other tyrants with Walpole and his administration. For example, in *Jonathan Wild* he often equates the exploits of Wild with those of Caesar and Alexander the Great. Because his contemporaries often identified Wild with Walpole, Fielding may have employed the classical exempla to reinforce his message about political corruption. During the Jacobite rebellion of 1745, Fielding focuses on the Catilinarian conspiracy; here events from the Roman Republic support his attacks on the Jacobites and his arguments about the threat faced by the English government. He identifies the Pretender with Caesar and Alexander and equates this threat with that faced by Rome from Catiline. Thus, Fielding's use of classical symbols reflects his political sentiments and the influence of the classical historians, who considered their work literature instead of science and who used historical exempla to illustrate general truths about mankind and their society.

Weinbrot has also noted another indication that eighteenth-century writers were uncomfortable with the Augustan age: they are often ambivalent about the Augustan poets Horace and Virgil, who wrote great poetry but used their talents to serve a tyrant.[55] Unlike Pope and some of his contemporaries, however, Fielding never expresses any reservations about either writer. Fielding's comments about Virgil are adulatory, especially compared with his reservations about Homer. For example, in the *Champion* he criticizes

Homer for excess, but he praises Virgil: "This was a Fault from which *Virgil* was entirely clear, and yet *Augustus* in his Orders to *Tucca* and *Varius*, concerning the Edition of his Works, gives them full Leave to retrench any Superfluities therein, but by no means to insert any Addition. Such an esteem had that polite Prince of Conciseness, and such a Detestation of all Redundancy in Writing" (15 March 1739–40, 2:3). Fielding is unreserved about Virgil's conciseness; he also does not hesitate to associate the greatness of his achievement with the emperor, who also receives praise for avoiding excess. Thus, Fielding uses the *Aeneid* as the model for *Amelia* and includes other Virgilian imitations in the *Vernon-iad*, *A Journey from this World to the Next*, *Jonathan Wild* and other parts of the *Miscellanies*. No wonder that he places Virgil at the head of his troops in the Paper War.[56] Fielding rarely mentions the politics of Horace or Virgil.

Fielding's attitude toward these Augustan writers also directed his choice of satiric personae. Fielding's persona is Horatian rather than Juvenalian. Most of his satire focuses on foibles rather than individuals, and he is not so concerned with vice as with minor flaws. Fielding writes as a member of the establishment; thus, his perspective is much more congenial with that of Horace, who was supported by his emperor, than with that of Juvenal, whose satires reflect his isolation from society. Consequently, while Fielding often attacks the same targets as Pope and Swift, he does so with far less venom. Furthermore, Fielding can laugh at himself; he sees his own flaws and, therefore, includes himself in the society that he criticizes.

Pope often stood outside the mainstream and, therefore, found the Juvenalian stance more compatible with his situation and perspective. As a Roman Catholic, Pope was automatically excluded by his religion from traditional education and religion; Fielding went to Eton and made friends with many who eventually joined the inner circles of the government—among them, George Lyttleton and William Pitt.[57] Having received the patronage of the Duke of Bedford in 1748 to become a magistrate in London, Fielding could not share the bitterness of Pope and Swift toward the government that supported him. Thus, during the Jacobite Rebellion of 1745, he defended the government against the opposition in the *True Patriot* and the *Jacobite's Journal*. Fielding could easily identify with a classical writer like Horace, who received the patronage of the emperor and criticized his society from the comfortable perspective of one who had a firm position inside it.

Fielding may also have drawn on the Augustan poets more often than Pope because of the genres in which the two primarily worked. Both Weinbrot and Christopher Ricks have noted the dilemma confronted by a poet working in a genre perfected by classical writers: while admiring the work of his predecessors, a poet like Pope or Dryden needs to challenge their productions and surpass them with his own.[58] Because Fielding chose a genre essentially unknown to the ancients, he could show his appreciation for classical authors without encountering the same conflict that faced Pope and Dryden when they imitated classical forms. Thus, Fielding, free from the oppression of classical genres, can refer constantly to ancient rhetoric, philosophy, and history without confronting its political and generic problems. While Fielding admires some classical poets unreservedly, however, he does challenge one classical genre in his fiction—the epic. His use of epic terminology and his allusions to Homer and Virgil suggest that he considers his new species the heir to the epic tradition, but his novels also challenge that tradition because his mock heroics both imitate and undercut the classical genre.

Although Fielding does not write in a classical genre, his work strongly reflects his close ties to the classical tradition. He shows that he believes that classical writers and critics were superior to the moderns in their taste and learning; he also finds their philosophy and their history more meaningful than that of many of his contemporaries. The classics guide his own desire to compose novels that do more than simply entertain his audiences and influence him as he develops rules for his new genre. Furthermore, the classics affect his attitude toward the writers of his own age, for, when measured against ancient writers, many moderns fell very short of the mark. Fielding considers the classical tradition important because it serves as a standard of good taste, provides a measure of literary value, and stresses that all writers have an ethical responsibility to their audiences. He is not concerned about the authenticity of the classical tradition or whether ancient civilization was more primitive than his own, since these issues did not affect the validity of classical "wisdom." Whether Bentley or any other scholar found a new fact about Homer was unimportant; it would hardly diminish the classical tradition from which he drew.

Fielding is not concerned whether the ancient world was exactly as he conceives it or even whether the texts he read were genuine. For him the classical tradition is important because it teaches us about taste and provides a source of wisdom, not generic models. He often finds the ancient writers more congenial to his outlook than his own contemporaries, who are so preoccupied with petty details that they misinterpret what they see. At the same time, Fielding demonstrates that he knows about the divergent thinking on Augustus, Homer, and other controversial figures of the ancient world; he cautions that no historical account is factually accurate, that each results from the ethical choices or prejudices of the author. For him the classical writers are less entities in themselves than exempla to be used to teach a lesson. Thus, Fielding is cautious about others who see his own age only through the classical past and judge all their experience against Homer and Virgil.

What kind of ancient was Henry Fielding? He regards his work as a continuation of the classical tradition begun by Homer and continued by Aristotle, Cicero, Virgil, and Horace. Unlike Pope and Scriblerians, he emphasizes his ties with Augustus, Horace, and the Maecenean circle. And like the great historians of the ancient world, Fielding uses historical and literary characters to encourage his readers to be more perceptive in assessing both literature and human behavior.

POSTSCRIPT

Literary Politics in the Mid-Eighteenth Century and the Genealogy of the Novel

> I am running on further than I intended, so pleasant it is to talk of one's self; I will however controll this Pleasure, and conclude like Horace.
> *Verbum non amplius addam.*
> —*Covent-Garden Journal*

Twentieth-century critics and scholars have assumed that by the mid-eighteenth century the controversy over the importance of classical literature was a dead issue; consequently, they have concentrated on the "modernity" of readers, writers, and critics in this period and have dismissed evidence of the classical tradition in literature as an insignificant holdover from the past. This study has shown that Fielding used the classics deliberately to portray both his characters and his narrator and that he addresses the ongoing controversy between the ancients and moderns by self-consciously selecting ancestors from classical antiquity; it also raises broader questions involving the politics of readers, writers, and critics in the eighteenth century and challenges modern theories about the genealogy of the English novel. Since Fielding clearly defined his readers, his work, and his role as a writer and critic in reference to classical antiquity, we must consider how this new perspective on his work changes some of our standard assumptions about eighteenth-century readers and writers and the impulses that prompted the novel. Does this new view of Fielding alter our definition of the eighteenth-century reader? What does his use of the classical tradition reveal about relationships among Fielding and other authors? Finally, how does this new information affect recent theories about the origins of the English novel—particularly those of Ian Watt, Michael McKeon, and J. Paul Hunter?

The evidence suggests that Fielding—and probably other writers in the eighteenth century—had a far more complex conception of their "audience" than most modern scholars have recognized and that they designed works that could anticipate multiple responses. Moreover, Fielding's interest in the classical tradition defines his relationships with his contemporaries more clearly, emphasizing his affinities with authors working in other genres and his differences from other novelists of this period, particularly Defoe and Richardson. Thus, my research indicates that modern theorists of the novel have erred in dismissing the role of the classics in the development of the novel; it also suggests the difficulty of finding a single theory that successfully accounts for all forms of fiction in this century.

CLASSICAL REFERENCES AND THE EIGHTEENTH-CENTURY AUDIENCE

Although reader-response critics have acknowledged the individuality of readers for years, most critics of eighteenth-century novels—like John Preston, Raymond Stephanson, and Wolfgang Iser—view the readers in the eighteenth century as a fairly homogeneous group, sharing a common education and beliefs; consequently, they have tacitly assumed that writers like Fielding geared their novels to a single ideal "reader."[1] This position is attractive, if mistaken, because it simplifies an analysis of the reader's response to a given text and of the techniques used by an author to elicit that reading. As my analysis of the quotations in the novels suggests, however, Fielding's audience is far more diverse than reader-response critics have assumed. Fielding provides many signals—both explicit and implicit—that show he was writing for more than one "reader"; the classical allusions provide one way in which we can get some picture of the variety of audiences Fielding manipulated simultaneously.

In chapter 1 I demonstrated that Fielding's prospective readers can be divided into three groups if we look only at their training in the classics—those highly skilled in Latin and Greek, those with a smattering of Latin restricted to Lily's grammar and various translations, and those whose knowledge of classical literature (if any) came entirely from English translations. Fielding's choice of classical references indicates that he directs his novels to all of these audiences. For the well-educated "classical" reader, he often leaves untranslated short Latin and Greek phrases and exploits the original contexts of his quotations. He also addresses another group of classical readers, who, remembering their lessons in Lily or the *Epigrammatum Delectus*, would recognize the quotations he draws from those sources. To accommodate readers who were classically illiterate, he alludes to ancient authors more frequently in his fiction than he actually quotes them and selects ancients readily available in popular translations: Dryden's Virgil, Creech's Lucretius, Pope's Homer, and Francis's Horace all figure prominently in the novels.[2] In addition to direct addresses to his "classical" and "English" readers, then, Fielding demonstrates clearly that he is aware that his audience was composed of people with widely different educational levels and prejudices.[3]

Fielding's attempt to cater to three audiences indicates that he anticipated more than a single response to his fiction. Readers who shared his knowledge of the classics would probably recognize the misuse of classical references as one signature of a given character and could identify with the narrator of *Joseph Andrews, Tom Jones,* or *Amelia,* appreciating the way he skillfully exploits allusions to ancient literature. Readers with only a smattering of Latin might initially identify with characters who rely heavily on Latin tags because that level of learning would most closely match their own, but they would be entrapped, because Fielding often links faulty learning and dubious morals. Fielding's least educated audience, who could be annoyed at untranslated quotations or would simply skip the classical references altogether, might misread characters who misuse classics—as have some modern critics. Such readers might be blinded to characters' positive attributes by their hostile reaction to classical allusions and quotations; without other clues to personality, such an audience would probably rely more heavily on the narrator for guidance, thereby reinforcing his authority.

My brief analysis of the possible responses of Fielding's audience shows that reader-response critics should acknowledge that the reading public in the eighteenth-century was sufficiently diverse that writers like Fielding could design novels that evoked a range of reactions. Fielding's use of the classics suggests both that knowledge of ancient literature varied from reader to reader and that, far from being passé, the classical tradition still interested many people. While classical learning provides one obvious way of distinguishing different readers, other criteria might be used to define various audiences: economic status, political alliances, or religion, for example. Such analyses of the eighteenth-century reading public could alter our view of its response to the novel and the audience assumed or created by individual authors.

Fielding's efforts to tailor his work to a wide variety of readers also sheds light on the dynamics of being a professional writer in the mid-eighteenth century. Although Fielding was well educated and identified with the Scriblerians and learned essayists like Addison and Steele, he was not writing for a coterie who shared his educational background. Because he had to earn his living from his pen, even after becoming a magistrate, he had to expand the market for his novels by appealing to the largest possible audience. With romance elements and classical references geared to each of his "audiences," he could increase the likelihood that more people would buy his books. Thus, Fielding's use of the classics indicates how much the writing profession had changed from the beginning of the century to the 1740s.

Fielding's Career and his Role in the Development of the Novel

While the diversity of classical allusions suggests that scholars need to rethink their assumption that the eighteenth-century reading public was fairly homogeneous and classically uneducated, it also suggests that we should reevaluate Fielding's literary alliances and his place in the early history of the novel. Ian Watt and Michael McKeon have argued that Fielding is an anomaly, whose career as a novelist is outside the main line of development represented by Defoe and Richardson. The classical allusions reveal that, on the contrary, Fielding has important affinities with other eighteenth-century writers and that his work grew out of an equally popular, though different, tradition from that of Defoe and Richardson. They also suggest the importance of the ancient/modern controversy in the development of the eighteenth-century novel.

Fielding scholars have long recognized that his topical-political allusions place his plays and journalism firmly in the controversies of the eighteenth century and relate his works to his contemporaries in the theater and in the periodical press. His references to ancient literature also ground his novels in the critical issues that concerned contemporary writers, critics, and scholars and suggest that, to Fielding, the significance of the classical past was still a vibrant issue. Fielding's interest in these critical controversies enhances our awareness that he shares many concerns with other learned writers of this period—for example, Dryden, Addison, Steele, Pope, Swift, and Gay. All had similar training in the classics and a lifelong interest in classical literature. As I pointed out in chapter 2, all use Horace extensively, either in their choice of mottoes or in imitations or translations. Fielding's novels and periodicals are full of complimentary references to these writers, and his opinions often echo theirs on classical literature.[4] In his fiction Fielding frequently turns to Dryden's and Pope's translations of the epic poets, and many of his characters refer to their works. Fielding agrees with Addison, Pope, and other Scriblerians that classical literature is important as a literary standard and that classical criticism is valuable in developing judgment. Like Pope and Swift, Fielding deplores the way in which the moderns debased classical tradition, choosing some of the same moderns as the targets of his satires. Hunter has discussed how Fielding patterned his career after that of Virgil; Fielding's efforts connect him to Dryden and Pope, whose choice of genres was determined by the work of the epic poet.[5] Thus, Fielding's reliance on classical texts demonstrates the ties between his fiction and the efforts of his contemporaries working in other genres.

While Fielding's affinities to these writers show that his novels reflect the concerns of many educated people in this period, his approach to the classics also highlights the differences between him and others who shared his classical background and belief in the classical tradition. For example, his use of the classics clarifies the ambivalence that characterizes his relations with the Scriblerians. Though he clearly admires Pope, Swift, and Gay, Fielding does not completely share their pessimistic view of society and politics; standing firmly inside the political establishment, Fielding uses the classics to satirize types, not individuals. While he acknowledges with the Scriblerians that classical learning is declining, and with it, literary taste and morality, he does not believe that the situation is hopeless. In his essays and novels, Fielding attempts to defend the classical tradition and make it more appealing to his readers. Because his literary choices are often responses—either positive or negative—to these writers, Fielding demonstrates that his novels are closely tied with their work; they also show that his work is much more part of the mainstream than critics of the novel have traditionally considered it.

His connection with writers who were known for work in genres other than fiction suggests that Fielding developed his novels from these genres rather than those usually associated with the early history of the novel. Certainly his own work in journalism supports Thomas Lockwood's theory about the connection between the periodical essay and his fiction.[6] As I have demonstrated, the narrator of *Jonathan Wild* is very similar to the pedantic persona in some of Fielding's journalism; Fielding also uses similar methods to exploit the classics in his periodical literature and in the chapters discussing theory in *Tom Jones* and *Joseph Andrews*. The essays in his journalism and fiction share identical critical and moral concerns and rely on the same classical authorities. In fact, some of his discussions of critical issues echo treatments done in his journalism.[7] In both, he uses ancient authorities to lend credibility to his argument and to introduce his own reflections. The similarities reveal that Fielding's concept of fiction came, at least in part, from the periodical essay; investigation of other genres in which he worked—plays, poetry, travel literature, law—could also prove fruitful.

This new view of the connection between Fielding and other eighteenth-century writers suggests that we should also reconsider Fielding's place in the development of the novel. Both Ian Watt and Michael McKeon have examined Fielding's novels primarily in conjunction with other major fiction writers of the period—particularly Defoe and Richardson. Fielding's classical references indicate, however, that he is much more closely related to Dryden, Addison, and the Scriblerians than these writers. His attitude toward classical literature reflects the traditional education he received at Eton and Leyden University—training that aligns him with the Scriblerians—while emphasizing his differences from Defoe and Richardson, who had primarily a Puritan educational and religious background. Fielding's reliance on classical authorities emphasizes that his attitude toward the ancient world was more positive than that of novelists raised in an environment hostile to the influence of "heathen" culture. Consequently, attempts to link the three authors in a common genealogy share the same problem.

One cannot deny that Fielding reacted to the works of Defoe and Richardson—and to those of a host of other eighteenth-century writers—and that he drew on genres such as romance and spiritual autobiography, which also influenced others. As Watt has demonstrated, however, Defoe and Richardson entirely rejected the relevance of classical tradition in their fiction and argued against relying heavily on that tradition because of its supposed immorality.[8] Unlike them, Fielding drew on the classics in developing his conception of the novel as a form and used classical authority extensively in his criticism and his discussions of morality. When he openly acknowledges his debt to ancient literature, he self-consciously distances himself from Defoe and Richardson and associates himself with others who drew from the classical tradition. By identifying his fiction with classical forms, Fielding calls attention to the differences between his "literary" novels and those of his contemporaries, and he establishes a legitimate genealogy based on another tradition.

Whatever their differences, both Watt and McKeon have assumed that all eighteenth-century writers of fiction responded to the same set of social and economic forces. For Watt, eighteenth-century fiction springs from the rise of the middle class and the demand for realism. Because Fielding's frequent use of the classics does not conform to this theory, Watt belittles the references to antiquity and argues that Fielding's allusions to epic do not represent the mainstream opinion in the eighteenth century, which he associates with Defoe and Richardson. But Fielding's references to ancient literature prove that he reflects the literary concerns of many of his educated contemporaries. Although Fielding does not agree with Defoe and Richardson about the place of classical literature, his views represent a more established, though still popular, opinion than theirs does, thereby showing that his work springs from equally valid, though different, sources than that of Puritan writers.

While McKeon addresses some of the difficulties created by Watt's approach to the novel, he, too, devalues the importance of Fielding's classical allusions and quotations. His argument assumes that all novels of the eighteenth century—Defoe's, Richardson's, and Fielding's—are either reactions or counterreactions to the romance. Because he must establish that Fielding's novels are, in effect, related to the romance, McKeon dismisses the classical references in the novels as mere ornament and sides with critics who ignore the importance of epic in Fielding's concept of the novel as a genre.[9] My study demonstrates that Fielding's use of classical literature is, on the contrary, far more extensive, deliberate, and systematic than McKeon's theory can allow.

The classical tradition challenges these theories and suggests that we must revise our understanding of the origins and development of the novel in the eighteenth century. Both Watt and McKeon assume that they can find some common ground uniting all eighteenth-century novels, maintaining that Fielding's concept of fiction must be like Defoe's and Richardson's. Therefore, both ignore or belittle those features of Fielding's novels that distinguish his work from that of the other writers. My analysis of Fielding's classical references suggests that Fielding was not working with the same assumptions that guided Defoe and Richardson. As his use of classical literature indicates, the classical tradition played an important role in the development of the novel, and studies of his theory of the novel should acknowledge his similarities with writers in other genres who also derived their work from classical literary tradition. Histories of the novel must recognize that the genre could have many different genealogies. Thus, we must ask if any single theory can ever explain the emergence of every type of novel in the eighteenth century.[10]

Like many of his contemporaries, Fielding so respected classical tradition that it determined the shape of his fiction, his mode of argument, and his moral and critical concerns. In his novels he relied on classical theory to define his new genre and used classical authority as a means of establishing his credibility with audiences and providing a starting point for his own thoughts. He argued that classical learning was essential for the effective writer and critic, for ancient literature provided the standard against which he measured modern literature and culture, which he frequently found deficient both artistically and morally. He continued the ancient-modern controversy by attacking those who had trivialized the ancient world through mindless debates. In order to legitimate his choice of fiction as a vehicle for his ideas, he deliberately alluded to classical works to show that he believed his novels to be an outgrowth of ancient, rather than modern, tradition.

Despite his obvious appreciation of classical tradition and his desire to associate his work with it, Fielding realized that problems arose when one invoked that tradition. He did not uncritically regard the classical world or classical learning, recognizing that the moral values presented in epics and in Stoic literature were not readily applicable in a Christian environment; he knew that classical learning divorced from experience resulted in pedantry and bad judgment. Because he appealed to a broader audience than did Dryden, Pope, and Swift, Fielding also realized that fewer of his readers shared his knowledge of classical literature and that, consequently, references to the ancients had less authority than earlier in the century. Like Pope and Swift, he acknowledged that among many writers classical learning had so degenerated that much of it had lost its meaning, motivating him to establish a new line of authority.

Unlike earlier writers, Fielding attempted to rectify this situation, resurrecting the classical tradition by incorporating it into a literary form, the novel, that appealed to modern audiences. He made it an integral part of his characterization and narrative persona in order to enhance his readers' awareness of the artifice underlying his creation and to force them to question their assumptions about literature and authorship. He translated the lessons communicated by Horace, Virgil, Aristotle, and Homer into a form that would appeal to and influence his eighteenth-century readers. By imitating and challenging the greatest authors of antiquity, he both defined his "new species" more clearly and attempted to preserve the most valuable elements of the classical world for his modern readers.

APPENDIX A
Tables for Chapter 1

Table A-1. Latin Authors Recommended in
Six Guides for a Gentleman's Reading

Latin Authors

Author	Brokesby	Felton	Blackwall	Waterland	Clarke	Boswell
Ammianus	x					x
Aulus Gellius			x			
Caesar	x		x	x	x	x
Catullus			x	x		
Cicero	x	x	x	x	x	x
Claudian			x			
Columella	x					
Curtius				x	x	x
Eutropius				x		
Festus	x					
Florus			x	x	x	x
Aulus Hirtius			x			
Horace		x	x	x	x	x
Justin			x	x	x	x
Juvenal			x	x		x
Livy	x	x	x	x	x	x
Lucan			x	x		
Lucretius				x		
Manilius				x		
Martial				x		
Nepos			x	x	x	x
Ovid			x	x		x
Persius				x		
Phaedrus				x		
Plautus		x	x	x		x

138   APPENDIX A

Author	Brokesby	Felton	Blackwall	Waterland	Clarke	Boswell
Pliny (Elder)			x			x
Pliny (Younger)			x	x		x
Propertius			x	x		
Quintilian			x		x	
Sallust		x	x	x	x	x
Seneca				x		
Silius Italicus			x			
Statius			x			
Suetonius	x		x	x	x	x
Tacitus	x		x	x	x	x
Terence		x	x	x	x	x
Tibullus			x	x		
Valerius Flaccus			x			
Varro	x					
Velleius						x
Virgil		x	x	x	x	x
Totals	9	7	27	29	14	20

Greek Authors

Author	Brokesby	Felton	Blackwall	Waterland	Clarke	Boswell
Aelian			x			
Aeschines						x
Aeschylus			x			
Alcaeus		x				
Anacreon		x	x		x	
Antoninus				x		x
Apollonius Rhodius			x			
Aratus			x			
Aristophanes			x	x		x
Aristotle		x	x	x	x	
Arrian			x		x	x
Calaber			x			
Callimachus			x	x		
Demosthenes		x	x	x		x
Dio Cassius	x					x
Diodorus Siculus			x		x	x

APPENDIX A   139

Author	Brokesby	Felton	Blackwall	Waterland	Clarke	Boswell
Diogenes Laertius				x		
Dionysius Periegetes			x	x		
Dionysius of Halicarnassos			x		x	x
Epictetus				x		x
Euripides			x	x		x
Herodian	x		x	x		
Herodotus		x	x	x	x	x
Hesiod			x	x		
Homer		x	x	x	x	x
Isocrates				x		x
Longinus			x	x	x	x
Lucian			x	x		x
Lycophron			x			
Nicander			x			
Nonus			x			
Oppian			x			
Orpheus		x	x			
Pindar		x	x			x
Plato		x	x	x		x
Plutarch	x		x	x	x	x
Polyaenus			x			
Polybius	x		x		x	x
Sappho		x				
Simonides		x				
Sophocles			x	x		x
Steisichorus		x				
Strabo		x				
Theocritus		x	x	x		x
Theognis		x				
Theophrastus				x		
Thucydides	x	x	x	x	x	x
Xenophon	x	x	x	x	x	x
Totals	6	15	37	23	11	24

Table A-2. Latin Authors in the *ESTC*

Author	Latin Editions	Latin/English Editions	English Editions	Total
Horace	25	57	32	114
Works	19	3	0	22
Ars poetica	1	2	3	6
Carmen seculare	0	0	1	1
Epistulae (sel.)	0	14	2	16
Epodes	0	3	0	3
Odes	0	2	1	3
Odes (sel.)	0	15	12	27
Satires (sel.)	0	8	3	11
Selections	5	10	10	25
Ovid	26	13	19	58
Works	2	0	0	2
Amores and Heroides	3	2	4	9
Ars amatoria	0	2	2	4
Fasti	2	0	0	2
Metamorphoses	5	5	2	12
Meta. (sel.)	1	1	4	6
Tristia	7	2	2	11
Selections	6	1	5	12
Cicero	38	2	12	52
Works	2	0	0	2
Academica	2	0	0	2
Ad familiares	2	0	0	2
De finibus	3	0	1	4
De legibus	1	0	0	1
De natura deorum	2	0	1	3
De officiis	3	0	0	3
De oratore	3	0	1	4
De senectute	0	0	2	2
Epistulae	5	1	2	8
Orations	3	0	3	6
Philippics	1	0	0	1
Philosophical Works	4	0	1	5

APPENDIX A 141

Author	Latin Editions	Latin/English Editions	English Editions	Total
Cicero (cont.)				
Rhetorical Works	2	0	0	2
Tusculan Disputations	2	0	1	3
Selections	3	1	0	4
Virgil	18	12	16	46
Works	15	2	3	20
Aeneid	0	0	3	3
Aeneid (sel.)	0	2	8	10
Eclogues	1	6	0	7
Georgics	0	2	1	3
Georgics and Eclogues	0	0	1	1
Selections	2	0	0	2
Sallust	15	4	4	23
Terence	15	4	1	20
Phaedrus	12	6	1	19
Persius	11	2	3	16
Cornelius Nepos	8	2	3	13
Pliny (Younger)	4	0	9	13
Juvenal	10	1	1	12
Justinus	7	2	2	11
Cato	2	4	4	10
Tibullus	6	0	4	10
Caesar	6	1	1	8
Martial	6	1	1	8
Seneca	1	2	5	8
Orations (sel.)	0	0	1	1
Moralia (sel.)	1	2	3	6
Tragedies (sel.)	0	0	1	1
Trogus	6	1	1	8
Eutropius	4	3	0	7
Florus	5	1	0	6
Lucretius	3	2	1	6
Propertius	5	0	1	6
Suetonius	1	1	4	6
Tacitus	2	0	4	6
Catullus	3	0	2	5

Author	Latin Editions	Latin/English Editions	English Editions	Total
Claudian	0	1	4	5
Quintus Curtius	4	0	1	5
Aulus Hirtius	4	0	1	5
Velleius Paterculus	3	0	2	5
Livy	3	0	1	4
Lucan	2	0	2	4
Petronius	3	0	1	4
Plautus	2	1	1	4
Statius	1	0	2	3
Columella	1	0	1	2
Pliny the Elder	1	0	1	2
Apicius	1	0	0	1
Pomponius Mela	1	0	0	1
Quintilian	1	0	0	1
Prudentius	0	0	1	1
Vegetius	0	0	1	1
Vitruvius	0	0	1	1
Totals	266	123	151	540

Table A-3. Greek Authors in the *ESTC*

Author	Gr.	Gr./Lat.	Eng./Lat.	Lat.	Gr./Eng.	Eng.	Total
Homer	4	6	0	0	0	16	26
Works	1	1	0	0	0	0	2
Batracho-myomachia	0	0	0	0	0	4	4
Iliad	2	4	0	0	0	6	12
Odyssey	1	1	0	0	0	3	5
Selections	0	0	0	0	0	3	3
Aesop	0	4	4	1	0	16	25
Xenophon	4	11	0	0	0	9	24
Works	0	1	0	0	0	0	1
Agesilaus	0	1	0	0	0	0	1
Anabasis	0	1	0	0	0	2	3
Apologia	0	1	0	0	0	0	1
Cyropaedia	1	2	0	0	0	1	4
Hieron	0	1	0	0	0	1	2
Memorabilia	0	2	0	0	0	3	5
Oeconomicus	0	1	0	0	0	1	2
Symposium	1	0	0	0	0	1	2
Selections	2	1	0	0	0	0	3
Euclid	0	1	0	3	0	9	13
Anacreon	0	6	0	0	1	5	12
Plutarch	2	4	0	0	1	5	12
Moralia	1	1	0	0	0	2	4
Vitae	0	2	0	0	0	3	5
Selections	1	1	0	0	1	0	3
Cebes	1	7	0	0	0	3	11
Epictetus	0	5	0	1	0	5	11
Hippocrates	0	5	0	2	0	4	11
Plato	1	6	0	0	0	4	11
Parmenides	0	1	0	0	0	0	1
Phaedo	0	0	0	0	0	1	1
Republic	0	1	0	0	0	0	1

Author	Gr.	Gr./Lat.	Eng./Lat.	Lat.	Gr./Eng.	Eng.	Total
Plato (cont.)							
Symposium	1	0	0	0	0	0	1
Selections	0	4	0	0	0	3	7
Sophocles	1	4	0	0	0	6	11
Works	0	4	0	0	0	1	5
Ajax	0	0	0	0	0	1	1
Electra	0	0	0	0	0	2	2
Oedipus	0	0	0	0	0	1	1
Philoctetes	0	0	0	0	0	1	1
Selected Plays	1	0	0	0	0	0	1
Theophrastus	0	5	0	0	1	5	11
Demosthenes	0	7	0	0	0	2	9
De corona	0	1	0	0	0	1	2
De legatione	0	1	0	0	0	0	1
In Midiam	0	1	0	0	0	0	1
Selections	0	4	0	0	0	1	5
Isocrates	2	3	0	1	0	3	9
Lucian	2	5	0	0	0	2	9
Aristotle	1	4	0	1	0	2	8
Ethics	0	1	0	1	0	1	3
Poetics	0	2	0	0	0	1	3
Rhetoric	0	1	0	0	0	0	1
Selections	1	0	0	0	0	0	1
Euripides	1	5	0	0	0	2	8
Sappho	0	4	0	0	1	3	8
Pindar	0	1	0	0	0	6	7
Musaeus	0	1	0	0	0	5	6
Phaleris	0	1	0	0	0	5	6
Pythagoras	0	2	0	0	0	4	6
Bion	0	2	0	0	0	3	5
Prodicus	1	3	0	0	0	1	5
Theocritus	0	3	0	0	0	2	5
Thucydides	1	1	0	0	0	3	5
Aeschines	0	3	0	0	0	1	4
In Ctesiphontem	0	1	0	0	0	1	2

APPENDIX A 145

Author	Gr.	Gr./Lat.	Eng./Lat.	Lat.	Gr./Eng.	Eng.	Total
Aeschines (cont.)							
De legatione	0	1	0	0	0	0	1
Selections	0	1	0	0	0	0	1
Aristophanes	0	1	0	0	0	3	4
Clouds	0	0	0	0	0	1	1
Plutus	0	0	0	0	0	2	2
Plutus and Nubes	0	1	0	0	0	0	1
Dionysius Periegetes	0	4	0	0	0	0	4
Longinus	0	2	0	0	0	2	4
Maximus Tyrius	0	3	0	0	0	1	4
Moschus	0	2	0	0	0	2	4
Apollonius of Perga	0	1	0	2	0	0	3
Archimedes	0	0	0	1	0	2	3
Callimachus	0	1	0	0	0	2	3
Dionysius of Halicarnassos	1	2	0	0	0	0	3
Herodian	0	2	0	0	0	1	3
Herodotus	1	1	0	0	0	1	3
Hesiod	0	2	0	0	0	1	3
Hierocles	0	2	0	0	0	1	3
Lysias	0	3	0	0	0	0	3
Origen	0	1	0	0	0	2	3
Theognis	0	3	0	0	0	0	3
Aeschylus	1	1	0	0	0	0	2
Artemidorus	0	0	0	0	0	2	2
Colluthus	0	0	0	0	0	2	2
Dio Cassius	0	0	0	0	0	2	2
Menander	0	1	0	1	0	0	2
Oppian	0	0	0	0	0	2	2
Polybius	0	0	0	0	0	2	2
Sibyl	0	0	0	0	1	1	2
Tryphiodorus	0	1	0	0	0	1	2
Xenophon the Ephesian	0	1	0	0	0	1	2
Appian	0	0	0	0	0	1	1
Aretaeus	0	1	0	0	0	0	1
Aristaenetus	0	0	0	0	0	1	1
Aristeas	0	0	0	0	0	1	1

Author	Gr.	Gr./Lat.	Eng./Lat.	Lat.	Gr./Eng.	Eng.	Total
Aristides	0	1	0	0	0	0	1
Arrian	0	0	0	0	0	1	1
Cleanthes	0	1	0	0	0	0	1
Demetrius of Phalerum	0	1	0	0	0	0	1
Epicurus	0	0	0	0	0	1	1
Heliodorus	0	0	0	0	0	1	1
Longus	0	0	0	0	0	1	1
Lycophron	0	1	0	0	0	0	1
Lycurgus	0	1	0	0	0	0	1
Naumachius	0	0	0	0	1	0	1
Orpheus	0	0	0	0	0	1	1
Suidas	0	1	0	0	0	0	1
Theodosius	0	1	0	0	0	0	1
Totals	24	151	4	13	6	170	368

Table A-4. Latin Editions with the Greatest Number of Issues in the *ESTC*

Latin only

Text	Number of Issues
Phaedrus (Delphin, ed. P. Danet)	9
Virgil, *Works* (Delphin, ed. C. Ruaus)	9
Cicero, *Sel. Orations, De senectute, De Amicitia* (Delphin, ed. Merouville)	7
Horace, *Works* (Delphin, ed. L. Desprez)	7
Ovid, *Heroides* (Delphin)	7
Ovid, *Metamorphoses* (Delphin)	7
Persius and Juvenal (Delphin, ed. Prateus)	7
Terence (Delphin, ed. N. Camus)	6
Cicero, *De natura deorum* (ed. J. Walker)	5
Cicero, *Tusculan Disputations* (ed. J. Davis)	5
Martial (Westminster)	5
Caesar (Delphin, ed. J. Godovinus)	4
Cornelius Nepos (Delphin, ed. N. Courtin)	4
Ovid, *Tristia* (ed. J. Minellius)	4
Phaedrus (ed. Samuel Hoadly)	4
Sallust (Delphin, ed. D. Crispinus)	4
Trogus (Stationers' Company)	4
Velleius Paterculus (ed. Michael Maittaire)	4
Caesar (ed. S. Clarke)	3
Cicero, *De oratore* (ed. Zachery Pearce)	3
Cicero, *De oratore* (Delphin, ed. J. Proust)	3
Eutropius (In usum scholarum Edinburgh)	3
Horace, *Eclogues* (ed. William Baxter)	3
Horace, *Works* (ed. Richard Bentley)	3
Justinus (Delphin, ed. P. J. Cantel)	3
Justinus (in usum schola mercatorum scissorum)	3
Justinus (Stationers' Company)	3
Pomponius Mela (ed. J. Reinoldius)	3
Cornelius Nepos	3
Ovid, *Tristia* (Delphin)	3
Terence (Cambridge)	3
Terence (ed. J. Minelli)	3
Virgil, *Works* (ed. J. Minellius)	3

Latin with English Translation

Text	Number of Issues
Cato, *Distiches* and Seneca (trans. C. Hoole)	11
Eutropius (literal trans. by J. Clarke)	6
Horace, *Sober Advice from Horace* (Pope)	6
Cornelius Nepos (literal trans. by J. Clarke)	6
Florus (literal trans. by J. Clarke)	4
Horace, *Satires, Epistles, Ars Poetica* (trans. S. Dunster)	4
Horace, *Works* (Poetical trans. Philip Francis)	4
Horace, *Art of Cookery* and *Ars Poetica* (trans. William King)	4
Justinus (literal trans. by J. Clarke)	4
Sallust (trans. J. Clarke)	4
Horace, Epistle 1.1 (trans. Pope)	3
Horace, Epistle 2.2 (trans. Pope)	3
Horace, *Odes, Epistles, Carmen Seculare* in 24 parts (trans. several hands)	3
Horace, *Odes, Epodes, and Carmen Seculare* (prose by David Watson)	3
Horace, *Satires, Epistles, Ars Poetica* (after David Watson)	3
Persius and Juvenal (trans. Thomas Sheridan)	3
Phaedrus (ed. Jonas Brown)	3
Virgil, *Georgics* (trans. John Martyn)	3
Virgil, *Georgics* bk. 2 (trans. William Benson)	3

English Translations

Text	Number of Issues
Seneca, *Morals* (R. L'Estrange)	12
Ovid, *Heroides and Amours* (trans. eminent hands, incl. Dryden and Pope)	10
Ovid, *Ars amatoriae* (trans. Dryden et al.)	9
Terence (trans. Echard and R. L'Estrange)	8
Caesar and Hirtius (trans. M. Bladen)	7
Ovid, *Metamorphoses* (trans. Dryden)	6
Persius and Juvenal (trans. Dryden)	6
Horace, *Odes, Satires, Epistles* (Creech)	5
Horace, *Odes, Satires* (trans. most eminent hands, incl. Congreve, Dryden, Milton)	5

English Translations (cont.)

Text	Number of Issues
Justinus (trans. T. Brown)	5
Sallust (trans. J. Rowe)	5
Trogus (trans. T. Brown)	5
Virgil, *Works* (trans. Dryden)	5
Lucan (trans. N. Rowe)	4
Ovid in *Fables Ancient and Modern* (trans. Dryden)	4
Ovid, *Metamorphoses* (trans. Sewell)	4
Petronius (trans. several hands)	4
Cicero, *Orations* (trans. W. Guthrie)	3
Claudian, *De raptu proserpinae* (trans. J. Hughes)	3
Horace *Odes* 2.1 (J. Swift)	3
Quintus Curtius (trans. John Digby)	3
Lucretius (trans. T. Creech)	3
Pliny the Younger, *Epistles* (trans. W. Melmoth)	3
Sallust and Cicero (trans. T. Gordon)	3
Tacitus (trans. T. Gordon)	3
Virgil, *Works* (trans. J. Trapp)	3

Table A-5. Greek Editions with the Greatest Number of Issues in the *ESTC*

Greek with Latin Translations

Text	Number of Issues
Lucian, *Select Dialogues* (ed. E. Leeds)	6
Dionysius Periegetes (ed. E. Wells)	5
Homer, *Iliad* (pub. T. Wood)	5
Lucian, *Select Dialogues* (ed. W. Dugard)	5
Xenophon, *Cyropaedia* (ed. T. Hutchinson)	5
Aesop, Cebes, Lucian, Isocrates (ed. J. Davidson and J. Traill)	4
Longinus (ed. J. Hudson)	4
Longinus (ed. Z. Pearce)	4
Aeschines, *In Ctesiphontem* (trans. P. Foulkes and J. Friend)	3
Anacreon (ed. J. Barnes)	3
Cebes, *Tabula* (ed. T. Johnson)	3
Dionysius of Halicarnassos, *De compositione verborum* (ed. J. Upton)	3
Epictetus *Enchiridion*, Cebes *Tabula*, Prodicus *Hercules*, Theophrastus (ed. J. Simpson)	3
Homer, *Iliad* (ed. S. Clarke)	3
Poetae minores graeci (incl. Hesiod, Theocritus, Moschus, Bion, Musaeus, Theognis, Phocylides, Pythagoras, ed. R. Winterton)	3
Sophocles, *Ajax and Electra*, (ed. T. Johnson)	3
Xenophon, *Memorabilia* (ed. B. Simpson)	3

English Translations

Text	Number of Issues
Homer, *Iliad* (trans. A. Pope)	10
Euclid and Archimedes (trans. I. Barrow)	9
Epictetus (trans. E. Walker)	8
Euclid (trans. J. Keil et al.)	6
Euclid (trans. Milliet de Chales)	5
Euclid (trans. W. Whiston)	5
Aristotle, *Poetics* (trans. T. Goulston)	4
Epictetus (trans. G. Stanhope)	4
Euclid (trans. I. Barrow)	4

English Translations (cont.)

Text	Number of Issues
Herodotus (trans. I. Littlebury)	4
Homer in *Fables Ancient and Modern* (trans. Dryden)	4
Homer, *Iliad* (trans. Ozell)	4
Longinus (trans. J. Craggs)	4
Longinus (trans. W. Smith)	4
Plato (abridged by M. Dacier, trans. several hands)	4
Plutarch, *Lives* (trans. several hands, incl. Dryden)	4
Pythagoras (trans. N. Rowe)	4
Xenophon, *Memorabilia* (trans. E. Bysshe)	4
Xenophon, *Symposium* (trans. J. Welwood)	4
Euclid (trans. E. Stone)	3
Longinus (trans. Welsted)	3
Lucian (trans. several eminent hands, incl. Dryden)	3

APPENDIX B
Tables for Chapter 2

Table B-1. Latin Authors in the *Champion*

Author	Allusions	Quotations	Total
Horace	5	48	53
Virgil	7	16	23
Ovid	3	10	13
Cicero	2	10	12
Juvenal	1	9	10
Pliny the Elder	1	3	4
Quintilian	2	1	3
Silius Italicus	1	2	3
Tacitus	3	0	3
Aulus Gellius	1	1	2
Lucan	1	1	2
Martial	0	2	2
Seneca	2	0	2
Terence	0	2	2
Livy	0	1	1
Lucretius	0	1	1
Plautus	1	0	1
Sallust	0	1	1
Suetonius	0	1	1
Totals	30	109	139

Table B-2. Greek Authors in the *Champion*

Author	Allusions	Quotations	Total
Homer	10	2	12
Plato	6	1	7
Plutarch	4	0	4
Aristotle	1	2	3
Aeschylus	1	0	1
Josephus	1	0	1
Longinus	0	1	1
Lucian	1	0	1
Pausanias	1	0	1
Sophocles	1	0	1
Totals	26	6	32

Table B-3. Latin Authors in the *True Patriot*

Author	Allusions	Quotations	Total
Horace	1	10	11
Cicero	0	7	7
Juvenal	1	6	7
Virgil	1	4	5
Ovid	1	4	5
Livy	0	3	3
Sallust	0	3	3
Lucretius	0	2	2
Martial	0	2	2
Seneca	1	1	2
Silius Italicus	0	1	1
Totals	5	43	48

Table B-4. Greek Authors in the *True Patriot*

Author	Allusions	Quotations	Total
Aristotle	0	2	2
Euripides	0	2	2
Homer	2	0	2
Pythagoras	1	1	2

Author	Allusions	Quotations	Total
Aesop	1	0	1
Lucian	1	0	1
Plato	1	0	1
Plutarch	1	0	1
Totals	7	5	12

Table B-5. Latin Authors in the *Jacobite's Journal*

Author	Allusions	Quotations	Total
Horace	5	31	36
Ovid	5	13	18
Cicero	3	9	12
Juvenal	0	8	8
Virgil	1	5	6
Livy	4	1	5
Quintilian	3	1	4
Martial	0	3	3
Suetonius	1	2	3
Tacitus	1	2	3
Lucretius	0	2	2
Plautus	0	2	2
Terence	1	1	2
Apuleius	1	0	1
Claudian	0	1	1
Jerome	0	1	1
Pliny the Younger	0	1	1
Priscian	1	0	1
Seneca	0	1	1
Silius Italicus	0	1	1
Totals	26	85	111

Table B-6. Greek Authors in the *Jacobite's Journal*

Author	Allusions	Quotations	Total
Aristotle	7	5	12
Plutarch	4	1	5
Homer	3	1	4
Diogenes Laertius	1	1	2
Plato	1	1	2

Author	Allusions	Quotations	Total
Thucydides	1	1	2
Demosthenes	0	1	1
Diodorus Siculus	1	0	1
Euripides	0	1	1
Herodotus	1	0	1
Longinus	1	0	1
Menander	0	1	1
Polybius	1	0	1
Totals	21	13	34

Table B-7. Latin Authors in the *Covent-Garden Journal*

Author	Allusions	Quotations	Total
Horace	14	42	56
Virgil	5	11	16
Cicero	4	8	12
Juvenal	2	10	12
Ovid	3	9	12
Tacitus	3	4	7
Seneca	4	2	6
Quintilian	3	1	4
Suetonius	3	1	4
Valerius Maximus	3	1	4
Livy	2	1	3
Martial	0	3	3
Terence	1	2	3
Lucretius	0	2	2
Plautus	0	2	2
Pliny the Elder	1	1	2
Tibullus	0	2	2
Claudian	0	1	1
Lucan	0	1	1
Petronius	1	0	1
Phaedrus	0	1	1
Priscian	1	0	1
Propertius	0	1	1
Silius Italicus	0	1	1
Totals	50	107	157

Table B-8. Greek Authors in the *Covent-Garden Journal*

Author	Allusions	Quotations	Total
Homer	10	6	16
Aristotle	7	3	10
Plato	6	2	8
Longinus	7	0	7
Plutarch	4	2	6
Lucian	5	0	5
Diodorus Siculus	3	1	4
Aristophanes	3	0	3
Dio Cassius	2	1	3
Thucydides	1	2	3
Demosthenes	2	0	2
Herodotus	2	0	2
Menander	0	2	2
Aeschines	1	0	1
Anacreon	0	1	1
Bion	0	1	1
Cleobolus	0	1	1
Herodian	0	1	1
Pausanias	1	0	1
Pindar	0	1	1
Stobaeus	1	0	1
Strabo	1	0	1
Totals	56	24	80

APPENDIX C
Tables for Chapter 3

Table C-1. Latin Authors in *Jonathan Wild*

Author	Allusions	Quotations	Total
Virgil	8	1	9 (27%)
Horace	0	3	3 (9%)
Ovid	0	2	2 (6%)
Cicero	1	0	1 (3%)
Claudian	0	1	1 (3%)
Lucan	0	1	1 (3%)
Lucretius	0	1	1 (3%)
Nepos	1	0	1 (3%)
Persius	0	1	1 (3%)
Pliny the Elder	0	1	1 (3%)
Sallust	1	0	1 (3%)
Suetonius	1	0	1 (3%)
Total	12	11	23 (68%)

Table C-2. Greek Authors in *Jonathan Wild*

Author	Allusions	Quotations	Total
Homer	3	0	3 (9%)
Aristotle	3	0	3 (9%)
Plato	2	0	2 (6%)
Herodotus	1	0	1 (3%)
Plutarch	1	0	1 (3%)
Sophocles	1	0	1 (3%)
Total	11	0	11 (32%)

Table C-3. Latin Authors in *Joseph Andrews*

Author	Allusions	Quotations	Total
Virgil	3	3	6 (11%)
Horace	1	4	5 (9%)
Cicero	4	0	4 (7%)
Ovid	0	3	3 (5%)
Seneca	2	0	2 (4%)
Juvenal	1	0	1 (2%)
Nepos	1	0	1 (2%)
Velleius Paterculus	1	0	1 (2%)
Persius	0	1	1 (2%)
Pliny the Elder	0	1	1 (2%)
Totals	13	12	25 (44%)

Table C-4. Greek Authors in *Joseph Andrews*

Author	Allusions	Quotations	Total
Homer	8	1	9 (16%)
Aeschylus	7	0	7 (12%)
Aristotle	6	0	6 (11%)
Plato	3	0	3 (5%)
Aristophanes	2	0	2 (4%)
Apollonius Rhodius	1	0	1 (2%)
Euripides	1	0	1 (2%)
Plutarch	1	0	1 (2%)
Sophocles	1	0	1 (2%)
Theocritus	0	1	1 (2%)
Totals	30	2	32 (56%)

Table C-5. Latin Authors in *Tom Jones*

Author	Allusions	Quotations	Total
Horace	13	22	35 (21%)
Virgil	11	13	24 (14%)
Cicero	11	3	14 (8%)
Ovid	4	8	12 (7%)
Juvenal	1	8	9 (5%)
Terence	0	8	8 (5%)

Author	Allusions	Quotations	Total
Seneca	3	0	3 (2%)
Lucretius	1	1	2 (1%)
Persius	0	2	2 (1%)
Pliny the Elder	0	2	2 (1%)
Catullus	0	1	1 (.6%)
Livy	1	0	1 (.6%)
Lucan	0	1	1 (.6%)
Martial	0	1	1 (.6%)
Quintilian	0	1	1 (.6%)
Suetonius	0	1	1 (.6%)
Tibullus	0	1	1 (.6%)
Totals	45	73	118 (70%)

Table C-6. Greek Authors in *Tom Jones*

Author	Allusions	Quotations	Total
Homer	22	0	22 (13%)
Aristotle	9	1	10 (6%)
Plato	6	0	6 (4%)
Demosthenes	2	0	2 (1%)
Longinus	2	0	2 (1%)
Plutarch	2	0	2 (1%)
Aristophanes	1	0	1 (.6%)
Arrian	1	0	1 (.6%)
Herodotus	1	0	1 (.6%)
Lucian	1	0	1 (.6%)
Stobaeus	1	0	1 (.6%)
Thucydides	1	0	1 (.6%)
Totals	49	1	50 (30%)

Table C-7. Latin Authors in *Amelia*

Author	Allusions	Quotations	Total
Virgil	5	7	12 (17%)
Horace	2	6	8 (11%)
Ovid	5	3	8 (11%)
Cicero	2	1	3 (4%)
Juvenal	1	2	3 (4%)
Claudian	1	1	2 (3%)

Author	Allusions	Quotations	Total
Martial	1	1	2 (3%)
Silius Italicus	2	0	2 (3%)
Lucan	0	2	2 (3%)
Livy	1	0	1 (1%)
Statius	1	0	1 (1%)
Suetonius	0	1	1 (1%)
Terence	0	1	1 (1%)
Valerius Maximus	0	1	1 (1%)
Totals	21	26	47 (66%)

Table C-8. Greek Authors in *Amelia*

Author	Allusions	Quotations	Total
Homer	9	4	13 (18%)
Aristotle	4	0	4 (6%)
Plato	2	0	2 (3%)
Thucydides	0	2	2 (3%)
Lucian	1	0	1 (1%)
Phocylides	0	1	1 (1%)
Simonides	0	1	1 (1%)
Total	16	8	24 (34%)

Notes

Preface

1. See Ian Watt's discussion of the audience for eighteenth-century novels in *The Rise of the Novel* (Berkeley and Los Angeles: University of California Press, 1957), 35–59. For the arguments of those who are interested only in Fielding's use of romance and other contemporary genres, see, for example, Homer Goldberg, "Comic Prose Epic or Comic Romance: The Argument of the Preface to *Joseph Andrews*," *Philological Quarterly* 43 (1964): 193–215; and Sheridan Baker, "Fielding's Comic Epic-in-Prose Romances Again," *Philological Quarterly* 58 (1979): 64–65.

2. For Defoe's and Richardson's attitude toward the classical tradition, see Ian Watt, "Defoe and Richardson on Homer: A Study of the Relation of Novel and Epic in the Early Eighteenth Century," *Review of English Studies*, n.s., 3 (1952): 325–40. Frederic Blanchard's presentation of the reaction to Fielding's novels appears to support the view that Fielding's contemporaries attacked or ignored his fiction. See *Fielding the Novelist: A Study in Historical Criticism* (New Haven: Yale University Press, 1926), 1–139.

3. See, for example, Watt, *Rise of the Novel*, 239–89; and Michael McKeon, *The Origins of the English Novel, 1600–1740* (Baltimore: Johns Hopkins University Press, 1987).

4. Bernard Shea, "Classical Learning in the Novels of Henry Fielding" (Ph.D. diss., Harvard University, 1952).

5. Caroline Goad, *Horace in the English Literature of the Eighteenth Century*, Yale Studies in English 58 (New Haven: Yale University Press, 1918), 191–212; Charles A. Knight, "Fielding and Aristophanes," *Studies in English Literature, 1500–1900* 21 (1981): 481–98.

6. Levi R. Lind, "Lucian and Fielding," *Classical Weekly* 29 (1936): 84–86; Henry Knight Miller, *Essays on Fielding's "Miscellanies": A Commentary on Volume One* (Princeton: Princeton University Press, 1961), 365–419; and Christopher Robinson, *Lucian and His Influence in Europe* (London: Duckworth, 1979), 198–235.

7. See, for example, Ronald Paulson, *Satire and the Novel in Eighteenth-Century England* (New Haven: Yale University Press, 1967), 132–41; Kevin Berland, "Indirect Ethical Discourse: Fielding, Dialogue, and Dialectic" (Ph.D. diss., McMaster University, 1983).

Chapter 1. Classical Learning and Novel Readers, 1701–1750

1. For the limited view of classical education, see, for example, the three standard works on classical education in England: M. L. Clarke, *Classical Education in Britain, 1500–1900*

NOTES TO CHAPTER 1

(Cambridge: Cambridge University Press, 1959), 46–73; M. L. Clarke, *Greek Studies in England, 1700–1830* (1945; Amsterdam: Adolf M. Hakkert, 1986), 10–39; and R. M. Ogilvie, *Latin and Greek: A History of the Influence of the Classics on English Life from 1600 to 1918* (New York: Archon, 1969), 37–45. The only attempt to revise this view has been Penelope Wilson's "Classical Poetry and the Eighteenth-Century Reader," in *Books and their Readers in Eighteenth-Century England*, ed. Isabel Rivers (Leicester, U.K.: Leicester University Press, 1982), 69–96. While Wilson does provide some sense of the diverse types of classical learning, she relies largely on anecdotal material. As the title of her article indicates, she is concerned exclusively with poetry and does not discuss the classical canon in the eighteenth century.

2. For a fuller discussion of the curriculum of Eton and other schools, see Clarke, *Classical Education*, 46–60 and Clarke, *Greek Studies in England*, 10–24.

3. H. C. Maxwell Lyte, *A History of Eton College, 1440–1875* (London: Macmillan, 1875), 311–19 summarizes this account. A complete transcription of this manuscript appears in *Etoniana*, no. 7 (3 July 1906): 97–108 and no. 8 (30 November 1906): 113–19. Although scholars are not certain about the specific year in which this manuscript was written and how much of it was by Thomas James, all agree that it presents an accurate picture of an Eton curriculum c. 1766. Martin C. Battestin also discusses the Eton curriculum in *Henry Fielding: A Life* (London: Routledge, 1989), 41–44.

4. Clarke, *Classical Education*, 46–60; Clarke, *Greek Studies in England*, 10–12.

5. C. G. Allen, "The Sources of 'Lily's Latin Grammar': A Review of the Facts and Some Further Suggestions," *Library*, 5th ser., 9 (1954): 85.

6. These figures and others have been drawn from a search of the on-line version of the British Library *ESTC* done from February through June, 1990.

7. We know about this practice because of the criticisms leveled at it; for example, see Francis Brokesby, *Of Education With respect to Grammar Schools, and the Universities* (London, 1701), 64–65, 72; John Clarke, *An Essay upon the Education of Youth in Grammar-Schools* (London, 1720), 11, 13, 26–27; *Of Education* (London, 1734), 6; Robert Ainsworth, *The Most Natural and Easy Way of Institution*, 2d ed. (London, 1736), 20–21; and James Barclay, *A Treatise on Education: or, An easy method of acquiring Language* (Edinburgh, 1743), 81–82, 86–89. One of the few positive references to this practice appears in John Boswell, *A Method of Study: or, An Useful Library*, 2 vols. (London, 1737), 1:3–5.

8. William Lily, *A Short Introduction of Grammar Compiled and set forth for the bringing up of all those that intend to attain to the knowledge of the Latin Tongue* (London: Roger Norton, 1690).

9. This book had royal sanction and was specifically named in the patent for the King's Printer of Greek, Latin, and Hebrew. The term "form" designates different classes of students grouped according to their proficiency in Latin and Greek. If the form grew too large, it might be subdivided. *A Bill of Eton College and School, 1745*, compiled by E. C. Hawtrey (Eton: E. P. Williams, 1843), lists three forms in the lower school; the upper school contained the fourth form, a midlevel called the remove, and the fifth and sixth forms.

10. William Camden, *Institutio Graecae Grammatices Compendiaria. In usum Regiae Scholae Westmonasteriensis* (1595; Menston, England: Scolar Press, 1969). The other Greek authors cited are Pindar (two times), Aristophanes, Isocrates, Dionysius of Halicarnassus, Theognis, Aratus, and Mimnermus (once each).

11. *Epigrammatum Delectus Ex omnibus Tum Veteribus, tum Recentioribus Poetis Accuratè decerptus . . . In usum Scholae Etonensis*, 7th ed. (London, 1711). Separate sections appear for the following authors: Horace (120 quotations), Seneca (119), Virgil (86), Terence (63), Ovid (61), Juvenal (53), Plautus (42), Lucan (41), Claudian (25), Persius (21), Lucretius (7), Manilius (8), Statius (5), and Silius Italicus (2).

12. For an account of this collection, published in Eton in 1766, see Clarke, *Classical Education*, 195. The full titles of the others are as follows: *Electa Minora Ex Ovidio, Tibullo, et*

Propertio. Usui Scholae Etonensis (London and Eton, 1705); *Poetae minores Graeci, selecti et emendati . . . In usum scholarum,* ed. Ralph Winterton (London, 1728).

13. The full titles of these works are *Poikile Historia. Sive Novus Historiarum Fabellarumque Delectus: Cum Notis & Versione. In Usum Scholae Etonensis* (London and Eton, 1701) and *Treis tragodiai, Aischylou Choephoroi, Sophokleous Elektra, Euripidou Elektra. In usum Scholae Regiae Westmonasteriensis* (Oxford, 1729).

14. In addition to the authors listed, who were covered regularly, students were also supposed to read in their leisure hours Cicero's *De officiis,* Ovid, Roman and Greek history, and Potter's and Kennett's books of antiquities. For two weeks in the year they left off their other studies and read Greek plays, a hundred lines at a time, and Demosthenes.

15. *Etoniana,* 102.

16. Clarke, *Classical Education,* 53.

17. See references to this practice in Brokesby, *Of Education,* 76 and Barclay, *A Treatise,* 25. Clarke, *Classical Education,* 57–60 also discusses the use of old copies.

18. *Guardian,* no. 94 (29 June 1713): 336.

19. John Locke, *Some Thoughts Concerning Education,* ed. James L. Axtell (Cambridge: Cambridge University Press, 1968), 268. For other comments, see the *Spectator,* ed. Donald Bond, 5 vols. (Oxford: Clarendon, 1965), 1:115; and the list in Richard S. Tompson, *Classics or Charity? The Dilemma of the Eighteenth-Century Grammar School* (Manchester, U.K.: Manchester University Press, 1971), 36–44.

20. Isaac Watts, "A Discourse on the Education of Children and Youth," in *Works,* 6 vols. (London, 1753), 5:377–78.

21. Nicholas Hans, *New Trends in Education in the Eighteenth Century* (1951; London: Routledge and Kegan Paul, 1966), 63–64, 117–35.

22. Clarke, *Classical Education,* 61–73; Clarke, *Greek Studies in England,* 25–34.

23. The full titles of the guides not previously cited are as follows: Henry Felton, *A Dissertation On Reading the Classics, And Forming a Just Style* (London, 1713); Anthony Blackwall, *An Introduction to the Classics,* 2d ed. (London, 1719; New York: Garland, 1971); Daniel Waterland, *Advice to a Young Student. With a method of Study for the Four First Years* (London, 1730); and John Clarke, *An Essay upon Study* (London, 1731; New York: Garland, 1970).

24. The most comprehensive lists are those of Blackwall (sixty-four authors), Waterland (fifty-two), and Boswell (forty-four). Each of the others recommends fewer than thirty authors: Clarke lists twenty-five, Felton, twenty-two, and Brokesby, fifteen. For the full list of authors, see appendix A, table A-1.

25. Watts, "A Discourse," 5:377.

26. *Spectator,* 3:317–19; see also no. 307 (21 February 1712), 3:105–9; Locke, *Some Thoughts,* 268; *Proposals for the Reformation of Schools & Universities* (1704), 4; *A Gentleman's Library* (London, 1715), 41–42; and Brokesby's suggestions about trade schools (*Of Education,* 36–37). Tompson, *Classics or Charity?,* 36–48 also covers this material.

27. Hans, *New Trends,* 63–81.

28. Irene Parker, *Dissenting Academies in England* (Cambridge: Cambridge University Press, 1914), 51–76; Herbert McLachlan, *English Education Under the Test Acts, Being the History of the Non-Conformist Academies, 1662–1820* (Manchester, U.K.: Manchester University Press, 1931), 17–35.

29. An account of the school written in Dr. Jenning's hand c. 1720–21 is at Dr. Williams's Library, London (MS. 12.40. [122]). Doddridge wrote a letter to Thomas Saunders in November 1728 describing the curriculum at Kibworth during the same period. See *The Correspondence and Diary of Philip Doddridge, D.D.,* ed. John Doddridge Humphreys, 5 vols. (London: Henry Colburn and Richard Bentley, 1829), 2:462–73. The curriculum is also summarized in Parker, *Dissenting Academices,* 143–46 and MacLachlan, *English Education,* 134–39.

30. "Constitutions Orders & Rules relating to the Academy at Northampton" (1743) in Dr. Williams's Library, London, MS. L2/4. See also Doddridge's letter to a friend (25 August 1750) in *Letters to and from the Rev. Philip Doddridge, D.D. Late of Northampton: Published from the originals: with Notes Explanatory and Biographical*, ed. Thomas Stedman (Shrewsbury, U.K., 1790). See also Parker, *Dissenting Academies*, 87–92; MacLachlan, *English Education*, 143–47.

31. Job Orton, *Memoirs of the Life, Character, and Writings of the Late Reverend Philip Doddridge, D.D. of Northampton* (Salop, 1766), 89–92; Stedman, *Letters to . . . Doddridge*, 295.

32. Richard Steele, *The Ladies Library, by a Lady*, 3 vols. (London, 1714), 1:22–23.

33. Clarke, *Essay upon Study*, 251–59.

34. William Law, *A Serious Call to a Devout and Holy Life* (1728), ed. Paul G. Stanwood (New York: Paulist Press, 1978), 262.

35. Samuel Richardson's letter to Lady Bradshaigh in *The Correspondence of Samuel Richardson*, ed. Anna Laetitia Barbauld, 6 vols. (London: Richard Phillips, 1804), 6:79. For similar comments from Hickes and Swift, see Myra Reynolds, *The Learned Lady in England 1650–1760* (Boston and New York: Houghton Mifflin, 1920), 290–93, 344–48. Dorothy Gardiner, *English Girlhood at School* (Oxford: Oxford University Press, 1929), 380–83, 433–34 discusses similar reactions from eighteenth-century writers.

36. For a discussion of this type, see Gardiner, *English Girlhood*, 378–83; Reynolds, *Learned Lady*, 372–400; and Jean Hunter, "The 18th-Century Englishwoman: According to the Gentleman's Magazine," in *Woman in the Eighteenth Century and Other Essays* (Toronto and Sarasota: Samuel Stevens Hakkert and Co., 1976), 77–79.

37. Henry Fielding, *Amelia*. Battestin includes a detailed discussion of this type on pp. 255–56 of *Henry Fielding: A Life*.

38. Lady Mary Wortley Montagu, *The Complete Letters of Lady Mary Wortley Montagu*, ed. Robert Halsband, 3 vols. (Oxford: Clarendon Press, 1965–67), 3:21–22.

39. Rosamond Bayne-Powell, *The English Child in the Eighteenth Century* (New York: E. P. Dutton, 1939), 109–11; Reynolds, *Learned Lady*, 259–67; Hans, *New Trends*, 197; and Gardiner, *English Girlhood*, 333–60.

40. Clarke, *Essay upon Study*, 253–61.

41. Daniel Bellamy, *The young ladies miscellany; or Youth's innocent and rational amusement* (London, 1723), 131–32, 143, 187–89.

42. *Spectator*, no. 37 (12 April 1711), 1:152–59.

43. Gardiner, *English Girlhood*, 426–33.

44. Erasmus Darwin, *A Plan for the Conduct of Female Education in Boarding Schools* (Yorkshire, 1797; New York: Johnson Reprint Corp., 1968), 17–18, 29–38, 118–25. Although he clearly advocates using translations, he does not give specific editions in many instances.

45. Bayne-Powell, *English Child*, 57–61.

46. Watts, "An Essay towards the encouragement of Charity-Schools," in *Works*, 2:739.

47. *An Account of the Charity-Schools Lately Erected in England, Wales, and Ireland* (London, 1706), 7–8; and Mary G. Jones, *The Charity School Movement: A Study of Eighteenth-Century Puritanism in Action* (Cambridge: Harvard University Press, 1938), 5, 57, 73–83, 85–93.

48. David Cressy, *Literacy and the Social Order: Reading and Writing in Tudor and Stuart England* (Cambridge: Cambridge University Press, 1980), 30–34. Also see J. Paul Hunter's discussion of Cressy's material on literacy in *Before Novels: The Cultural Contexts of Eighteenth-Century Fiction* (New York: W. W. Norton, 1990), 69–85.

49. Cressy, *Literacy*, 142–53.

50. Samuel Richardson, *Pamela or, Virtue Rewarded* (1740; London: Penguin Books, 1980), 63.

51. To determine what books were read frequently in the first half of the eighteenth century, I have used the results of an on-line search done between February and June, 1990 on the British Library *ESTC*. I chose this source over contemporary handbooks like Edward

Harwood's *View of the Various Editions of the Greek and Roman Classics, with Remarks* (1775) and Lewis Bruggemann's *View of the English Editions, Translations and Illustrations of the Ancient Greek and Latin Authors with Remarks* (1797) for several reasons. Harwood's bibliography is a guide only to the best editions available, so that it does not give us a complete listing of all editions of a given author. Although Bruggemann's list is more comprehensive, it does not distinguish between translations, editions only in Latin and Greek, and editions that include some type of translation. When I compared Bruggemann's entries with those of the *ESTC*, I found discrepancies in publication dates and format that call its accuracy into question. Finally, the *ESTC* lists only editions and translations that the compilers were able to examine. While we must recognize that this list does not represent all of those books available in the eighteenth century (some have not survived), it does give us the most accurate picture of those that it includes.

52. Clarke, *Essay on Study*, 266–350. Also see the lists in Paul Kaufman, "Reading Vogues at English Cathedral Libraries of the Eighteenth Century," *Bulletin of the New York Public Library* 67 (1963): 643–72; 68 (1964): 48–64, 110–32, 191–202. Although the number of foreign editions definitely identified by Kaufman exceeds the number of English editions, enough works have no place of publication that an accurate assessment is not possible.

53. For an account of these acts, see Harry Ransom, *The First Copyright Statute: An Essay on An Act for the Encouragement of Learning, 1710* (Austin: University of Texas Press, 1956), 96; and John Feather, *The Provincial Book Trade in Eighteenth-Century England* (Cambridge: Cambridge University Press, 1985), 7–9.

54. Giles Barber, "Book Imports and Exports in the Eighteenth Century," in *Sale and Distribution of Books from 1700*, ed. Robin Myers and Michael Harris (Oxford: Oxford Polytechnic Press, 1982), 77–83. Barber's only relevant comment is that classical texts formed one of the largest segments of the import and export markets.

55. Because of the limited number of editions, Aristotle was known not in the original, but by reputation. Throughout the eighteenth century his name lent credibility to several handbooks on midwifery and astronomy, among which were *Aristotle's compleat master-piece. In three parts. Displaying the secrets of nature, in the generation of man.... To which is added, a treasure of health; or, the family-physician* (thirteen separate printings), *Aristotle's compleat and experienc'd midwife* (six printings), and *Aristotle's book of problems, with other astronomers, astrologers, physicians, and philosophers* (eight printings). Aristotle's *Poetics* was frequently mentioned by epic theorists like Boileau, Le Bossu, and Dryden, but readers knew his work primarily through these intermediaries and not through the works themselves.

56. Richard D. Altick, *The English Common Reader* (Chicago: University of Chicago Press, 1957), 49–53; Marjorie Plant, *The English Book Trade: An Economic History of the Making and Sale of Books* (1939; London: Allen and Unwin, 1965), 54–55, 245.

57. Altick, *English Common Reader*, 59–65.

58. For an account of these early libraries, see Alan McKillop, "English Circulating Libraries, 1725–50," *Library*, 4th ser., 14 (1934): 477–85; and Devendra P. Varma, *The Evergreen Tree of Diabolical Knowledge* (Washington, D.C.: Consortium Press, 1972), 9, 30.

59. Benjamin Mackerell, *A New Catalogue of the Books in the Public Library of the City of Norwich, In the Year 1732* (Norwich, 1732).

60. William Bathoe, *A New Catalogue Of the Curious and Valuable Collection of Books*. We know that the catalog dates from 1757 because of an advertisement appearing on the back page for a catalog and description "just published" of King Charles I's collection, which first appeared in 1757.

61. John Noble, *A New Catalogue Of the Large and Valuable Collection of Books* (London, 1767).

62. Kaufman, "Reading Vogues," 648–55.

63. Because Kaufman could not always identify specific editions or works from the notations, only general figures for authors can be determined with any accuracy. Another problem is that he does not clearly distinguish between editions in the original languages and in translation.

64. The complete list of loans appears in Kaufman, "Reading Vogues," 657–72; 48–64, 110–32, 191–202.

65. Ibid., 650–53.

Chapter 2. Fielding, the Classical Scholar

1. See, for example, Wilbur Cross, *The History of Henry Fielding*, 3 vols. (1918; rpt., New York: Russell and Russell, 1963), 1:22–24, 29, 41–48, 65–72; Goad, *Horace in the English Literature*, 191–94; F. Holmes Dudden, *Henry Fielding: His Life, Works, and Times*, 2 vols. (Oxford: Clarendon Press, 1952), 1:11–15, 25–26; Miller, *Essays*, 339–44; Christopher Robinson, *Lucian and his Influence in Europe* (London: Duckworth, 1979), 198–235; and Charles A. Knight, "Fielding and Aristophanes," *Studies in English Literature, 1500–1900* 21 (1981): 481–98. Only Cross asserts—without stating any evidence—that Fielding's ability in Greek was limited. For the importance of Lucian to Fielding, see, for example, Paulson, *Satire and the Novel*, 132–41 and Miller, *Essays*, 365–419.

2. Cross, *History of Henry Fielding*, 1:42–48. For a similar discussion, see Dudden, *Henry Fielding*, 1:11–15. Miller, *Essays*, 339, disagrees with Cross's argument about Fielding's attendance in the sixth form, arguing that Cross's reasoning is circular. See also Battestin, *Life*, 41–44.

3. Cross, *History of Henry Fielding*, 1:66.

4. John Edwin Sandys, *A History of Classical Scholarship*, 3 vols. (Cambridge, 1958; rpt., New York: Hafner Publishing, 1964), 2:444–47.

5. See, for example, the "scholarly" introductions and footnotes to *The Tragedy of Tragedies* (1731) and *The Vernon-iad* (1741).

6. A facsimile of this catalog appears in vol. 7 of A. N. L. Munby's *Sale Catalogues of Libraries of Eminent Persons*, ed. Hugh Amory (London: Mansell, 1973), 7:123–58. See the discussions of the library in Cross, *History of Henry Fielding*, 3:77–83 and Dudden, *Henry Fielding*, 2:1059–64.

7. Amory, *Sale Catalogues*, 123–24; 130–31.

8. Henry Fielding, *The Journal of a Voyage to Lisbon* (London, 1755), vii–viii. I have consulted the censored edition, in which the innkeeper at Ryde is named Mrs. Humphrys.

9. See *Miscellanies*, 1:80–81, 84–117, 205–11.

10. Henry Fielding and William Young, *Plutus, the God of Riches. A Comedy. Translated from the Original Greek of Aristophanes: With Large Notes Explanatory and Critical* (London, 1742).

11. All references come from *Ovid's Art of Love Paraphrased, and Adapted to the Present Time. With Notes. And A most Correct Edition of the Original. Book I* (London, 1747). See also *Covent-Garden Journal*, no. 58 (8 August 1752): 313–15.

12. John Dryden, preface to *Ovid's Epistles, Translated by Several Hands* (1680) in *The Works of John Dryden*, 20 vols. in progress (Berkeley: University of California Press, 1956–), 1:114–15.

13. For example, see *Covent-Garden Journal*, no. 5 (18 January 1752): 41 and no. 43 (30 May 1752): 242–43.

14. *Covent-Garden Journal*, no. 42 (26 May 1752): 242. Also see the use of "paraphrase" in the original title and preface of *The Lover's Assistant*.

15. Henry Fielding, *Miscellanies*, 1:92–93.

16. Contemporary allusions also replace the ancient ones at lines 1–4, 49–50, 53–54, 78–94, 95, 119, 126, 134, 141–42, 169, 177, 183, 187, 189, 191, 232, 240–41, 256–63, 286–301, 327–28, 353–54, 363, 366, 378–83, 387–91, 392–95, 414, 436–37, 441–42, 446–47, and 451. Throughout his version of book 1 of Ovid's *Ars Amatoria*, he substitutes eighteenth-century allusions for the ancient ones in a similar fashion.

17. *Covent-Garden Journal*, no. 33 (22 April 1752): 202; no. 49 (20 June 1752): 268. Other

examples of this practice appear in the mottoes of the following issues: no. 5 (18 January 1752): 41; no. 10 (4 February 1752): 72; no. 11 (8 February 1752): 79; no. 14 (18 February 1752): 99; no. 17 (29 February 1752): 119; no. 28 (7 April 1752): 176; no. 30 (14 April 1752): 187; no. 35 (2 May 1752): 211; no. 36 (5 May 1752): 214; no. 37 (9 May 1752): 217; no. 43 (30 May 1752): 242–43; no. 53 (4 July 1752): 289; and no. 70 (11 November 1752): 368. Only the mottoes of nos. 28 and 35 are in Greek.

18. See the discussion of this correspondence in Battestin, *Life*, 368, 700; and in Clive T. Probyn, *The Sociable Humanist: The Life and Works of James Harris 1709–1780* (Oxford: Oxford University Press, 1991), 111–12. The letters are reprinted in *The Correspondence of Henry and Sarah Fielding*, ed. Martin C. Battestin and Clive T. Probyn (Oxford: Clarendon Press, 1993), 29–30.

19. Miller, *Essays*, 347–62. When he compared the text of Fielding's version to the Latin translation by Wolfius in Fielding's library, Miller discovered that in places Fielding followed Wolfius's Latin rather than the original.

20. Cross, *History of Henry Fielding*, 1:364–65; Miller, *Essays*, 343; and Knight, "Fielding and Aristophanes," 484–87.

21. *Jacobite's Journal*, no. 13 (27 February 1748): 172–78.

22. Ibid., no. 38 (20 August 1748): 371.

23. Fielding also uses mock classical references in the following essays: *Champion*, 17 November 1739, 1:7–12; 25 December 1739, 1:123–30; 28 February 1739–40, 1:314–19; 20 May 1740, 2:236–40; 31 May 1740, 2:279–85; *True Patriot*, no. 9 (31 December 1745): 164–71; *Jacobite's Journal*, no. 6 (9 January 1748): 121–27; no. 12 (20 February 1748): 162–67; no. 23 (7 May 1748): 266–70; and *Covent-Garden Journal*, no. 9 (1 February 1752): 60–71; no. 11 (8 February 1752): 79–84; no. 24 (24 March 1752): 154–58; and no. 59 (15 August 1752): 318–22.

24. Fielding also uses classical authors in a more serious way in *Champion*, 15 January 1739–40, 1:186–88; 15 March 1739–40, 2:1–5; 27 March 1740, 2:37–39; *True Patriot*, no. 8 (24 December 1745): 158–60; *Jacobite's Journal*, no. 22 (30 April 1748): 256–61; no. 45 (8 October 1748): 403–9; no. 46 (15 October 1748): 409–13; and *Covent-Garden Journal*, no. 10 (4 February 1752): 72–77; and no. 66 (14 October 1752): 347–51.

25. Other mistakes of this kind appear in *Champion*, 4 March 1739–40, 1:328, where he identifies Horace as the author of a motto by Juvenal; *True Patriot*, no. 17 (18 February 1746): 225, where he misquotes Sallust; *Jacobite's Journal*, no. 15 (12 March 1748): 199, where he gives an altered version of a line from Seneca; and *Covent-Garden Journal*, no. 66 (14 October 1752): 347, where he misquotes Livy.

26. *The History of Our Own Times*, with introduction and notes by Thomas Lockwood (Delmar, N.Y.: Scholars' Facsimiles and Reprints, 1985), no. 2 (15–30 January 1741): 48.

27. Henry Fielding, *The Vernon-iad. Done into English, From the original Greek of Homer. Lately found at Constantinople. With notes in usum; &c. Book the first* (London, 1741), 1–2. The other lines match up as follows:

Vernoniad	*Aeneid*
1–14	1–11
15–26	12–22
33–40	23–28
41–46	34–37
95–119	37–49
126–59	52–64
164–80, 221–60	65–80
267–76	81–90

28. Henry Fielding, *A Journey from this World to the Next*, in *Miscellanies*, 2:106–7. Italics reversed.

29. In collecting my data for the discussion that follows, I counted every instance where Fielding refers to a Latin or Greek author by name or where he quotes a classical writer verbatim in the original. I also included translations of classical authors when Fielding identifies his source or the English so closely parallels the original that the source is unmistakable. Because of attribution problems, I have restricted my survey to those journals to which Fielding undoubtedly contributed. Since we cannot be certain how much of the peripheral material in each journal was written by Fielding, I have chosen to use only the leaders attributed to him by Coley and Goldgar. For the *Champion* I consulted the collected edition and those issues reprinted by the Augustan Reprint Society. Therefore, the tabulation of references in the periodicals provides a large sample of Fielding's use of classical authors but is by no means exhaustive.

30. For an account of the change in the reading public, see Ian Watt, *The Rise of the Novel* (Berkeley: University of California Press, 1957), 35–59 and J. Paul Hunter, *Before Novels* (New York: W. W. Norton, 1990), 61–88.

31. *Covent-Garden Journal*, no. 52 (30 June 1752): 288–89.

32. See Miller, *Essays*, 370; Robinson, *Lucian*, 198. Baker items nos. 19, 28, 44, 260, 368, 417, 554, 620, and 630 are works by Lucian.

33. Robinson, *Lucian*, 198–203.

34. *True Patriot*, no. 1 (5 November 1746): 336; and *Covent-Garden Journal*, no. 10 (4 February 1752): 74–75. In no. 60 (22 August 1752): 323, he also mentions his wit.

35. *Covent-Garden Journal*, no. 1 (4 January 1752): 18–19.

36. Ibid., no. 52 (30 June 1752): 285–89.

37. *True Patriot*, no. 1 (5 November 1745): 336.

38. *Covent-Garden Journal*, no. 52 (30 June 1752): 288–89.

39. Charles B. Woods suggests that Lucian may have influenced the puppet show. See Woods, *The Author's Farce*, Regents Restoration Drama Series (Lincoln: University of Nebraska Press, 1966), xiv. For imitations in the periodicals, see the *Champion*, 24 May 1740, 2:253–59.

40. Although many critics have noted that the first third of *A Journey from This World to the Next* is loosely based on Lucian, the editors of the Wesleyan edition argue persuasively that Plato is a more influential source for this work. For the traditional view, see Claude Rawson, ed., *A Journey from This World to the Next* (London: Dent; New York: Dutton, 1973), viii, xxiii–xxvi. On the influence of Plato, see Bertrand A. Goldgar, "Myth and History in Fielding's *Journey from This World to the Next*," *Modern Language Quarterly* 47 (1986): 236–39; and *Miscellanies*, 2:xxviii–xxxi.

41. For a discussion of other "dialogues of the dead," see Miller, *Essays*, 365–66, 393–96; and Frederick M. Keener, *English Dialogues of the Dead: A Critical History, an Anthology, and a Checklist* (New York: Columbia University Press, 1973), 21–23, 49–74, 279–84.

42. Miller, *Essays*, 367–69, 374; Robinson, *Lucian*, 218–35.

43. See Miller's statements in *Essays*, 370–71, and Robinson's in *Lucian*, 234–35.

44. He mentions Horace over three times more often than any other ancient writer. Although only 69 references appear in the essays themselves, the number far surpasses that for Virgil, next in frequency, who only appears 50 times in all.

45. *Covent-Garden Journal*, no. 3 (11 January 1752): 30. For other complimentary references to Horace, see *Jacobite's Journal*, no. 8 (23 January 1748): 136; *Covent-Garden Journal*, no. 1 (4 January 1752): 18 and no. 3 (11 January 1752): 28.

46. *Jacobite's Journal*, no. 16 (19 March 1748): 209. See also *Jacobite's Journal*, no. 16 (19 March 1748): 209 and no. 33 (16 July 1748): 346; and *Covent-Garden Journal*, no. 7 (25 January 1752): 57.

47. He quotes or alludes to this passage in the *Champion,* 29 April 1740, 2:157; 25 December 1739, 1:130; and *Covent-Garden Journal,* no. 51 (27 June 1752): 282.

48. *Covent-Garden Journal,* no. 4 (14 January 1752): 34 and no. 26 (31 March 1752): 169. Fielding also refers to Horace's criticism in the *Champion,* 27 November 1739, 1:33 and 1 March 1739–40, 1:322; *Jacobite's Journal,* no. 8 (23 January 1748): 138; *Covent-Garden Journal,* no. 15 (22 February 1752): 110 and no. 19 (7 March 1752): 130.

49. *Champion,* 6 March 1739–40, 1:338.

50. *Jacobite's Journal,* no. 8 (23 January 1748): 136–38.

51. Ibid., no. 15 (12 March 1748): 198–99; and *Covent-Garden Journal,* no. 23 (21 March 1752): 150.

52. *Champion,* 15 March 1739–40, 2:4–5.

53. *Covent-Garden Journal,* no. 72 (25 November 1752): 381.

54. See, for example, the *Champion,* 26 January 1739–40, 1:219; 10 June 1740, 2:316; and *Covent-Garden Journal,* no. 69 (4 November 1752): 364.

55. *Champion,* 26 February 1739–40, 1:307, 308.

56. Ibid., 4 December 1739, 1:60; *True Patriot,* no. 18 (25 February 1746): 234; and *Covent-Garden Journal,* no. 60 (22 August 1752): 327.

57. For the importance of Horace to these writers, see Goad, *Horace,* 26–65, 128–90.

58. *Champion,* 1 March 1739–40, 1:326. For the imitation of the *Freeholder,* see *Jacobite's Journal,* no. 36 (6 August 1748): 359–62.

59. See, for example, his discussions of Colley Cibber in the *Champion,* 22 April 1740, 2:132 and 29 April 1740, 2:157–58; and of his enemies in the *Champion,* 27 November 1739, 1:37; *True Patriot,* no. 7 (17 December 1745): 152; and *Jacobite's Journal,* no. 26 (28 May 1748): 293.

60. See, for example, his comments in the *Champion,* 25 December 1739, 1:123–30; 29 January 1739–40, 1:226–27; *Jacobite's Journal,* no. 22 (30 April 1748): 256–61; and *Covent-Garden Journal,* no. 42 (26 May 1752): 239–42.

Chapter 3. Classical Epic and the "New Species of Writing"

1. Ethel M. Thornbury, *Henry Fielding's Theory of the Comic Prose Epic,* University of Wisconsin Studies in Language and Literature 30 (1931; rpt., New York: Russell and Russell, 1966); Martin C. Battestin, *The Moral Basis of Fielding's Art: A Study of Joseph Andrews* (Middletown: Wesleyan University Press, 1959), 40–41, 86–88, 104, 151–52; E. T. Palmer, "Fielding's *Joseph Andrews*: A Comic Epic in Prose," *English Studies* 52 (1971): 331–39; Leon Gottfried, "The Odyssean Form," in *Essays on European Literature in Honor of Liselotte Dieckmann,* ed. P. Hohendahl, H. Lindenberger, and E. Schwarz (St. Louis: Washington University Press, 1972), 19–43; J. Paul Hunter, *Occasional Form: Henry Fielding and the Chains of Circumstance* (Baltimore: Johns Hopkins University Press, 1975), 16–17, 130–40, 185.

2. For detailed discussion of the position of the "romance" theorists, see Homer Goldberg, "Comic Prose Epic or Comic Romance: The Argument of the Preface to *Joseph Andrews,*" *Philological Quarterly* 43 (1964): 193–215; and Sheridan Baker, "Fielding's Comic Epic-in-Prose Romances Again," *Philological Quarterly* 58 (1979): 63–81. These articles give useful, though biased, summaries of the previous criticism on this issue. The only recent addition to this debate is James Lynch, *Henry Fielding and the Heliodoran Novel: Romance, Epic, and Fielding's New Province of Writing* (Rutherford, N.J.: Fairleigh Dickenson University Press, 1986), which covers much of the same ground as Baker, Goldberg, and Henry Knight Miller, *Henry Fielding's*

Tom Jones and Romance Tradition, University of Victoria English Literary Studies 6 (Victoria: University of Victoria Press, 1976).

3. See Baker, "Fielding's Comic," 64–67; Hunter, *Occasional Form*, 131; J. Paul Hunter, *Before Novels: The Cultural Contexts of Eighteenth-Century Fiction* (New York: W. W. Norton, 1990), 18–21; Ian Watt, *The Rise of the Novel: Studies in Defoe, Richardson and Fielding* (Berkeley: University of California Press, 1957), 257–59; and Claude Rawson, *Henry Fielding and the Augustan Ideal under Stress* (London: Routledge and Kegan Paul, 1972), 147–70.

4. For example, see Paulson's discussion of the influence of Lucian and other classical satirists in *Satire and the Novel in Eighteenth-Century England*, 132–41, 161–64.

5. I have not included *Shamela* in this tabulation. Because it is a close parody of Richardson, *Shamela* has very few references to classical authors; most are Williams's miscitations of Latin writers, the significance of which I will discuss in chapter 4. I have chosen to use the second edition of *Jonathan Wild*, published in 1754, rather than the first edition, which appeared in volume three of the *Miscellanies* (1743); Fielding added several references to classical authors in the second edition, but the first edition has no references that are unique to it.

6. For a complete list of authors, see appendix C.

7. See George Sherburn, "Fielding's *Amelia*: An Interpretation," *ELH* 3 (1936): 1–14; Lyall Powers, "The Influence of the *Aeneid* on Fielding's *Amelia*," *Modern Language Notes* 71 (1956): 330–36; and Maurice Johnson, *Fielding's Art of Fiction: Eleven Essays on Shamela, Joseph Andrews, Tom Jones, and Amelia* (Philadelphia: University of Pennsylvania Press, 1961), 139–56. Although Joseph F. Bartolomeo argues that Fielding makes the analogy to the *Aeneid* to mount a clever defense of "a tepidly received novel," the parallels that other critics have outlined between *Amelia* and Virgil's epic suggest that Fielding's remarks were more than just a rhetorical device. See Joseph F. Bartolomeo, *A New Species of Criticism: Eighteenth-Century Discourse on the Novel* (Newark: University of Delaware Press, 1994), 71.

8. Fielding also cites Horace and Aristotle when discussing epic theory in the following: the title page, which quotes Horace's comment in the *Ars Poetica* about Homer (lines 141–42); bk. 11, chap. 1, 2:569–70, where they are listed with epic theorists Le Bossu and Dacier; bk. 5, chap. 1, 1:210, in which Fielding alludes to Horace's rules about the five-act structure of plays in connection with unity; bk. 9, chap. 1, 1:490 and 491, where Fielding supports his comments about the need for genius and learning in authors with allusions to Horace (*Ars*, lines 408–18); and bk. 10, chap. 1, 2:527, where Fielding justifies the mixed character with a quotation from Horace (*Ars*, lines 352–53). Other references are connected with Horace's critical pronouncements in the *Ars*: bk. 4, chap. 14, 1:208, and bk. 7, chap. 6, 1:344, where Fielding mentions Horace's strictures on what material is suitable for description (*Ars*, lines 149–50); and bk. 9, chap. 2, 1:494, where Fielding says that the author who makes his reader weep, must first weep himself (*Ars*, lines 102–3).

9. See *Tom Jones*, bk. 13, chap. 1, 1:686, where Fielding groups Lucian with Aristophanes, Cervantes, Rabelais, Molière, Shakespeare, Swift, and Marivaux; and *Amelia*, bk. 8, chap. 5, pp. 325–26.

10. See Thornbury, *Henry Fielding's Theory*, and Lynch, *Henry Fielding and the Heliodoran Novel*, 17–19. Arthur L. Cooke, "Henry Fielding and the Writers of Heroic Romance," *PMLA* 62 (1947): 984–94, mentions Fielding's concern with probability, unity, characters, and moral purpose, but he suggests that Fielding and the writers of seventeenth-century heroic romances share these interests. As I will show, Fielding repeatedly argued that these are the very areas in which the romance and his new genre differed.

11. René Le Bossu, *Treatise of the Epick Poem* (1695), in *Le Bossu and Voltaire on the Epic*, introduced by Stuart Curran (Gainesville, Fla.: Scholars' Facsimiles and Reprints, 1970), 6.

12. For a detailed discussion of the theory of the epic in the eighteenth century, see A. F. B. Clark, *Boileau and the French Classical Critics in England, 1660–1830* (Paris: Librarie Ancienne Edouard Champion, 1925), 232–55, 286–88; and H. T. Swedenberg Jr., *The Theory of the Epic*

in England, 1650–1800, University of California Publications in English 15 (1944; rpt., Milwood, N.Y.: Kraus Reprint Co., 1977), 16–27, 43–57.

   13. See John Dryden, dedication of the *Aeneis,* in *The Works of John Dryden* (Berkeley: University of California Press, 1987), 5:267–341; Alexander Pope, preface to *The Iliad of Homer,* ed. Maynard Mack, in *The Poems of Alexander Pope* (London: Methuen, 1967), 7:3–25 and *The Odyssey of Homer,* ed. Maynard Mack, in *The Poems of Alexander Pope* (London: Methuen, 1967), 9:3–24.

   14. For a discussion of the critical theories of these men, see A. F. B. Clark, *Boileau,* 275–79; and M. L. Clarke, *Greek Studies in England, 1700–1830* (1945; rpt. Amsterdam: Adolf M. Hakkert, 1986), 136–38.

   15. For a discussion of the meaning of "comic epic" in this passage, see W. L. Renwick, "Comic Epic in Prose," *Essays and Studies* 32 (1946): 40–43; and Claude Rawson, *Satire and Sentiment, 1660–1830* (Cambridge: Cambridge University Press, 1994), 146–47. Bartolomeo (*New Species of Criticism,* 70–71) discusses the interpretive problems created by the narrative voice in this passage. See also Abraham Adams's discussion of the *Iliad* in *Joseph Andrews,* bk. 3, chap. 2, pp. 196–99, where he uses categories similar to those of Le Bossu.

   16. See Swedenberg, *Theory of the Epic,* 216–19.

   17. See also *Tom Jones,* bk. 4, chap. 1, 1:150, where Fielding refers to "those idle Romances which are filled with Monsters, the Productions, not of Nature, but of distempered Brains."

   18. See A. F. B. Clark, *Boileau,* 308–10; Swedenberg, *Theory of the Epic,* 266–70.

   19. *Jonathan Wild,* bk. 2, chap. 12, p. 112; *Tom Jones,* bk. 17, chap. 1, 2:875–76.

   20. See Swedenberg, *Theory of the Epic,* 306–8.

   21. See also *Jonathan Wild,* bk. 3, chap. 11, p. 167, where Fielding argues that the readers of romance like to be deceived; bk. 4, chap. 4, p. 198, where he talks about the extravagancies of romance; *Joseph Andrews,* bk. 3, chap. 1, p. 185, where he equates historians with romance writers who are not concerned with the truth; pp. 185–86, in which he refers to works that readers justly consider romances because "the Writer hath indulged a happy and fertile Invention"; and *Tom Jones,* bk. 9, chap. 1, 1:489, where he says that he has avoided the term romance because he wants to make sure that his readers understand that his novels have some truth.

   22. See, for example, Paulson, *Satire and the Novel,* 106–7; Hunter, *Occasional Form,* 130. Although Thornbury discusses the mock-heroic description of the fight involving Molly Seagrim, she argues that it is not mock-heroic but comic; she maintains that the battle is fitted to the importance of the characters and reflects their seriousness about the fight (*Henry Fielding's Theory,* 128–30).

   23. For a discussion of the mock-heroic as imitation and critical parody, see Ulrich Broich, *The Eighteenth-Century Mock-Heroic Poem,* trans. David Henry Wilson (Cambridge: Cambridge University Press, 1990), 1–6, 50–67. Although Broich observes that the serious epic is never consciously mocked in mock-heroics as in a critical parody, he concludes by admitting that such parodies often have the inadvertent effect of putting the classical epic in a "comic light" (66–67).

   24. Rawson, *Henry Fielding and the Augustan Ideal Under Stress,* 147–70, esp. 159–60.

   25. See *Joseph Andrews,* bk. 1, chap. 12, pp. 55–56; bk. 1, chap. 8, pp. 37–38; and bk. 3, chap. 4, p. 225; and *Tom Jones,* bk. 9, chap. 2, 1:495.

   26. See, for example, *Joseph Andrews,* bk. 1, chap. 8, pp. 37–38; *Tom Jones,* bk. 1, chap. 6, 1:47–48; bk. 4, chap. 2, 1:154–55; bk. 5, chap. 11, 1:259; and bk. 9, chap. 2, 1:495.

   27. *Joseph Andrews,* bk. 2, chap. 9, pp. 138–39, the battle between Adams and Fanny's intended ravisher; bk. 3, chap. 6, pp. 237–43, between Joseph, Adams, and the dogs; bk. 3, chap. 10, pp. 256–59, between Joseph and Adams and the emissaries of the Squire; *Tom Jones,* bk. 2, chap. 4, 1:89–90, between Mr. and Mrs. Partridge over Jenny Jones; bk. 4, chap. 8,

1:177–84, involving Molly Seagrim and the townspeople; bk. 5, chap. 11, 1:259–63, involving Tom, Thwackum, and Blifil over Molly; and bk. 9, chap. 3, 1:501–4, involving Partridge, Jones, the Innkeeper, and his wife over the honor of Mrs. Waters.

28. See also the parody of the libation in the *Iliad* in *Tom Jones*, bk. 9, chap. 4, 1:508.

29. Sheridan Baker, "The Idea of Romance in the Eighteenth-Century Novel," *Papers of the Michigan Academy of Science, Arts, and Letters* 49 (1964): 507–22. For a detailed discussion of the adoption of courtly language in *Pamela* and *Clarissa*, see Carey McIntosh, *Common and Courtly Language: The Stylistics of Social Class in 18th-Century English Literature* (Philadelphia: University of Pennsylvania Press, 1986), 77–78, 118–30.

30. See Paulson, *Satire and the Novel*, 22–41, 89–92, 111–21.

31. See Watt, *Rise of the Novel*, 240–47.

32. Alexander Pope, preface to *The Iliad of Homer*, 13–14.

33. Rawson, *Henry Fielding and the Augustan Ideal Under Stress*, 150–61.

34. Johnson, *Fielding's Art of Fiction*, 155–56.

35. Powers, "Influence of the *Aeneid*," 334–36.

36. Dryden, *Aeneis*, 6:806.

37. For a full discussion of Dryden's ambivalence towards the Homeric hero, see William Frost, *Dryden and the Art of Translation*, Yale Studies in English 128 (New Haven: Yale University Press, 1955), 62–69; and Judith Sloman, *Dryden: The Poetics of Translation* (Toronto: University of Toronto Press, 1985), 126–36.

38. See *Miscellanies*, 1:21–22, lines 67–90, and Miller's note.

CHAPTER 4. CLASSICAL ALLUSION AND THE JUDGMENT OF CHARACTER

1. Of the reader-response studies, the most useful are the following: Wolfgang Iser, *The Implied Reader: Patterns of Communication in Prose Fiction from Bunyan to Beckett* (Baltimore: Johns Hopkins University Press, 1974), 29–56; Alan T. McKenzie, "The Processes of Discovery in *Tom Jones*," *Dalhousie Review* 54 (1974–75): 720–40; Hunter, *Occasional Form*, 95–114, 152–61; Susan P. McNamara, "Mirrors of Fiction Within *Tom Jones*: The Parodox of Self-Reference," *Eighteenth-Century Studies* 12 (1979): 372–90; Raymond Stephanson, "The Education of the Reader in Fielding's *Joseph Andrews*," *Philological Quarterly* 61 (1982): 243–58; and Stephen C. Berendt, "Art as Deceptive Intruder: Audience Entrapment in Eighteenth-Century Verbal and Visual Art," *Papers on Language and Literature* 19 (1983): 37–52.

2. See Christopher Robinson, *Lucian and his Influence in Europe* (London: Duckworth, 1979), 227–30.

3. John Coolidge, "Fielding and 'Conservation of Character,'" *Modern Philology* 57 (1960): 245–59.

4. Robert Alter, *Fielding and the Nature of the Novel* (Cambridge: Harvard University Press, 1968), 81–84; Hunter, *Occasional Form*, 111–14.

5. Henry Fielding, *An Apology for the Life of Mrs. Shamela Andrews* (1741; rpt., New York: Garland, 1974), 21; and *Joseph Andrews*, bk. 1, chap. 14, p. 63.

6. See the suspicion aroused by Jenny Jones's Latin in *Tom Jones*, bk. 1, chap. 6, 1:48–49; bk. 2, chap. 3, 1:81–84; bk. 2, chap. 4, 1:88, and Mrs. Atkinson's learning in *Amelia*, bk. 7, chap. 4, pp. 281–82. Other examples of negative responses to learning appear in the following: *Joseph Andrews*, bk. 4, chap. 9, p. 312, where Didapper greets Adams's Latin by exclaiming that he does not understand Welch; *Amelia*, bk. 11, chap. 2, pp. 459–60, where the lord declares to Harrison that he does not consider learning necessary for a soldier, and bk. 6, chap.

7, pp. 258–59, where Mrs Atkinson frightens Amelia when she emphatically repeats several lines of Virgil in Latin.

7. See the scenes in *Joseph Andrews*, bk. 2, chap. 11, pp. 146–47, where a wit "defeats" Adams; and *Amelia*, bk. 9, chap. 9, pp. 395–98, where a group of wits at the park intrude on the Booths' party.

8. See also the silent reaction of the author to Booth's lengthy discussion of a variety of classical authors in *Amelia*, bk. 8, chap. 5, pp. 326–27.

9. See *Amelia*, bk. 9, chap. 8, pp. 388–89; bk. 10, chap. 1, pp. 407–10; bk. 10, chap. 4, pp. 425–27; and bk. 12, chap. 8, pp. 528–29.

10. In addition to Harrison's responses, see those of Adams and Partridge.

11. See *Amelia*, bk. 9, chap. 3, pp. 365–66; bk. 10, chap. 1, pp. 407–10; bk. 10, chap. 4, pp. 425–27; and bk. 12, chap. 8, pp. 528–29.

12. Glenn Hatfield, *Henry Fielding and the Language of Irony* (Chicago: University of Chicago Press, 1968), 39–178.

13. *Tom Jones*, bk. 4, chap. 10, 1:188, 189; bk. 12, chap. 2, 2:622.

14. Another lawyer who uses legal jargon is Squire Western's advisor in *Tom Jones*, bk. 4, chap. 4, 1:164.

15. Other figures who use classics in this way are Squire Western, the Man of the Hill, the lord whom Harrison consults, and the author whom Booth meets in the sponging house.

16. Eric Rothstein, "The Framework of *Shamela*," *ELH* 35 (1968): 381–402; and Leo Braudy, *Narrative Form in History and Fiction: Hume, Fielding, and Gibbon* (Princeton: Princeton University Press, 1970), 134–43.

17. See Cicero, *De oratore*. George Kennedy includes a useful discussion of this work in *The Art of Rhetoric in the Roman World, 300 B.C. to A.D. 300* (Princeton: Princeton University Press, 1972), 205–30.

18. Braudy, *Narrative Form*, 134–43.

19. For instance, *in futuro* (bk. 1, chap. 6, p. 26); *ab effectu* (bk. 2, chap. 12, p. 114); *terra firma* (bk. 2, chap. 13, p. 117); and *Quomodo* (bk. 3, chap. 11, p. 166).

20. Another example is a quotation from Lucretius that the narrator applies to the Ordinary, who has retired from the gallows to safeguard himself at Wild's execution (bk. 4, chap. 14, p. 254). In Lucretius the lines refer to the Epicurean philosophical withdrawal from the world; here the Ordinary withdraws to protect himself from the mob. See also the use of quotations in bk. 1, chap. 3, p. 9; bk. 1, chap. 14, pp. 56–57; bk. 3, chap. 11, pp. 167–68; and bk. 4, chap. 13, p. 238.

21. Coolidge, "Fielding and 'Conservation,'" 245–59. For the exemplary interpretation of Adams, see, for example, Martin C. Battestin, *The Moral Basis of Fielding's Art* (Middletown, Conn.: Wesleyan University Press, 1959), 94–114; Kevin Berland, "Satire and the *Via Media*: Anglican Dialogue in *Joseph Andrews*," in *Satire in the Eighteenth Century*, ed. J. D. Browning, Publications of the McMaster University Association for Eighteenth-Century Studies 10 (New York: Garland, 1983), 83–99; and Iser, *Implied Reader*, 40–45.

22. Alter, *Fielding and the Nature of the Novel*, 81–84; Hunter, *Occasional Form*, 111–14.

23. References to Adams's Aeschylus appear in bk. 2, chap. 2, pp. 95, 96; bk. 2, chap. 7, p. 130; bk. 2, chap. 11, pp. 148–49; bk. 2, chap. 12, pp. 154–55; and bk. 3, chap. 2, p. 192.

24. Adams uses short phrases in bk. 2, chap. 2, p. 93; bk. 2, chap. 8, p. 133; bk. 2, chap. 10, p. 140; bk. 2, chap. 13, p. 161; bk. 2, chap. 14, p. 163; bk. 2, chap. 17, p. 180; bk. 3, chap. 5, pp. 230, 231; bk. 4, chap. 10, pp. 314–15; and bk. 4, chap. 12, p. 325. The three that appear in standard sources are in bk. 2, chap. 8, p. 134; bk. 2, chap. 17, p. 181; and bk. 3, chap. 5, p. 232. On p. 231 he uses a proverbial expression drawn from Horace. Other ancient quotations appear in bk. 2, chap. 2, p. 93; bk. 3, chap. 2, p. 193; bk. 4, chap. 9, p. 312; and bk. 4, chap. 15, p. 339.

25. Later in the discussion, he implies that he is similar to the ancient schoolmaster Chiron; again the recondite allusion would probably be beyond Joseph's learning.

26. The quotations appear on the following pages: bk. 8, chap. 4, 1:414–15; bk. 8, chap. 5, 1:421; bk. 8, chap. 12, 1:461–62; bk. 8, chap. 13, 1:471; bk. 9, chap. 6, 1:514; bk. 10, chap. 4, 2:540; bk. 10, chap. 5, 2:543; bk. 12, chap. 3, 2:626, 629; bk. 12, chap. 4, 2:630–31, 633; bk. 12, chap. 5, 2:636; bk. 12, chap. 13, 2:676, 677; and bk. 16, chap. 5, 2:855, 856.

27. He uses the following eight tags more than once: *Infandum, Regina, jubes renovare dolorem* (bk. 8, chap. 6, 1:424; bk. 8, chap. 9, 1:438; bk. 12, chap. 3, 2:628; bk. 14, chap. 3, 2:752); *Mens sana in corpore sano* (bk. 12, chap. 4, 2:633; bk. 12, chap. 5, 2:636); *Mors omnibus communis* (bk. 8, chap. 6, 1:423; bk. 12, chap. 3, 2:629); *Non omnia possumus omnes* (bk. 8, chap. 4, 1:414; bk. 10, chap. 5, 2:543); *Non sum qualis eram* (bk. 15, chap. 12, 2:829; bk. 18, chap. 5, 2:935); *Nemo omnibus horis sapit* (bk. 12, chap. 13, 2:677; bk. 16, chap. 5, 2:856); *Proh Deum atque Hominum Fidem* (bk. 8, chap. 5, 1:417, 421); and *Tempus edax Rerum* (bk. 8, chap. 5, 1:421; bk. 8, chap. 13, 1:471).

28. Similarly he applies the phrase *Hiatus in manuscriptis* incongruously to Tom's wound (bk. 8, chap. 4, 1:415).

29. Bk. 12, chap. 10, 2:659–60, where he quotes *Odes* 1.22.17–24 without a translation for Dowling; and bk. 12, chap. 3, 2:629, where he quotes *Odes* 3.2.13–16 and translates for Partridge.

30. See, for example, bk. 8, chap. 9, 1:440–41.

31. See Hugh Amory, "Magistrate or Censor? The Problem of Authority in Fielding's Later Writings," *Studies in English Literature, 1500–1900* 12 (1972): 512–18; Martin Battestin, "The Problem of *Amelia*: Hume, Barrow, and the Conversion of Captain Booth," *ELH* 41 (1974): 614; and Eric Rothstein, *Systems of Order and Inquiry in Later Eighteenth-Century Fiction* (Berkeley: University of California Press, 1975), 187, 198–99.

32. The Greek authors are Aristotle (bk. 3, chap. 10, p. 137; bk. 9, chap. 5, p. 375), Homer (bk. 10, chap. 4, pp. 425–27; bk. 12, chap. 3, p. 504; bk. 12, chap. 8, p. 528), Phocylides (bk. 9, chap. 8, p. 388), and Thucydides. The Latin authors are Cicero (bk. 3, chap. 10, p. 137–38), Horace (bk. 10, chap. 1, p. 409; bk. 10, chap. 4, p. 426; bk. 12, chap. 8, p. 528), Juvenal (bk. 10, chap. 4, p. 427), Livy (bk. 11, chap. 2, p. 462), Ovid (bk. 10, chap. 3, chap. 10, p. 137; bk. 10, chap. 1, p. 408), and Virgil (bk. 10, chap. 1, p. 408; bk. 12, chap. 3, p. 505).

33. In their other two encounters both Harrison and Atkinson reinforce the reader's initial impressions of their attitudes. When Harrison cites a passage in Greek during a discussion of adultery and Mrs. Atkinson responds by admitting that she knows some Greek, he makes a series of recondite antifeminine allusions (bk. 10, chap. 4, pp. 425–29). These references can have only two possible effects: if Mrs. Atkinson understands them, she will be insulted; if, however, as Harrison probably expects, she does not know the passages, he will have demonstrated her actual ignorance once again and his own superiority. As before, Harrison's display of learning does not achieve the result he desires; Fielding says, "from this Day, she considered [him] as a conceited Pedant." He also assails her again at the end of the novel and tweaks her with repeated references to the "Delphin" editions of various books (bk. 12, chap. 8, pp. 528–29).

34. The only exception appears when he says to Amelia that Bath is a little too "on the *Qui vive*" (bk. 5, chap. 6, p. 213).

35. While critics have noted that the narrative persona of *Amelia* is not identical with the narrator of the other two novels, all three use classics in much the same way.

36. The narrator also uses general allusions in *Joseph Andrews*, bk. 1, chap. 7, p. 36, where he refers to Adonis, Hercules, and Cupid; bk. 1, chap. 17, p. 85, where Adams is compared to Hercules; bk. 3, chap. 5, p. 232, where he says that Adams would not yield to Alexander; bk. 3, chap. 11, p. 267, where Adams is similar to Socrates; and bk. 4, chap. 7, p. 303, where the narrator says that Didapper is not of the Herculean race. In *Tom Jones* he states that Mrs.

Honour loved men "as Socrates was a Lover of Mankind" (bk. 5, chap. 4, 1:223). In *Amelia*, bk. 1, chap. 5, p. 40, he compares the Gambler's pockets to the pitchers of Belides, and Trent's wife and the Peer to Jupiter and Semele (bk. 11, chap. 3, p. 470).

37. See also *Joseph Andrews*, bk. 1, chap. 2, p. 21; bk. 3, chap. 6, p. 237.

38. He also uses the following common phrases: in *Joseph Andrews*, the phrase *è contra, totis viribus* (bk. 1, chap. 15, p. 69); in *Tom Jones* the phrases *Arbiter Deliciarum* (bk. 13, chap. 7, 2:712), *Foro Conscientiae* (bk. 4, chapt, 11, 1:192), *in sensu praedicto* (bk. 7, chap. 14, 1:386), *Nolo Episcopari* (bk. 1, chap. 11, 1:68), *Quantum* (bk. 11, chap. 9, 2:611), and *viva voce* (bk. 2, chap. 6, 1:98); in *Amelia*, the phrases *Materia Medica* (bk. 1, chap. 6, pp. 42–43), *Opus est Interprete* (bk. 1, chap. 2, p. 23), and *Verbum sapienti* (bk. 1, chap. 4, p. 35).

39. For Fielding's more learned readers, it would also suggest the treachery and defeat that ended the relationship of Caesar and Pompey and marks the relationship between Mrs. Ellison and Mrs. Atkinson. Fielding also provides contextual clues in *Joseph Andrews*, where he prefaces his description of Fanny with short quotations from Ovid and Horace (bk. 2, chap. 12, p. 152); and in *Amelia*, when he quotes Claudian (bk. 1, chap. 3, pp. 30–31), Juvenal (bk. 6, chap. 1, pp. 232–33), Ovid (bk. 1, chap. 2, p. 20), and Virgil (bk. 4, chap. 5, p. 171).

40. See also his paraphrases in *Tom Jones*, bk. 3, chapt 2, 1:120; bk. 4, chap. 13, 1:202; bk. 8, chap. 1, 1:404.

41. Eric Rothstein, "Virtues of Authority in *Tom Jones*," *The Eighteenth Century: Theory and Interpretation* 28 (1987): 107–17.

CHAPTER 5. THE ANCIENTS, THE MODERNS, AND THE ENGLISH NOVEL

1. See Ian Watt, *The Rise of the Novel: Studies in Defoe, Richardson, and Fielding* (Berkeley: University of California Press, 1957), 239–89; Michael McKeon, *The Origins of the English Novel, 1600–1740* (Baltimore: Johns Hopkins University Press, 1987), 382–409; Martin C. Battestin, "Fielding's Definition of Wisdom: Some Functions of Ambiguity and Emblem in *Tom Jones*," *ELH* 35 (1968): 188–217; and Henry Knight Miller, *Essays*.

2. See Howard Weinbrot, *Augustus Caesar in "Augustan" England: The Decline of a Classical Norm* (Princeton: Princeton University Press, 1978); "Augustan Imitation: The Role of the Original," in *Proceedings of the Modern Language Association Neoclassicism Conferences 1967–1968*, ed. Paul J. Korshin (New York: AMS Press, 1970), 53–70; and "History, Horace, and Augustus Caesar: Some Implications for Eighteenth-Century Satire," in *Eighteenth-Century Satire: Essays on Text and Context from Dryden to Peter Pindar* (Cambridge: Cambridge University Press, 1988), 21–33.

3. The seminal work on the ancients and moderns is R. F. Jones, *Ancients and Moderns: A Study of the Rise of the Scientific Movement in Seventeenth-Century England*, 2d ed. (St. Louis: Washington University Studies, 1961). Joseph M. Levine revises Jones in "Ancients, Moderns, and History: The Continuity of English Historical Writing in the Later Seventeenth Century," in *Studies in Change and Revolution*, ed. Paul Korshin (Menston, England: Scolar Press, 1972), 43–75; idem, "Ancients and Moderns Reconsidered," *Eighteenth-Century Studies* 15 (1981): 72–89; idem, "The Battle of the Books and the Shield of Achilles," *Eighteenth-Century Life* 9 (1984): 33–61; and idem, *The Battle of the Books: History and Literature in the Augustan Age* (Ithaca: Cornell University Press, 1991), 1–263. See also the discussion of the ancient-modern controversy in Kirsti Simonsuuri, *Homer's Original Genius: Eighteenth-century Notions of the Early Greek Epic, 1688–1798* (Cambridge: Cambridge University Press, 1979), 29–78.

4. Levine, "Ancients and Moderns Reconsidered," 76–79.

5. Ibid., 82–83. The controversy over the shield of Achilles in the *Iliad* epitomizes the

modern preoccupation with the truth of ancient accounts. See Levine, "Battle of the Books," 33–61 and idem, *Battle of the Books*, 125–31, 145–47, 165–66, 212–17, 234–36.

6. Similar comments appear in the *Champion*, 1 March 1739–40, 1:321–22; *True Patriot*, no. 7 (17 December 1745): 152; *Jacobite's Journal*, no. 5 (2 January 1748): 121; no. 26 (28 May 1748): 293; no. 33 (16 July 1748): 346; and *Covent-Garden Journal*, no. 48 (16 June 1752): 265.

7. See *Covent-Garden Journal*, no. 10 (4 February 1752): 72–77; no. 19 (7 March 1752): 129–34; no. 46 (9 June 1752): 255–59; no. 51 (27 June 1752): 280–85; *Tom Jones*, bk. 9, chap. 1, 1:487–89.

8. See also the *Champion*, 1 March 1739–40, 1:321–32; *True Patriot*, no. 7 (17 December 1745): 152; *Jacobite's Journal*, no. 5 (2 January 1748): 121; no. 26 (28 May 1748): 293; *Covent-Garden Journal*, no. 40 (19 May 1752): 232–33; no. 46 (9 June 1752): 256–57; and the unflattering portrait of the author whom Booth encounters in *Amelia* (bk. 8, chap. 5, pp. 326–27).

9. *Champion* , 22 April 1740, 2:129–32; 29 April 1740, 2:157–64; 3 May 1740, 2:173–77; 6 May 1740, 2:180–86; 10 May 1740, 2:200–204; and 17 May 1740, 2:224–29.

10. For other references to Cibber, see *Shamela* and *Covent-Garden Journal*, no. 17 (29 February 1752): 121.

11. See especially his discussion of the comic prose epic in *Joseph Andrews*, preface, 3–5.

12. For the first, see *Covent-Garden Journal*, no. 24 (24 March 1752): 156; and *A Journey from this World to the Next*, bk. 1, chap. 8, pp. 37–38 in *Miscellanies*, vol. 2. For the second, see the *Champion*, 15 November 1739, 1:4.

13. For example, see the *Champion*, 15 March 1739–40, 2:4; *Tom Jones*, bk. 11, chap. 1, 2:570.

14. See, for example, Fielding's comment in the *True Patriot*, no. 23 (1 April 1746): 258: "I have somewhere heard of a Geographer who received no other Pleasure from the *Aeneid* of *Virgil*, than by tracing out the Voyage of *Aeneas* in the Map. To which I may add a certain Coach-maker, who having sufficient *Latin* to read the story of *Phaeton* in the *Metamorphosis*, shook his Head that so fine a Genius for making Chariots as *Ovid* had, was thrown away on making Poems."

15. See his essay on commentators and antiquarians in the *Champion*, 15 March 1739–40, 2:3–5, where he classifies such work as form of excess to be avoided.

16. *Amelia*, bk. 10, chap. 1, pp. 408–10; Fielding also mentions Bentley's *ingentia fata* in the *Champion*, 27 November 1739, 1:33 and 31 May 1740, 2:270–80.

17. See *Joseph Andrews*, bk. 2, chap. 1, pp. 90–91. In *Journey from This World to the Next* Fielding asks Homer about this theory of divisions. Homer's reply demonstrates how contrary Bentley's theory runs to common sense: "He smiled at my question, and asked me whether there appeared any connexion in the poem; for if there did he thought I might answer myself" (bk. 1, chap. 8, pp. 37–38 in *Miscellanies*, vol. 2).

18. Fielding's satires and novels are full of mock scholarship: for example, see the *Champion*, 31 May 1740, 2:270–80; 7 June 1740, 2:307–13; and no. 139 (2 October 1740): 34–35; *True Patriot*, no. 23 (1 April 1746): 259; *Jacobite's Journal*, no. 6 (9 January 1748): 122; no. 23 (7 May 1748): 267–68; no. 38 (20 August 1748): 371–84; *Covent-Garden Journal*, no. 9 (1 February 1752): 66–71; no. 31 (18 April 1752): 192–96; no. 37 (9 May 1752): 217–21; *Jonathan Wild*, bk. 2, chap. 6, p. 91; *Amelia*, bk. 10, chap. 1, pp. 408–10; and the notes throughout *The Tragedy of Tragedies*, *The Vernon-iad*, and *A Journey from This World to the Next*.

19. See "Several Papers relating to the Terrestrial Chrysipus, Golden-Foot, or Guinea," in *Miscellanies*, 1:191–204; and the travel narrative in *Jonathan Wild*, bk. 4, chaps. 7–9, 11, pp. 208–28, 231–37.

20. *Joseph Andrews*, bk. 2, chap. 1, p. 185; similar remarks appear in the *Champion*, 15 March 1739–40, 2:4; *Jonathan Wild*, bk. 1, chap. 2, p. 5; and *Tom Jones*, bk. 4, chap. 1, 1:151.

21. The instances in which Fielding mentions the ancients and shows his preference for them are too numerous to mention. I include only a few examples here: *Jacobite's Journal*, no.

37 (13 August 1748): 363; *Covent-Garden Journal,* no. 1 (4 January 1752): 17–19; no. 6 (21 January 1752): 47–48; no. 19 (7 March 1752): 129; no. 40 (19 May 1752): 232; *Joseph Andrews,* bk. 1, chap. 1, pp. 18–19; and *Tom Jones,* bk. 12, chap. 1, 2:620.

22. For similar comments about the greatness of ancient critics, see *Jacobite's Journal,* no. 37 (13 August 1748): 363; *Covent-Garden Journal,* no. 15 (22 February 1752): 110.

23. See, for example, his comments about Milton in *Covent-Garden Journal,* no. 19 (7 March 1752): 129; no. 24 (24 March 1752): 159; and *Tom Jones,* bk. 9, chap. 1, 1:492.

24. *Tom Jones,* bk. 12, chap. 1, 2:620–21; bk. 14, chap. 1, 2:740. Fielding also attacks those who borrow from the ancients without truly understanding their meaning: see, for example, the *Champion,* 1 March 1739–40, 1:323.

25. See, for example *Covent-Garden Journal,* no. 10 (4 February 1752): 75: "If a Man, for Instance, should be overlooked with Prosperity, or Adversity, (both of which cases are liable to happen to us) who is there so very wise, or so very foolish, that, if he was a Master of Seneca and Plutarch, could not find great Matter of Comfort and Utility from their Doctrines?" Fielding expresses similar sentiments on the comfort to be derived from classical authors in "Of the Remedy of Affliction for the Loss of Friends," in *Miscellanies,* 1:212–25.

26. *Covent-Garden Journal,* no. 4 (14 January 1752): 37; see also the Ordinary's attack on Greek philosophy in *Jonathan Wild,* bk. 4, chap. 13, pp. 249–50; and Dr. Harrison's remarks about the reputation of Aristotle in *Amelia,* bk. 3, chap. 10, p. 137.

27. *Covent-Garden Journal,* no. 3 (11 January 1752): 30. For a similar comment praising Aristotle as a critic, see *Tom Jones,* bk. 11, chap. 1, 2:570–71.

28. Frederick Ribble, "Aristotle and the 'Prudence' Theme of *Tom Jones,*" *Eighteenth-Century Studies* 15 (1981): 26–47.

29. *Amelia,* bk. 8, chap. 10, pp. 350–51; bk. 4, chap. 10, pp. 174–75 (where Fielding himself calls Aristotle a "mental Physician"). Harrison mentions Aristotle in bk. 3, chap. 10, p. 137 and bk. 12, chap. 8, p. 528.

30. See *Covent-Garden Journal,* no. 10 (4 February 1752): 77 for Cicero's comments on taste, which Bertrand Goldgar suggests Fielding took from Pope's *Essay on Criticism,* lines 19–20. Fielding's comment about the wit in Cicero's writing appears in *Covent-Garden Journal,* no. 18 (3 March 1752): 124.

31. See Miller, *Essays,* 67–68, where he discusses the influence of Cicero and Aristotle on Fielding's concept of good nature; also 153–58 and 230; and *Miscellanies,* 1:xviii–xxvii, where Miller notes the similarities between the ideas expressed in Fielding's essays and Cicero's philosophy.

32. For a full discussion of the controversy over Homer, see Levine, "Battle of the Books," 35–49; idem, *Battle of the Books,* 122–244; and Simonsuuri, *Homer's Original Genius,* 37–78. Levine, *Battle of the Books,* explores Dacier's views on Homer on pp. 122–45.

33. For a full discussion of this controversy, see Simonsuuri, *Homer's Original Genius,* 29–61; Levine, "Battle of the Books," 36–42; and idem, *Battle of the Books,* 181–244.

34. *Covent-Garden Journal,* no. 1 (4 January 1752): 18–19; *Tom Jones,* bk. 12, chap. 1, 2:620–21. See also his remarks about Homer's "majestic air" in the *Champion* (13 December 1739), 1:91; and Adams's praise of Homer in *Joseph Andrews,* bk. 3, chap. 2, pp. 196–99.

35. For Fielding's comments about Homer's learning, see, for example, *True Patriot,* no. 8 (24 December 1745): 158; and *Tom Jones,* bk. 9, chap. 1, 1:492; bk. 14, chap. 1, 2:740.

36. Fielding points out Homer's originality in *Covent-Garden Journal,* no. 24 (24 March 1752): 24; and *Joseph Andrews,* preface, 4–5. Among his other compliments, Adams praises Homer for both his learning and his originality in *Joseph Andrews,* bk. 3, chap. 2, pp. 196–99.

37. James William Johnson, "The Classics and John Bull, 1660–1714," in *England in the Restoration and Early Eighteenth Century: Essays on Culture and Society,* ed. H. T. Swedenberg Jr. (Berkeley: University of California Press, 1972), 1–26; and Howard Weinbrot, *Augustus Caesar in "Augustan" England,* esp. pp. 120–81. Other critics, particularly Howard Erskine-Hill, have

argued that Weinbrot has overstated his case for a negative view of Augustus and the writers of the Maecenean circle. See Howard Erskine-Hill, *The Augustan Idea in English Literature* (London: Edward Arnold, 1983), 234–349. Reuben Brower's position appears in *Alexander Pope: The Poetry of Allusion* (Oxford: Oxford University Press, 1959), esp. 163–87, 282–318. For Weinbrot's response to Erskine-Hill and Brower, see "The Emperor's Old Toga: Augustanism and the Scholarship of Nostalgia," *Modern Philology* 83 (1986): 286–97; and *Britannia's Issue: The Rise of British Literature from Dryden to Ossian* (Cambridge: Cambridge University Press, 1993), 19–47.

38. Weinbrot, *Augustus Caesar in "Augustan" England*, 58, 231.

39. Fielding, "Of True Greatness," lines 199–200, in *Miscellanies*, 1:27. See also *Jacobite's Journal*, no. 48 (29 October 1748): 422.

40. Addison Ward, "The Tory View of Roman History," *Studies in English Literature, 1500–1900* 4 (1964): 413–56.

41. For Caesar's reputation in the eighteenth century and the controversy about his career, see ibid., 414–29.

42. *Jonathan Wild*, bk. 1, chap. 1, pp. 3–4. See also bk. 4, chap. 15, pp. 260–61; *Champion*, 22 March 1739–40, 2:29; "An Essay on Nothing," in *Miscellanies*, 1:188.

43. *True Patriot*, no. 2 (12 November 1745): 117; *Jonathan Wild*, bk. 1, chap. 1, p. 2. For other references to the two Bruti, see *Champion*, 4 December 1739, 1:61; *True Patriot*, no. 17 (18 February 1746): 226; *Jacobite's Journal*, no. 8 (23 January 1748): 138; no. 17 (26 March 1748): 210; no. 28 (11 June 1748): 306; *Miscellanies*, preface, 1:3; "Liberty," lines 15–16, p. 36; "Of the Remedy of Affliction for the Loss of Friends," p. 213; *Tom Jones*, bk. 4, chap. 4, 1:162–63; and *Amelia*, bk. 1, chap. 3, pp. 30–31; bk. 3, chap. 9, p. 130.

44. Ward, "Tory View," 414–15.

45. He mentions this speech more than once in the *Champion*, 15 January 1739–40, 1:186–87. In *Joseph Andrews* Adams also refers to Cicero's eulogium of Pompey's valor; unfortunately, he mentions in the same passage that Pompey behaved like a coward after the Battle of Pharsalia (bk. 2, chap. 9, p. 136).

46. *Champion*, 3 January 1739–40, 1:154. Fielding also uses passages from the Catilinarian speeches as mottoes in the *True Patriot*; see no. 10 (7 January 1746): 171; and no. 29 (13 May 1746): 289. Adams quotes Cicero's *O Tempora! O Mores!* when he relates the behavior of a beau he meets in the *True Patriot*, no. 13 (28 January 1746): 203. These mottoes suggest that Fielding associates the Jacobite Rebellion in 1745 with the Catilinarian conspiracy.

47. For a discussion of Cicero's reputation and the response to Middleton's biography, see Ward, "Tory View," 425–46.

48. *A Journey from this World to the Next*, bk. 1, chap. 9, in *Miscellanies*, 2:44. Although Weinbrot uses this passage as evidence to prove that Fielding was ambivalent about Augustus, Fielding never states why he prefers Hooke to Echard. See Weinbrot, *Augustus Caesar in "Augustan" England*, 58.

49. See *Jonathan Wild*, bk. 1, chap. 1, pp. 3–4; bk. 1, chap. 3, p. 13; bk. 1, chap. 5, p. 19; bk. 1, chap. 14, p. 59; bk. 4, chap. 4, p. 200; bk. 4, chap. 13, p. 239; bk. 4, chap. 15, pp. 260–61.

50. Fielding, "Of True Greatness," lines 55–65 and 92, in *Miscellanies*, 1:21–22. Other references to Alexander, all negative, appear in the following: *Champion*, 17 November 1739, 1:8; 5 January 1739–40, 1:160; 4 March 1739–40, 1:330; 22 March 1739–40, 2:29; 6 May 1740, 2:181; *Miscellanies*, "An Essay on Nothing," 1:188; "A Dialogue Between Alexander the Great and Diogenes the Cynic," 226–35; *Tom Jones*, bk. 6, chap. 9, 1: 303–4; *Covent-Garden Journal*, no. 19 (7 March 1752): 132; and *Amelia*, bk. 8, chap. 7, p. 337.

51. For references to Nero, see *Champion*, 5 January 1739–40, 1:160; *True Patriot*, no. 9 (31 December 1745): 166; *Jonathan Wild*, bk. 1, chap. 1, p. 2; *Joseph Andrews*, preface, 7; *Jacobite's Journal*, no. 3 (19 December 1747): 105, 106; *Tom Jones*, bk. 8, chap. 1, 1:402, 403, 406; and *Covent-Garden Journal*, no. 19 (7 March 1752): 132–33; no. 24 (24 March 1752): 155; no. 55 (18

July 1752): 301. For references to Caligula, see *Champion*, 18 December 1739, 1:107; 22 March 1739–40, 2:30; *Jacobite's Journal*, no. 3 (19 December 1747): 105, 106; *Covent-Garden Journal*, no. 19 (7 March 1752): 132–33; and *Tom Jones*, bk. 8, chap. 1, 1:402.

52. Ward, "Tory View," 415–24.

53. *Jacobite's Journal*, no. 28 (11 June 1748): 306. Fielding uses the same example in *Tom Jones*, bk. 4, chap. 4, 1:162–63. See also *Champion*, 4 March 1739–40, 1:330; *Joseph Andrews*, bk. 3, chap. 1, pp. 185–88.

54. For a discussion of the controversy between the ancients and the moderns over the writing of history, see Joseph Levine, "Ancients, Moderns, and History," 43–75; and idem, *Battle of the Books*, 267–90.

55. See, for example, Weinbrot, *Augustus Caesar in "Augustan" England*, 120–49.

56. See also other references about Virgil in Fielding: *Champion*, 31 May 1740, 2:282, where Fielding claims that Virgil would not have discussed the myth of the Hamadryades unless the superstition were still strong among the Romans, since the story is better suited to "the Extravagance of the *Metamorphoses*, than the sober Dignity of the *Aeneid*." In *Covent- Garden Journal*, no. 24 (24 March 1752): 159, he says that Homer's originality is the only advantage he can claim over Virgil and Milton.

57. See Battestin, *Life*, 39–46.

58. Weinbrot, "Augustan Imitation," 53–70; Christopher Ricks, "Allusion: The Poet as Heir," in *Studies in the Eighteenth Century III: Papers presented at the Third David Nichol Smith Memorial Seminar, Canberra 1973*, ed. R. F. Brissenden and J. C. Eade (Toronto: University of Toronto Press, 1976), 209–40; and Robert Folkenflik, "'Homo Alludens' in the Eighteenth Century," *Criticism* 24 (1982): 218–32.

POSTSCRIPT. LITERARY POLITICS IN THE MID-EIGHTEENTH CENTURY AND THE GENEALOGY OF THE NOVEL

1. Although Hunter, for example, speaks of various readers whom Fielding addresses, he argues that Fielding is trying to persuade only the "skeptical" reader in *Joseph Andrews*. See Hunter, *Occasional Form*, 95–111. See also Wolfgang Iser, *The Implied Reader. Patterns of Communication in Prose Fiction from Bunyan to Beckett* (Baltimore: Johns Hopkins University Press, 1974), 29–56; John Preston, "*Tom Jones* and the 'Pursuit of True Judgment,'" *ELH* 33 (1966): 315–26; idem, "Plot as Irony: The Reader's Role in *Tom Jones*," *ELH* 35 (1968): 365–80; and Raymond Stephanson, "The Education of the Reader in Fielding's *Joseph Andrews*," *Philological Quarterly* 61 (1982): 243–58.

2. Allusions account for 197 references (or 60 percent) in the novels; in his journalism they represent 221 citations (or 36 percent). For a complete listing, see the tables in chapters 2 and 3 and appendices B and C. He uses Dryden's Virgil in *Tom Jones*, bk. 5, chap. 4, 1:226; and *Amelia*, bk. 9, chap. 3, pp. 365–66; Creech's Lucretius in *Tom Jones*, bk. 2, chap. 1, 1:76; Pope's Homer in *Amelia*, bk. 9, chap. 3, pp. 365–66; bk. 10, chap. 4, pp. 425–27; and Francis's Horace in *Tom Jones*, bk. 8, chap. 13, 1:471–72; bk. 9, chap. 1, 1:488–89; bk. 11, chap. 1, 2:570; bk. 12, chap. 10, 2:659–60; and *Amelia*, bk. 10, chap. 4, p. 426.

3. For addresses to his English readers see, for example, *Joseph Andrews*, preface, 3; *Tom Jones*, bk. 2, chap. 8, 1:109; bk. 5, chap. 5, 1:229; and bk. 11, chap. 1, 2:566. He mentions his "classical" readers in *Joseph Andrews*, preface, 4; and *Tom Jones*, bk. 12, chap. 1, 2:619–20.

4. Fielding refers to these authors too often to make a complete list feasible. The following are examples only. He mentions Pope in *Jacobite's Journal*, no. 20 (16 April 1748): 235–36; *Covent-Garden Journal*, no. 3 (11 January 1752): 28; no. 13 (15 February 1752): 95–96; no. 15 (22 February 1752): 108; no. 18 (3 March 1752): 127; no. 23 (21 March 1752): 149, 153; no. 50

(23 June 1752): 273; and no. 59 (15 August 1752): 320–22. For Swift, see his obituary in *True Patriot*, no. 1 (5 November 1745): 336; and *Covent-Garden Journal*, no. 18 (3 March 1752): 125, 127. For Dryden, see *Covent-Garden Journal*, no. 18 (3 March 1752): 127; no. 23 (21 March 1752): 153. For Addison, see the *Champion*, 1 March 1739–40, 1:326; *True Patriot*, no. 2 (12 November 1745): 121; *Covent-Garden Journal*, no. 18 (3 March 1752): 127; and Coley's comments in the preface to the Wesleyan edition of *Jacobite's Journal*, pp. lvi–lvii. For the novels, see Fielding's use of translations by these authors listed in note 2.

 5. Hunter, *Occasional Form*, 15–19.

 6. Thomas Lockwood, "Matter and Reflection in *Tom Jones*," *ELH* 45 (1978): 226–35.

 7. For example, compare the strictures about the novel in the essays of *Tom Jones* with his comments about Charlotte Lennox's *Female Quixote* in *Covent-Garden Journal*, no. 24 (24 March 1752): 158–61; and his discussion of the need for learning in writers and critics in the *Champion*, 27 November 1739, 1:36–38; *Covent-Garden Journal*, no. 51 (27 June 1752): 280–85; and *Tom Jones*, bk. 9, chap. 1, 1:491–92; bk. 13, chap. 1, 2:687; bk. 14, chap. 1, 2:739–42.

 8. Watt, *Rise of the Novel*, 240–48.

 9. Michael McKeon, *The Origins of the English Novel, 1600–1740* (Baltimore: Johns Hopkins University Press, 1987).

 10. J. Paul Hunter, *Before Novels: The Cultural Contexts of Eighteenth-Century Fiction* (New York: W. W. Norton, 1990) indicates a number of possible sources for the novel, although, like Watt and McKeon, he stresses influences that reveal the "modernity" of the novel.

Bibliography

An Account of Charity-Schools Lately Erected in England, Wales, and Ireland. London: Joseph Downing, 1706.

"An Account of Eton Discipline in 1766 by Thomas James." *Etoniana*, no. 7 (3 July 1906): 97–108; no. 8 (30 November 1906): 113–19.

Ainsworth, Robert. *The Most Natural and Easy Way of Institution.* 2d ed. London: E. Curll and J. Wilford, 1736.

Allen, C. G. "The Sources of 'Lily's Latin Grammar': A Review of the Facts and Some Further Suggestions." *Library*, 5th ser., 9 (1954): 85–100.

Alter, Robert. *Fielding and the Nature of the Novel.* Cambridge: Harvard University Press, 1968.

Altick, Richard D. *The English Common Reader.* Chicago: University of Chicago Press, 1957.

Amory, Hugh. "Magistrate or Censor? The Problem of Authority in Fielding's Later Writings." *Studies in English Literature, 1500–1900* 12 (1972): 503–18.

Baker, Sheridan. "Fielding's *Amelia* and the Materials of Romance." *Philological Quarterly* 41 (1962): 437–49.

———. "Fielding's Comic Epic-in-Prose Romances Again." *Philological Quarterly* 58 (1979): 63–81.

———. "Henry Fielding and the Cliché." *Criticism* 1 (1959): 354–61.

———. "The Idea of Romance in the Eighteenth-Century Novel." *Papers of the Michigan Academy of Science, Arts, and Letters* 49 (1964): 507–22.

Ballard, George. *Memoirs of several ladies of Great Britain who have been celebrated for their writings or skill in the learned languages, arts and sciences.* Oxford, 1752.

Barber, Giles. "Book Imports and Exports in the Eighteenth Century." In *Sale and Distribution of Books from 1700*, edited by Robin Myers and Michael Harris, 77–105. Oxford: Oxford Polytechnic Press, 1982.

Barclay, James. *A Treatise on Education: or, An easy method of acquiring Language.* Edinburgh: James Cochran, 1743.

Bartolomeo, Joseph. *A New Species of Criticism: Eighteenth-Century Discourse on the Novel.* Newark: University of Delaware Press, 1994.

Bathoe, William. *A New Catalogue Of the Curious and Valuable Collection of Books: (Both English and French) Consisting of Several Thousand Volumes, By the best Authors, (Including all those that have been lately published) in almost every Branch of Polite Literature. Likewise Above the Fourteen Hundred different Sorts of Plays. Which are lent to Read, By the Year, Quarter, or single Book.* London, n.d.

Battestin, Martin C. "Fielding's Definition of Wisdom: Some Functions of Ambiguity and Emblem in *Tom Jones.*" *ELH* 35 (1968): 188–217.

———. *The Moral Basis of Fielding's Art: A Study of Joseph Andrews.* Middletown, Conn.: Wesleyan University Press, 1959.

———. "The Problem of *Amelia*: Hume, Barrow, and the Conversion of Captain Booth." *ELH* 41 (1974): 613–48.

———. *The Providence of Wit: Aspects of Form in Augustan Literature and the Arts.* Oxford: Clarendon Press, 1974.

Battestin, Martin C., with Ruthe R. Battestin. *Henry Fielding: A Life.* London: Routledge, 1989.

Battestin, Martin C., and Clive T. Probyn, eds. *The Correspondence of Henry and Sarah Fielding.* Oxford: Clarendon Press, 1993.

Bayne-Powell, Rosamond. *The English Child in the Eighteenth Century.* New York: E. P. Dutton, 1939.

Bellamy, Daniel. *The young ladies miscellany; or, Youth's innocent and rational amusement.* London, 1723.

Berendt, Stephen. "Art as Deceptive Intruder: Audience Entrapment in Eighteenth-Century Verbal and Visual Art." *Papers on Language and Literature* 19 (1983): 37–52.

Berland, Kevin. "Indirect Ethical Discourse: Fielding, Dialogue, and Dialectic." Diss., McMaster University, 1983.

———. "Satire and the *Via Media*: Anglican Dialogue in *Joseph Andrews*." In *Satire in the Eighteenth Century*, edited by J. D. Browning, 83–99. Publications of the McMaster University Association for Eighteenth Century Studies 10. New York: Garland, 1983.

Bissell, Frederick O., Jr. *Fielding's Theory of the Novel.* 1933. Reprint, New York: Cooper Square, 1969.

Blackwall, Anthony. *An Introduction to the Classics.* 2d ed. London, 1719; New York: Garland, 1971.

Blanchard, Frederic T. *Fielding the Novelist: A Study in Historical Criticism.* New Haven: Yale University Press, 1926.

Bond, Donald, ed. *The Spectator.* 5 vols. Oxford: Oxford University Press, 1965.

Booth, Wayne C. *The Rhetoric of Fiction.* 2d ed. Chicago: University of Chicago Press, 1983.

———. "The Self-Conscious Narrator in Comic Fiction Before *Tristram Shandy*." *PMLA* 67 (1952): 163–85.

Boswell, John. *A Method of Study; or, An Useful Library.* 2 vols. London, 1737.

Braudy, Leo. *Narrative Form in History and Fiction: Hume, Fielding, and Gibbon.* Princeton: Princeton University Press, 1970.

Broich, Ulrich. *The Eighteenth-Century Mock-Heroic Poem.* Translated by David Henry Wilson. Cambridge European Studies in English Literature. Cambridge: Cambridge University Press, 1990.

Brokesby, Francis. *Of Education. With respect to Grammar Schools, and the Universities.* London: John Hartley, 1701.

Bruggemann, Lewis. *A View of the English Editions, Translations and Illustrations of the Ancient Greek and Latin Authors with Remarks.* London, 1797.

Camden, William. *Institutio Graecae Grammatices Compendiaria. In usum Regiae Scholae Westmonasteriensis.* 1595; Menston, England: Scolar Press, 1969.

Clark, A. F. B. *Boileau and the French Classical Critics in England, 1660–1830.* Paris: Librarie Ancienne Edouard Champion, 1925.

Clarke, John. *An Essay upon Study.* London, 1731; New York: Garland, 1970.

———. *An Essay upon the Education of Youth in Grammar-Schools*. London: John Wyat, 1720.

Clarke, M. L. *Classical Education in Britain, 1500–1900*. Cambridge: Cambridge University Press, 1959.

———. *Greek Studies in England, 1700–1830*. Cambridge: Cambridge University Press, 1945. Reprint, Amsterdam: Adolf M. Hakkert, 1986.

Cooke, Arthur L. "Henry Fielding and the Writers of Heroic Romance." *PMLA* 62 (1947): 984–94.

Coolidge, John. "Fielding and 'Conservation of Character.'" *Modern Philology* 57 (1960): 245–59.

Crane, R. S. "The Concept of Plot and the Plot of *Tom Jones*." In *Critics and Criticism*, edited by R. S. Crane, 616–47. Chicago: University of Chicago Press, 1952.

Cressy, David. *Literacy and the Social Order: Reading and Writing in Tudor and Stuart England*. Cambridge: Cambridge University Press, 1980.

Cross, Wilbur. *The History of Henry Fielding*. 3 vols. New Haven: Yale University Press, 1918. Reprint, New York: Russell and Russell, 1963.

Darwin, Erasmus. *A Plan for the Conduct of Female Education in Boarding Schools*. Derby, 1797; New York: Johnson Reprint Corp., 1968.

Doddridge, Philip. "Constitutions Orders & Rules relating to the Academy at Northampton (1743)." Dr. Williams' Library, London. MS. L2/4.

———. *The Correspondence and Diary of Philip Doddridge, D. D.* Edited by John Doddridge Humphreys. 5 vols. London: Henry Colburn and Richard Bentley, 1829.

Dodsley, Robert. *The preceptor: containing A General Course of Education*. 2 vols. London: R. and J. Dodsley, 1758.

Dryden, John. *Ovid's Epistles, Translated by Several Hands* (1680). In *The Works of John Dryden*. Vol. 1. Berkeley: University of California Press, 1956.

———. *The Works of Virgil in English* (1697). In *The Works of John Dryden*, edited by William Frost and Vinton A. Dearing. Vols. 5 and 6. Berkeley: University of California Press, 1987.

Dudden, F. Homes. *Henry Fielding. His Life, Works, and Times*. 2 vols. Oxford: Clarendon Press, 1952.

Eighteenth-Century Short Title Catalogue. On-line version.

Electa Minora Ex Ovidio, Tibullo, et Propertio. Usui Scholae Etonensis. London: Tho. Newborough; Eton: Joan. Slatter, 1705.

Epigrammatum Delectus Ex omnibus Tum Veteribus, tum Recentioribus Poetis Accuratè dercerptus . . . In usum Scholae Etonensis. 7th ed. London: W. Innys, 1711.

Erskine-Hill, Howard. *The Augustan Idea in English Literature*. London: Edward Arnold, 1983.

Essay on the New Species of Writing Founded by Mr. Fielding (1751). Introduced by Alan D. McKillop. Augustan Reprint Society 95. Los Angeles: Augustan Reprint Society, 1962.

Essex, John. *The young ladies conduct: or, Rules for education under several heads; With instructions upon dress, both before and after marriage; and advice to young wives*. London: J. Brotherton, 1722.

Farrell, William J. "Fielding's Familiar Style." *ELH* 34 (1967): 65–77.

———. "The Mock-Heroic Form of *Jonathan Wild*." *Modern Philology* 63 (1966): 216–26.

Feather, John. *The Provincial Book Trade in Eighteenth-Century England*. Cambridge: Cambridge University Press, 1985.

Felton, Henry. *A Dissertation On Reading the Classics, And Forming a Just Style*. London: Jonah Bowyer, 1713.

Fielding, Henry. *Amelia.* Edited by Martin C. Battestin. Middletown, Conn.: Wesleyan University Press, 1983.

———. *An Apology for the Life of Mrs. Shamela Andrews.* London: A. Dodd, 1741. Reprint, New York: Garland, 1974.

———. *The Author's Farce.* Edited by Charles B. Woods. Regents Restoration Drama Series. Lincoln: University of Nebraska Press, 1966.

———. *The Champion.* 2d ed. 2 vols. London: H. Chapelle, 1743.

———. *The Covent-Garden Journal.* Edited by Gerard Edward Jensen. 2 vols. New Haven: Yale University Press, 1915.

———. *The Covent-Garden Journal, and a Plan of the Universal Register-Office.* Edited by Bertrand A. Goldgar. Oxford: Oxford University Press, 1988.

———. *The History of Our Own Times.* With introduction and notes by Thomas Lockwood. Delmar, N. Y.: Scholars' Facsimiles and Reprints, 1986.

———. *The Jacobite's Journal and Related Writings.* Edited by W. B. Coley. Middletown, Conn.: Wesleyan University Press, 1975.

———. *Joseph Andrews.* Edited by Martin C. Battestin. Middletown, Conn.: Wesleyan University Press, 1967.

———. *A Journey from this World to the Next.* In *Miscellanies.* Vol. 2. London: A. Millar, 1743.

———. *The Journal of a Voyage to Lisbon.* London: A. Millar, 1755.

———. *The Life of Mr. Jonathan Wild the Great.* 2d ed. London: A. Millar, 1754. Reprint, New York: Garland, 1974.

———. *The Lovers Assistant, or, New Art of Love* (1760). Edited by Claude E. Jones. Augustan Reprint Society 89. Los Angeles: Augustan Reprint Society, 1961.

———. *Miscellanies by Henry Fielding, Esq; Volume One.* Edited by Henry Knight Miller. Middletown, Conn.: Wesleyan University Press, 1972.

———. *Miscellanies by Henry Fielding, Esq; Volume Two.* Edited by Hugh Amory and Bertrand A. Goldgar. Middletown, Conn.: Wesleyan University Press, 1993.

———. *Ovid's Art of Love Paraphrased, and Adapted to the Present Time. With Notes. And A most Correct Edition of the Original. Book I.* London, 1747.

———. *Tom Jones.* Edited by Martin C. Battestin and Fredson Bowers. 2 vols. Middletown, Conn.: Wesleyan University Press, 1975.

———. *The True Patriot and Related Writings.* Edited by W. B. Coley. Middletown, Conn.: Wesleyan University Press, 1987.

———. *The Vernon-iad. Done into English, From the original Greek of Homer. Lately found at Constantinople. With Notes in usum, &c. Book the First.* London, 1741.

Fielding, Henry, and William Young. *Plutus, the God of Riches. A Comedy. Translated from the Original Greek of Aristophanes: With Large Notes Explanatory and Critical.* London: T. Waller, 1742.

Fielding, Sarah. *The Adventures of David Simple.* London, 1744. Reprint, New York: Garland Publishing, 1974.

Folkenflick, Robert. "'Homo Alludens' in the Eighteenth Century." *Criticism* 24 (1982): 218–32.

Frost, William. *Dryden and the Art of Translation.* Yale Studies in English 128. New Haven: Yale University Press, 1955.

Gardiner, Dorothy. *English Girlhood at School.* Oxford: Oxford University Press, 1929.

Gaskell, Philip. "Printing the Classics in the Eighteenth Century." *Book Collector* 1 (1952): 98–111.

A Gentleman's Library. London: W. Mears and J. Browne, 1715.

Goad, Caroline. *Horace in the English Literature of the Eighteenth Century*. Yale Studies in English 58. New Haven: Yale University Press, 1918.

Goldberg, Homer. *The Art of Joseph Andrews*. Chicago: University of Chicago Press, 1969.

———. "Comic Prose Epic or Comic Romance: The Argument of the Preface to *Joseph Andrews*." *Philological Quarterly* 43 (1964): 193–215.

Goldgar, Bertrand A. "Myth and History in Fielding's *Journey from This World to the Next*." *Modern Language Quarterly* 47 (1986): 235–52.

Gottfried, Leon. "The Odyssean Form." In *Essays on European Literature in Honour of Liselotte Dieckmann*, edited by P. Hohendahl, H. Lindenberger, and E. Schwarz, 19–43. St. Louis: Washington University Press, 1972.

The Guardian. Edited by John Calhoun Stephens. Lexington: University Press of Kentucky, 1982.

Hans, Nicholas. *New Trends in Education in the Eighteenth Century*. London: Routledge and Kegan Paul, 1951, 1966.

Harwood, Edward. *View of the Various Editions of the Greek and Roman Classics with Remarks*. London, 1775.

Hatfield, Glenn. *Henry Fielding and the Language of Irony*. Chicago: University of Chicago Press, 1968.

Hawtrey, E. C. *A Bill of Eton College and School, 1745*. Eton: E. P. Williams, 1843.

Howard, Susan K. "The Intrusive Audience in Fielding's *Amelia*." *Journal of Narrative Technique* 17 (1987): 286–95.

Hunter, Jean. "The 18th-Century Englishwoman: According to the Gentleman's Magazine." In *Woman in the 18th Century and Other Essays*, edited by Paul Fritz and Richard Morton, 73–88. Toronto and Sarasota: Samuel Stevens Hakkert and Co., 1976.

Hunter, J. Paul. *Before Novels: The Cultural Contexts of Eighteenth-Century Fiction*. New York: W. W. Norton, 1990.

———. *Occasional Form: Henry Fielding and the Chains of Circumstance*. Baltimore: Johns Hopkins University Press, 1975.

Irwin, William Robert. *The Making of Jonathan Wild: A Study in the Literary Method of Henry Fielding*. New York: Columbia University Press, 1941.

Iser, Wolfgang. *The Implied Reader: Patterns of Communication in Prose Fiction from Bunyan to Beckett*. Baltimore: Johns Hopkins University Press, 1974.

Jennings, John. "An Account of the Curriculum at Kibworth Academy, ca. 1720." Dr. Williams' Library. London. MS. 12.40 (122).

Johnson, James William. "The Classics and John Bull, 1660–1714." In *England in the Restoration and Early Eighteenth Century: Essay on Culture and Society*, edited by H. T. Swedenberg Jr., 1–26. Berkeley: University of California Press, 1972.

Johnson, Maurice, *Fielding's Art of Fiction: Eleven Essays on Shamela, Joseph Andrews, Tom Jones, and Amelia*. Philadelphia: University of Pennsylvania Press, 1961.

Jones, Mary G. *The Charity School Movement: a Study of Eighteenth-Century Puritanism in Action*. Cambridge: Harvard University Press, 1938.

Jones, R. F. *Ancients and Moderns: A Study of the Rise of the Scientific Movement in Seventeenth-Century England*. 2d ed. St. Louis: Washington University Studies, 1961.

Karl, Frederick. *The Adversary Literature: The English Novel in the Eighteenth Century, A Study in Genre*. New York: Farrar, Straus, and Giroux, 1974.

Kaufman, Paul. "Reading Vogues at English Cathedral Libraries of the Eighteenth Century." *Bulletin of the New York Public Library* 67 (1963): 643–72; 68 (1964): 48–64, 110–32, 191–202.

Keener, Frederick M. *English Dialogues of the Dead: A Critical History, an Anthology, and a Checklist.* New York: Columbia University Press, 1973.

Keith, William. *A Collection of Papers and other tracts written occasionally on various subjects.* London: J. Mechell, 1740.

Kennedy, George. *The Art of Rhetoric in the Roman World, 300 B.C. to A.D. 300.* Princeton: Princeton University Press, 1972.

Knight, Charles A. "Fielding and Aristophanes," *Studies in English Literature, 1500–1900* 21 (1981): 481–98.

Kropf, C. R. "Educational Theory and Human Nature in Fielding's Works." *PMLA* 89 (1974): 113–20.

Law, William. *A Serious Call to a Devout and Holy Life* (1728). Edited by Paul G. Stanwood. New York: Paulist Press, 1978.

Le Bossu, René. *Treatise of the Epick Poem* (1695). In *Le Bossu and Voltaire on the Epic.* Introduced by Stuart Curran. Gainesville, Fla.: Scholars' Facsimiles and Reprints, 1970.

Levine, Joseph. "Ancients, Moderns, and History: The Continuity of English Historical Writing in the Later Seventeenth Century." In *Studies in Change and Revolution*, edited by Paul Korshin, 43–75. Menston, England: Scolar Press, 1972.

———. "Ancients and Moderns Reconsidered." *Eighteenth-Century Studies* 15 (1981): 72–89.

———. *The Battle of the Books: History and Literature in the Augustan Age.* Ithaca: Cornell University Press, 1991.

———. "The Battle of the Books and the Shield of Achilles." *Eighteenth-Century Life* 9 (1984): 33–61.

Lily, William. *A Short Introduction of Grammar Compiled and set forth for the bringing up of all those that intend to attain to the knowledge of the Latin Tongue.* London: Roger Norton, 1690.

Lind, Levi R. "Lucian and Fielding." *Classical Weekly* 29 (1936): 84–86.

Locke, John. *Some Thoughts Concerning Education.* Edited by James L. Axtell. Cambridge: Cambridge University Press, 1968.

Lockwood, Thomas. "Matter and Reflection in *Tom Jones*." *ELH* 45 (1978): 226–35.

Lynch, James. *Henry Fielding and the Heliodoran Novel: Romance, Epic, and Fielding's New Province of Writing.* Rutherford, N.J.: Fairleigh Dickinson University Press, 1986.

Lyte, H. C. Maxwell. *A History of Eton College, 1440–1875.* London: Macmillan, 1875.

Mackerell, Benjamin. *A New Catalogue of the Books in the Public Library of the City of Norwich, In the Year 1732.* Norwich: William Chase, 1732.

Maresca, Thomas E. *Epic to Novel.* Columbus: Ohio State University Press, 1974.

McIntosh, Carey. *Common and Courtly Language: The Stylistics of Social Class in Eighteenth-Century English Literature.* Philadelphia: University of Pennsylvania Press, 1986.

McKee, John. *Literary Irony and the Literary Audience: Studies in the Victimization of the Reader in Augustan Fiction.* Amsterdam: Rodopi, 1974.

McKenzie, Alan T. "The Processes of Discovery in *Tom Jones*." *Dalhousie Review* 54 (1974–75): 720–40.

McKeon, Michael. *The Origins of the English Novel, 1600–1740.* Baltimore: Johns Hopkins University Press, 1987.

McKillop, Alan. "English Circulating Libraries, 1725–50." *Library*, ser. 4, 14 (1934): 477–85.

McLachlan, Herbert. *English Education Under the Test Acts, being the History of the Non-Conformist Academies, 1662–1820.* Manchester: Manchester University Press, 1931.

McMullin, B. J. "An Anatomy of the Foulis Press Duodecimo Ciceros of 1748 and 1749." *Papers of the Bibliographical Society of America* 74 (1980): 177–200.

McNamara, Susan P. "Mirrors of Fiction Within *Tom Jones*: The Parodox of Self-Reference." *Eighteenth-Century Studies* 12 (1979): 372–90.

Miller, Henry Knight. *Essays on Fielding's "Miscellanies": A Commentary on Volume One.* Princeton: Princeton University Press, 1961.

———. *Henry Fielding's Tom Jones and the Romance Tradition.* University of Victoria English Literary Studies 6. Victoria, B.C.: University of Victoria, 1976.

———. "Some Functions of Rhetoric in *Tom Jones*." *Philological Quarterly* 45 (1966): 209–35.

———. "The Voices of Henry Fielding: Style in *Tom Jones*." In *The Augustan Milieu*, edited by H. K. Miller, Eric Rothstein, and G. S. Rousseau, 262–88. Oxford: Clarendon Press, 1970.

Montagu, Lady Mary Wortley. *The Complete Letters of Lady Mary Wortley Montagu.* Edited by Robert Halsband. 3 vols. Oxford: Clarendon Press, 1965–67.

Munby, A. N. L. *Sale Catalogues of Libraries of Eminent Persons.* Edited by Hugh Amory. Vol. 7. London: Mansell, 1973.

Noble, John. *A New Catalogue Of the Large and Valuable Collection of Books, (Both English, and French) in John Noble's Circulating Library: Consisting of Several Thousand Volumes, by the Best Authors, In almost every Branch of Literature, Which are Lent to Read, By the Year, Quarter, or Single Book.* London, 1767.

Of Education. London: Thomas Wotton, 1734.

Ogilvie, R.M. *Latin and Greek: A History of the Influence of the Classics on English Life from 1600 to 1918.* New York: Archon, 1969.

Orton, Job. *Memoirs of the Life, Character, and Writings of the Late Reverend Philip Doddridge, D. D. of Northampton.* Salop: J. Cotton and J. Eddowes, 1766.

Osland, Diane. "Fielding's *Amelia*: Problem Child or Problem Reader?" *Journal of Narrative Technique* 10 (1980): 56–67.

Palmer, E. T. "Fielding's *Joseph Andrews*: A Comic Epic in Prose." *English Studies* 52 (1971): 331–39.

Parker, Irene. *Dissenting Academies in England.* Cambridge: Cambridge University Press, 1914.

Paulson, Ronald. *Satire and the Novel in Eighteenth-Century England.* New Haven: Yale University Press, 1967.

Pfeiffer, Rudolf. *History of Classical Scholarship from 1300 to 1850.* Oxford: Clarendon Press, 1976.

Plant, Marjorie. *The English Book Trade: An Economic History of the Making and Sale of Books.* London: Allen and Unwin, 1939, 1965.

Poikile Historia. Sive Novus Historiarum Fabellarumque Delectus: Cum Notis et Versione. In Usum Scholae Etonensis. London and Eton, 1701.

Pope, Alexander. *The Iliad of Homer* (1715–20). Edited by Maynard Mack. 2 vols. London: Methuen; New Haven: Yale University Press, 1967.

———. *The Odyssey of Homer* (1725–26). Edited by Maynard Mack. 2 vols. London: Methuen; New Haven: Yale University Press, 1967.

Powers, Lyall H. "The Influence of the *Aeneid* on Fielding's *Amelia*." *Modern Language Notes* 71 (1956): 330–36.

Preston, John. *The Created Self: The Reader's Role in Eighteenth-Century Fiction*. London: Heinemann, 1970.

———. "Plot as Irony: The Reader's Role in *Tom Jones*." *ELH* 35 (1968): 365–80.

———. "*Tom Jones* and the 'Pursuit of True Judgment.'" *ELH* 33 (1966): 315–26.

Probyn, Clive T. *The Sociable Humanist: The Life and Works of James Harris, 1709–1780*. Oxford: Oxford University Press, 1991.

Proposals for the Reformation of Schools & Universities. 1704.

Ransom, Harry. *The First Copyright Statute: An Essay on An Act for the Encouragement of Learning, 1710*. Austin: University of Texas Press, 1956.

Rawson, C. J. *Henry Fielding and the Augustan Ideal Under Stress*. London: Routledge and Kegan Paul, 1972.

———."Language, Dialogue, and Point of View in Fielding, Some Considerations." In *Quick Springs of Sense: Studies in the Eighteenth Century*, edited by Larry S. Champion, 137–56. Athens: University of Georgia Press, 1974.

———. *Satire and Sentiment, 1660–1830*. Cambridge: Cambridge University Press, 1994.

———. "Some Considerations on Authorial Intrusion and Dialogue in Fielding's Novels and Plays." *Durham University Journal* 64 (1971): 32–44.

Renwick, W. L. "Comic Epic in Prose." *Essays and Studies* 32 (1946): 40–43.

Reynolds, Myra. *The Learned Lady in England, 1650–1760*. Boston and New York: Houghton Mifflin, 1920.

Ribble, Frederick. "Aristotle and the 'Prudence' Theme of *Tom Jones*." *Eighteenth-Century Studies* 15 (1981): 26–47.

Richardson, Samuel. *The Correspondence of Samuel Richardson*. Edited by Anna Laetitia Barbauld. 6 vols. London: Richard Phillips, 1804.

———. *Pamela; or, Virtue Rewarded* (1740). London: Penguin Books, 1980.

Ricks, Christopher. "Allusion: The Poet as Heir." In *Studies in the Eighteenth Century III: Papers presented at the Third David Nicol Smith Memorial Seminar, Canberra 1973*, edited by R. F. Brissenden and J. C. Eade, 209–40. Toronto: University of Toronto Press, 1976.

Robinson, Christopher. *Lucian and his Influence in Europe*. London: Duckworth, 1979.

Rollin, Charles. *The Method of Teaching and Studying the Belles Lettres . . . designed more particularly for students in the universities*. Trans. from French. 5th ed. 4 vols. London: C. Hitch and L. Hawes, 1758.

Rothstein, Eric. "The Framework of *Shamela*." *ELH* 35 (1968): 381–402.

———. *Systems of Order and Inquiry in Later Eighteenth-Century Fiction*. Berkeley: University of California Press, 1975.

———. "Virtues of Authority in *Tom Jones*." *Eighteenth-Century Theory and Interpretation* 28 (1987): 99–126.

Sandys, John Edwin. *A History of Classical Scholarship*. 3 vols. Cambridge, 1958. Reprint, New York: Hafner Publishing, 1964.

Shea, Bernard. "Classical Learning in the Novels of Henry Fielding." Diss., Harvard University, 1952.

Sherburn, George. "Fielding's *Amelia*: An Interpretation." *ELH* 3 (1936): 1–14.

Simonsuuri, Kirsti. *Homer's Original Genius: Eighteenth-Century Notions of the Early Greek Epic, 1688–1798*. Cambridge: Cambridge University Press, 1979.

Sloman, Judith. *Dryden: The Poetics of Translation*. Toronto: University of Toronto Press, 1985.

Smart, Christopher. *Poems on Several Occasions*. London, 1763.

Stedman, Thomas, ed. *Letters to and from The Rev. Philip Doddridge, D. D. Late of Northampton: Published from the originals with Notes Explanatory and Biographical*. Shrewsbury: J. and W. Eddowes, 1790.

Steele, Richard. *The Ladies Library, by a Lady*. 3 vols. London: J. Tonson, 1714.

Stephanson, Raymond. "The Education of the Reader in Fielding's *Joseph Andrews*." *Philological Quarterly* 61 (1982): 243–58.

Swedenberg, H. T., Jr. *The Theory of the Epic in England, 1650–1800*. University of California Publications in English 15. Berkeley: University of California Press, 1944. Reprint, Milwood, N.Y.: Kraus Reprint Co., 1977.

Thomson, J. A. K. *The Classical Background of English Literature*. London: Allen and Unwin, 1948.

Thornbury, Ethel M. *Henry Fielding's Theory of the Comic Prose Epic*. University of Wisconsin Studies in Language and Literature 30. 1931. Reprint, New York: Russell and Russell, 1966.

Tompson, Richard S. *Classics or Charity? The Dilemma of the 18th Century Grammar School*. Manchester: Manchester University Press, 1971.

Town, Mr. *The Connoisseur*. 3d ed. 2 vols. London: R. Baldwin, 1757.

Treis tragodiai, Aischylou Choephoroi, Sophokleous Elektra, Euripidou Elektra. In usum Scholae Regiae Westmonasteriensis. Oxford: Clarendon Press, 1729.

Vander Motten, J. P. "Molly Seagrim in the Plains of Troy." *English Studies* 69 (1988): 249–53.

Varma, Devendra P. *The Evergreen Tree of Diabolical Knowledge*. Washington, D.C.: Consortium Press, 1972.

Ward, Addison. "The Tory View of Roman History." *Studies in English Literature, 1500–1900* 4 (1964): 413–56.

Waterland, Daniel. *Advice to a Young Student. With a method of Study for the Four First Years*. London: Crownfield, 1730.

Watt, Ian. "Defoe and Richardson on Homer: A Study of the Relation of Novel and Epic in the Early Eighteenth Century." *Review of English Studies*, n.s., 3 (1952): 325–40.

———. *The Rise of the Novel: Studies in Defoe, Richardson, and Fielding*. Berkeley: University of California Press, 1957.

Watts, Isaac. *Works*. 6 vols. London: Longman, Buckland, et alia, 1753.

Weinbrot, Howard. "Augustan Imitation: The Role of the Original." In *Proceedings of the Modern Language Association Neoclassicism Conferences, 1967–1968*, edited by Paul J. Korshin, 53–70. New York: AMS Press, 1970.

———. *Augustus Caesar in "Augustan" England: The Decline of a Classical Norm*. Princeton: Princeton University Press, 1978.

———. *Britannia's Issue: The Rise of British Literature from Dryden to Ossian*. Cambridge: Cambridge University Press, 1993.

———. "The Emperor's Old Toga: Augustanism and the Scholarship of Nostalgia," *Modern Philology* 83 (1986): 286–97.

———. "History, Horace, and Augustus Caesar: Some Implications for Eighteenth-Century Satire." In *Eighteenth-Century Satire: Essays on Text and Context from Dryden to Peter Pindar*, edited by Howard Weinbrot, 21–33. Cambridge: Cambridge University Press, 1988.

Wiesenfarth, Joseph. "'High' People and 'Low' in *Joseph Andrews*: A Study of Structure and Style." *College Language Association Journal* 16 (1973): 357–65.

Wilson, Penelope. "Classical Poetry and the Eighteenth-Century Reader." In *Books and their Readers in Eighteenth-Century England*, edited by Isabel Rivers, 69–96.Leicester: Leicester University Press; New York: St. Martin's Press, 1982.

Wilson, Thomas. *The true Christian method of educating the children both of the poor and rich*. London: Downing, 1724.

Winterton, Ralph, ed. *Poetae minores Graeci, selecti et emendati . . . In usum scholarum*. London, 1728.

Index

Achilles, 71, 74–75, 116–17
Adams, Abraham: classical learning of, 71–72, 89–90, 118; compared to narrator, 102–3; response to classics, 81–82, 84, 115; use of classics by, 79, 80, 89–92, 102; views of epic hero, 71–73
Addison, Joseph: connection with Fielding, 59, 61–62, 66–67, 104, 131, 132–33; discussion of epic, 67; translations by, 34; treatment of Brutus, 121; use of classics by, 108
Aelian, 21
Aeneas, 71–75
Aeschylus: editions of, 21, 35, 38; references to, by Fielding, 50, 64, 80, 82, 89–90
Aesop: editions of, 35; in school curricula, 22, 30, 31; translations of, 29
Ainsworth, Robert, 23, 41
Alcibiades, 85
Alexander the Great, 75, 121–24
Allestree, Richard, 30
Allworthy, Squire, 94
Allworthy, Bridget, 72, 101–2
Altick, Richard, 36, 38
Amelia, 76, 97, 114; with characters who use classics, 75, 96, 98, 99
Amelia: and *Aeneid*, 64, 73–76, 125; and epic hero, 117; classical references in, 65, 109, 113, 114; portrait of Mrs. Bennet, 28, 99; use of classics, by characters, 78–80, 83–84, 95–100, 122; —, by narrator, 100–101, 103, 131
Amory, Hugh, 40
Anacreon, 35
Anchises, 74
ancients, Fielding's attitudes toward, 105–6, 111–18, 126–27

ancients and moderns, debate between, 61–62, 105–11, 124, 127, 129; and epic, 115–18; and Fielding, 105–18, 126, 129, 135; and genealogy of the novel, 132
Andrews, Joseph, 79, 91, 100, 101, 118
Andrews, Pamela, 86, 88, 111
Andromache, 100
antiquarians, 49, 107–11, 124
Apuleius, 46, 49
Aratus, 162n. 10
aretalogi, 96, 103
Aristophanes: editions of, 41, 162n. 10; references to, by Fielding, 12, 47, 49, 55, 64, 117; translation of *Plutus*, 43, 45, 56
Aristotle, 59; and ancient/modern debate, 115; and epic, 65, 67, 70, 90; editions of, 35, 38, 41–42, 54, 165n. 55; influence on Fielding, 65, 112–13, 117, 127, 136; in school texts and guides, 20–21; references to, by Fielding, 47–49, 51–53, 55, 57, 64–65, 82, 84, 102, 112–14, 174n. 32
Atkinson, Serjeant, 99
Atkinson, Mrs. *See* Bennet, Mrs.
Attalus, 91
audience: classical learning of, 82–86, 88–94, 101, 130–31, 135; conditioning of, by Fielding, 130–31; concept of, in eighteenth century, 129–31; response to classical learning, 81–90, 93–94, 96, 102, 130
Augustan Age, 106, 118–20, 122–26; and eighteenth century, 105, 118–20
Augustus, 105–6, 118–20, 122–27
Aulus Gellius, 49

191

Baker, Samuel, sale catalog of Fielding's library, 40–42, 47, 50, 54
Baker, Sheridan, 71
Banier, Abbé Antoine, 42
Barnes, Joshua, 97
Bath, Colonel, 73, 75–76, 80–81, 84
Bathoe, William, circulating library catalog, 37, 38
Battestin, Martin C., 95, 105
Bayle, Pierre, 42
Bell, John, *Pantheon*, 29
Bellamy, Daniel, 29
Bellaston, Lady, 75, 85
Bennet, Mrs. (Mrs. Atkinson): classical learning of, 75, 80–81; use of classics by, 96–100
Bentley, Richard, 106, 111, 118; theories on epic, 67, 115–16, 126; references to, by Fielding, 49, 109
Bion, 20
Blackwall, Anthony, *Introduction to the Classics*, 24–25
Blifil, 79, 85
Booby, Lady, 79, 91, 101
Booth (in *Amelia*), 103, 118; and heroic ideal, 73, 75–76; knowledge and use of the classics, 83–84, 96–99, 122
Boswell, John, *Method of Study*, 24–25
Braudy, Leo, 86, 87
Brokesby, Francis, *Of Education*, 24–25
Brower, Reuben, 118–19
Brutus, 120–24
Bryant, Jacob, 29
Burmann, Pieter, 40, 46, 49

Caesar, Julius, 38; eighteenth-century reputation, 120–24; in curricula and handbooks, 22, 24, 27; references to, by Fielding, 101, 123
Cambridge University, 23–24
Camden, William, *Institutio Graecae grammatices compendiaria*, 20, 22
Canterbury Cathedral library, 37–38
Carlisle Cathedral library, 37–38
Carter, Elizabeth, translation of Epictetus, 29
Casaubon, I., 46
cathedral libraries, 37–38
Catiline, 121–22, 124
Cato the Elder, 87, 121–22
Cato the Younger, 33, 49
Cebes, 35, 36

Cervantes, Saavedra, Miguel de, 55, 65, 71
Champion: essay on ancient prolixity, 58, 124–25; imitation of Lucian, 56; satire, on Colley Cibber, 107–8; —, on Royal Society, 110
Chapone, Hester, 29
character: and epic, 69; judgment and presentation of, 77–85, 131
characters: response to, 81–85, 90–100, use of classics by, 79–85
charity schools, 30
Charke, Charlotte, 29
Cibber, Colley, 59, 72, 86, 107–9, 111
Cicero, 18, 31, 59; editions of, 33–34, 37–38, 42; eighteenth-century attitudes toward, 107, 115; influence on Fielding, 112–15, 117, 121–22, 127; in school curricula and handbooks, 20–22, 24, 27, 29; references to, by Fielding, 46, 50–53, 63–64, 82, 86, 90, 94, 96, 103, 113–15, 174 n. 32
circulating libraries, 36–38
Clarke, John, 24–25, 28–29, 32, 34
Clarke, Samuel, 35
classics: editions of, 31–36; in handbooks and curricula, 24–25; knowledge of, 107–9, 111, 112, 118, 130–31, 135–36; use of, 79–86, 88–89; references to, in Fielding, 50–54, 63–65; response to, among readers, 79–81
"classical" readers, 130–31
Claudian, 40, 49, 162 n. 11
clergy, use of classics by, in Fielding's novels, 81–83
Clive, Kitty, 44
coffeehouses, 36
Coley, W. B., 47
Congreve, William, translations by, 34
Coolidge, John, 78, 95
copyright, and the classics, 32
Covent-Garden Journal: attacks on antiquarians, 108; classical translations in, 43, 45, 60; paper war, 55, 113, 125; puff for Lucian translation, 55–56; satire, on Royal Society, 110
Creech, Thomas, translation of Lucretius, 130
Cressy, David, 30–31
critics, Fielding's guidelines for, 112–13
Croesus, 91, 101
Cross, Wilbur, 40

INDEX 193

D'Ablancourt, Nicolas Perrot, 54
Dacier, André, 67, 116
Dacier, Anne Lefevre, 47, 95, 115–18
Daedalus, 90
dame schools, curriculum of, 30
Darwin, Erasmus, *Plan for the Conduct of Female Education*, 29
Defoe, Daniel: concept of fiction, 62, 132–35; relationship to Fielding, 111, 130; views on classical past, 11, 72, 109
Delphin classics, 32, 34, 99
Demosthenes: editions of, in curricula and libraries, 38, 163n. 14; Fielding's translation of, 43, 45; references to, by Fielding, 55, 114
Dennis, John, 118
dialogues of the dead, 56
Dido, 75, 107
Diodorus Siculus, 47, 53
Diogenes, 20
Dionysius of Halicarnassos, 21, 162n. 10
dissenting academies, curriculum in, 26–28
doctors, use of classics by, in Fielding's novels, 83–84
Doddridge, Philip, 27–28
Dodsley, Robert, translation of Aesop, 29
Dowling (lawyer in *Tom Jones*), 95
Dryden, John: attitudes to epic, 66–67, 72–74; classical translations by, 29, 34, 36, 43, 54, 73–75; references to, by Fielding, 46, 49; relationship to Fielding, 61–62, 66, 74–75, 104, 125–26, 130, 132–33, 135
D'Urfey, Tom, 107
Durham Cathedral library, 37–38

Echard, Laurence, *Roman History*, 29, 85, 93
Eighteenth-Century Short Title Catalogue (ESTC), 19, 20, 32–36
Electa Minora Ex Ovidio, Tibullo, et Propertio, 20
Elysium, 100
"English" readers, addresses to, by Fielding, 131
epic: and mock heroics, 70–73; and romance, 111; debate over, 115–18; definition of, 66; heroic ideal in, 72–76, 84, 98, 102, 116, 135; learning in, 108; theory and Fielding's fiction, 61–70, 90, 112–13, 126
Epictetus, 29, 35–36

Epigrammatum Delectus: audience's knowledge of, 82, 130; citations from, in Fielding's novels, 82, 83–84, 87, 90, 93, 100; in school curricula, 20, 22
Epistles of Phalaris, 109
Erskine-Hill, Howard, 118–19
essay, influence on Fielding's fiction, 61
Eton College, classical curriculum of, 19–22, 50, 51; Fielding's education at, 40, 47–48, 125, 133; references to, by Fielding, 92
Euclid, 35–36, 86
Euripides, 21, 38, 49, 51
Eustathius, 49
Exeter Cathedral library, 37–38

Fabricius, commentaries of, 42
Fancourt, Samuel, circulating library catalog, 36–37
Farnaby, Thomas, *Index Grammaticus*, 22
Fellamar, Lord, 75, 85
Felton, Henry, *Dissertation on Reading the Classics*, 24–25
Fénelon, François de Salignac de La Mothe, *Télémaque*, 69
Ferrarius, 46
Fielding, Henry: ambivalence to epic hero, 72–76; and ancient/modern debate, 105–18, 132; and history, 127; attitudes, toward ancient historical figures, 119–27; —, toward ancient authors, 111–17; audience of, 11, 17–18, 31, 101; classical citations in, 50–54, 63–65; classical learning of, 39–42, 50; classical parodies by, 46–50; classical translations by, 43–45, 56; fiction, generic sources of, 61–62; narrative persona, authority of, 88, 104; Works: *Amelia*, 62; *Author's Farce*, 56; *Champion*, classical references in, 50–53, 57–58, 114–17, 120–21; *Covent-Garden Journal*, classical references in, 47, 50–54, 57–58, 113–14, 116–20; *Dialogue Between the Devil, the Pope, and the Pretender*, 122–23; *History of Our Own Times*, 48; *Jacobite's Journal*, classical references in, 47, 50–53, 113, 119, 121–22; *Jonathan Wild*, 62, 108, 121–22, 124; *Joseph Andrews*, 62; *Journal of a Voyage to Lisbon*, 41, 117; *Journey from This World to the Next*, 48–50, 56, 85, 116, 122, 125;

Fielding, Henry *(continued):*
  Miscellanies, vol. 1, 43, 45; *Shamela,* 79, 82–83, 86, 88–89, 99–100, 107, 111, 122; *Tom Jones,* classical references in, 62, 65, 114, 116–17; *Tragedy of Tragedies,* 40, 72; *True Patriot,* 47, 50–53, 55, 86, 120–21, 125; *Vernon-iad,* 40, 48–49, 125. *See also* individual works
Fielding, Sarah, 28, 29
Florus, 34
Fontanelle, Bernard le Bovier de, 56
Francis, Philip, translation of Horace, 130
Freeholder (Addison), 59

Galen, 83
Garth, Samuel, translation of *Metamorphoses,* 29
Gay, John, 132, 133
Gloucester Cathedral library, 37–38
Goad, Caroline, 12
Goodwill, Fanny, 71, 100
Gradus ad Parnassum, 93
Graevius, 46
grammar schools, 18–23, 162n. 7
Greek authors, editions of, 34–36
Grub-Street Journal, 109
Guardian (Steele), 21

Hans, Nicholas, 26
Harris, James, 45
Harrison, Dr.: and classical learning, 80–81, 95–99, 103, 109, 113, 118; as exemplary figure, 95; attitude toward epic hero, 75, 115; pedantry of, 96–97
Hatfield, Glenn, 81
Havercamp, Siegbert, 40
Hector, 74, 102
Hederich, Benjamin, *Greek Lexicon,* 41
Helen, 75, 85
hero, epic, 71–76, 102, 117
Herodotus, 21, 24–25, 38, 64, 88
Hesiod, 20, 42, 49
Hippocrates, 35, 83
history: and narrators of Fielding's novels, 87–88; influence on Fielding, 61, 110–11, 118–27; satires of, by Fielding, 86
Homer, 18; attitudes about, in eighteenth century, 67, 108–9, 115–18, 126; editions of, 34–38, 41–42; heroic code in, 72–75, 102; in school curricula and handbooks, 20–22, 24, 27, 29, 38;

influence on Fielding, 61, 108, 112–13, 124–26, 136; knowledge of, in eighteenth century, 29, 31, 80, 99; *Odyssey,* 12; parodies of, 71, 73; references to, by Fielding, 41, 46, 48, 50–55, 58, 64, 66, 69, 71, 73, 75, 80, 83, 90, 97, 107, 116–17, 125–26; translation of, by Dacier, 115; —, by Dryden, 36; —, by La Motte, 115–16; —, by Pope, 29, 66, 75, 85, 93, 109, 115–16, 130
Honour, Mrs., 94
Hooke, Nathaniel, *Roman History,* 122
Horace, 18, 31, 59; *Ars Poetica,* 57, 65; attitudes toward, in eighteenth century, 29, 105–6, 108, 119–20, 123, 132; editions of, 33–34, 37–38, 40–42; influence on Fielding, 40, 57–59, 65, 67, 70, 112, 117, 124–25, 127, 136; in school curricula and handbooks, 20–22, 24, 27; references to, by Fielding, 12, 43, 46–48, 50–53, 55, 57–58, 63–65, 80, 82, 87, 90, 93–95, 99, 103, 109, 113, 120; translation of, by Fielding, 45; —, by Francis, 130
Hunter, J. Paul, 129, 132

Icarus, 90
Iser, Wolfgang, 130
Isocrates, 34, 162n. 10

Jacobite rebellion (1745), 124, 125
Jacobite's Journal: Addison essay reprinted in, 59; attitude toward history in, 123–25; Court of Censorial Enquiry, 57; mock learning in, 46–47; narrator of, 86
James, Colonel, 76
Jennings, John, 27
Johnson, James William, 119
Johnson, Maurice, 73
Jonathan Wild: and epic, 68–69, 72–73, 75–76, 125; characters, use of classics by, 82, 84; mock heroics in, 70; narrator of, 86–89, 93, 99–100, 102, 107, 133
Jones, Jenny, 72, 92
Jones, R. F., 105, 113
Jones, Tom, 114; and heroic ideal, 72–73, 80; classical learning of, 94–95; use of classics by, 80, 93–94
Joseph Andrews: and epic, 65–70, 71–73, 76, 108; and history, 124; and romance, 69,

71, 111; attack on Conyers Middleton, 122; characters, judgment of, 78–84, 89–92; models for, 12, 133; narrator of, 100–103, 131
Josephus, 38
Justinus, editions of, 33–34, 40, 42
Juvenal: editions of, 33–34, 38, 42; in school curricula and handbooks, 20, 27, 162 n. 11; influence on Fielding, 125; references to, by Fielding, 46–48, 50–53, 63–65, 82–84, 99, 114, 119–20, 174 n. 32; translation of, by Dryden, 29; —, by Fielding, 44

Kaufman, Paul, 37–38
Kennett, B., 163 n. 14
Keyber, Conny, 86
Kibworth Academy, 27
King, William, 56
Knight, Charles, 12

La Motte, Antoine Houdar de la, 115–17
Langford, Abraham, 41
Latin authors, editions of, 32–34
Law, William, 28
lawyers, use of classics by, in Fielding's novels, 79, 83, 95
Leake, James, circulating library of, 36
"learned lady," satiric type, 28, 97, 99
Le Bossu, René: and epic, 66–67, 69–70, 90; mentioned by Fielding, 102, 112
L'Estrange, Roger, 29
Levine, Joseph, 105, 115
Leyden University, 40, 133
Lillo, George, 121
Lily, William, *Short Introduction of Grammar*, 19–20, 82, 130; used in Fielding's novels, 80, 82–84, 87, 90–91, 93–94, 100
Lipsius, 42
literacy, in eighteenth century, 30–31
Livy: editions of, 38; in school curricula and handbooks, 20, 24–25; references to, by Fielding, 46–48, 52–53, 82–83, 167 n. 25, 174 n. 32
Locke, John, 23
Lockwood, Thomas, 48, 133
Longinus, 59; editions of, 35–36; references to, by Fielding, 51, 53, 55, 57, 112
Lucan: editions of, 40; in school curricula and handbooks, 27, 162 n. 11; references to, by Fielding, 49, 63, 87–88, 98–99, 101, 122
Lucian: editions of, 34–36, 38, 41, 54; influence of, on Fielding, 12, 39–40, 54–57, 59, 63, 78; in school curricula and handbooks, 21–22; references to, by Fielding, 49, 53–55, 59, 65; translation of, proposed by Fielding, 55–56
Lucretius, 38; editions of, 40, 42, 130; in school curricula and handbooks, 27, 162 n. 11; references to, by Fielding, 173 n. 20
Lynch, James L., 66
Lyttleton, George, 122, 125

Maecenean circle, 118–19, 123–25, 127
Maittaire, Michael, 23
Mandeville, Bernard, 30
Manilius, 162 n. 11
Man of the Hill, 80, 93–94
Martial, 20, 49, 52
Mathews, Miss, 79, 83, 96, 98
Maximus Tyrius, 21
McKeon, Michael, 105, 129, 132–35
Melmoth, William, 29, 46
Middleton, Conyers, 86, 122
Miller, Henry Knight, 12, 54, 56–57, 105, 114
Milton, John, 66, 112
Mimnermus, 162 n. 10
Miscellanies, vol. 1: and *Aeneid*, 125; "Dialogue Between Alexander the Great and Diogenes the Cynic," 56; "Essay on Conversation," 114; "First Olynthiac of *Demosthenes*," 43, 45; influence of Cicero on, 114; "Interlude Between Jupiter, Juno, Apollo, and Mercury," 56; Lucian, imitations of, 56; "Of Celia," 109; "Of the Remedy of Affliction for the Loss of Friends," 114; "Of True Greatness," 75, 120, 121, 123; "Parody, for the First Aeneid," 43; "Part of *Juvenal's* Sixth Satire, Modernized in Burlesque Verse," 44; "Simile, from Silius Italicus," 43; satire, of Defoe, 111
mock heroics, 62, 70–73, 117, 126
mock learning, 48–49, 87–88, 109–10
moderns, 105–13, 117, 124, 126, 132. *See also* ancients and moderns

Montagu, Lady Mary Wortley, 28
Moschus, 20
Murphy (lawyer in *Amelia*), 79, 83, 84
Musaeus, 20

narrator, 77; bumbling, in *Jonathan Wild* and *Shamela*, 86–89, 93, 99–100, 107, 111, 133; intrusive, 95, 100–104, 131
neoclassical, as label for the eighteenth century, 105, 118–19
Nepos, Cornelius, 22, 33, 34, 88
Nero, 121, 123
Noble, John, circulating library of, 37, 38
Northampton Academy, 27–28
Northerton, 73, 80
Norwich, public library of, 37
novel, genealogy of, 129–30, 132–35

Odysseus, 71
Oedipus, 100
Ogilby, John, 29
Oliver, Parson (in *Shamela*), 86
Ordinary of Newgate (in *Jonathan Wild*), 82
Orosius, 40
Orton, Job, 27
Ovid: editions of, 33–34, 38, 40; in school curricula and handbooks, 20–22, 29; knowledge of, in the eighteenth century, 29, 31; references to, by Fielding, 46–53, 58, 63–64, 87, 93–94, 103, 117, 120, 174n. 32; translations of, 43
Oxford University, 23–24
Ozell, John, 35–36

paper war, 113, 116, 125
Partridge (in *Tom Jones*), 79–80, 92–94, 102–3
Paulson, Ronald, 71
Pausanias, 47, 49
Paris, 75
pedantry, 90–94, 96–99, 109–10, 133, 135
Penelope, 75
Perrault, Charles, 115
Persius, 33, 34, 42, 65, 162n. 11
Petronius, 40, 117
Phaedrus, 20, 33–34, 40
Phalaris, Epistles of. See *Epistles of Phalaris*
Phidias, 101
Phocylides, 20, 174n. 32
Pindar, 27, 162n. 10
Pitt, William, 125

Plant, Marjorie, 36
Plato: editions of, 35, 38, 41; influence on Fielding, 117, 168n. 40; references to, by Fielding, 53, 64, 82, 84, 85, 113
Plautus, 20, 27, 42, 49, 162n. 11
Pliny the Elder, 42, 63
Pliny the Younger, 20, 29, 33, 46
Plutarch: editions of, 34–36, 38, 41; in school curricula and handbooks, 20, 24–25, 29; references to, by Fielding, 46–47, 49, 53, 55, 64, 88
Poetae Graeci, 20–22
Poikile Historia, 21
Polyaenus, 21
Polybius, 41
Pompey, 101, 121
Pomponius Mela, 22
poor, classical education of , 30
Pope, Alexander, 126; ancient/modern debate, views on, 66, 72, 115–16, 118; attitude toward Augustus, 106, 119–20, 124–26; classical translations by, 29, 34–36, 109; references to, by Fielding, 49, 85, 93; relationship of, to Fielding, 57, 59, 62, 66–67, 75, 104, 127, 130, 132–33, 135
Potter, J., 42, 163n. 14
Powers, Lyall, 73
Praxiteles, 101
Preston, John, 130
Prideaux, Humphrey, 29
private academies, classical curriculum in, 23, 26
Pythagoras, 20, 51
professionals, use of classics by, in Fielding's novels, 81–85

Quintilian, 40, 52, 55, 59
Quixote, Don, 71

Rabelais, François, 55
Ragois, Claude, 29
Rapin, René, 67
Rawson, Claude, 70, 73
Ribble, Frederick, 113
Richardson, Samuel: and Fielding, 72, 111, 130; and genealogy of the novel, 62, 132–35; attitude towards classics, 11, 28, 72, 109; *Pamela*, 31, 88
Ricks, Christopher, 125
Robinhoodians, 110

Robinson, Christopher, 12, 54, 56–57, 78
Rollin, Charles, 29
romance, influence of, on Fielding, 61–62, 68–71, 73, 111, 131, 134; —, on the novel, 134–35; relation of, to history, 124
Roman Republic, eighteenth-century attitudes toward, 118–24
Rothstein, Eric, 86, 103–4
Rowe, Nicholas, 34
Royal Society, 46, 110

Sabine women, rape of, 75, 85
St. Paul's Cathedral library, 37–38
Sallust, 20, 24–25, 33, 48, 88
satire, 61, 65
Scarron, Paul, 65, 71
Scriblerians: attitude toward the classical world, 106–7, 109, 118, 120, 131; relationship to Fielding, 127, 132–33
Scriptores Romani, 20–21
Seagrim, Molly, 72, 83
Seneca the Younger: editions of, 29, 38, 42; in school curricula and handbooks, 20, 27, 29; references to, by Fielding, 52–53, 63, 114, 167 n. 25
Shea, Bernard, 11–12
Silius Italicus, 43, 162 n.11
Simonsuuri, Kirsti, 115
Slipslop, Mrs., 79
Smith, William, translation of Longinus by, 29
Snap, Laetitia, 87
Society for the Promotion of Christian Knowledge (S.P.C.K.), 30
Socrates, 81, 85, 93, 118, 121
Sophists, 114
Sophocles, 21, 35, 41,50
Spectator (Addison and Steele), 26, 29, 59, 66, 108
Spence, Joseph, 29
spiritual autobiography, 61, 134
Square (in *Tom Jones*), 84, 114
Statius, 162 n.11
Steele, Richard, 21, 28, 123, 131–32
Stephanson, Raymond, 130
Stobaeus, 47
Stoicism, 121
Suetonius: editions of, 40; in school curricula and handbooks, 24–25, 27; references to, by Fielding, 46–47, 88, 119

Supple, Parson (in *Tom Jones*), 82–83
Swift, Jonathan: attitude towards classical world, 109, 123; references to, by Fielding, 55; relationship of, to Fielding, 57, 59, 62, 104, 132–33, 135–36; satiric stance of, 125; translations by, 34

Tacitus: editions of, 20, 37–38; in school curricula and handbooks, 24, 27; references to, by Fielding, 47, 52–53, 119
Tate, Nahum, 34
Telltruth, Tom, 43, 118
Temple, Sir William, 107, 109
Terence: editions of, 33–34, 38; in school curricula and handbooks, 20, 22, 24, 27; knowledge of, in eighteenth century, 31; references to, by Fielding, 63
Theocritus, 20, 27, 42
Theognis, 20, 162 n. 10
Theophrastus, 35
Thomson, James, 121
Thornbury, Ethel M., 66
Thucydides: editions of, 37–38; in school curricula and handbooks, 24; references to, by Fielding, 53, 55, 64, 95–96
Thwackum (in *Tom Jones*), 94
Tibullus, 33, 43
Tom Jones: ancient/modern debate, references to, 107–8, 110, 112; and epic, 66–73, 75–76; and romance, 71; characterization in, 78, 79–85, 92–95; narrator of, 100–104, 131; prefatory essays in, 108, 133
Tow-wouse, Mrs., 79
translation, types of, 43
Trapp, Joseph, 49
Treis tragodiai, 21
Trott-Plaid, John, 46
Turnus, 73–74

Valerius Flaccus, 40
Valerius Maximus, 47
Varro, 42
Velleius Paterculus, 20, 40
Virgil: attitudes toward, in eighteenth century, 105–6, 118–19, 126; editions of, 33–34, 37–38, 42; epic hero, ambivalence toward, 72–74; in school curricula and handbooks, 20–22, 24, 27, 29; influence of, on Fielding, 61, 64,

Virgil *(continued):*
    73–76, 108, 115, 117, 124–25, 127, 132, 136; knowledge of, in eighteenth century, 18, 29, 31; parodies of, by Fielding, 43, 48–50, 71, 73; references to, by Fielding, 46–48, 50–53, 63–64, 73, 75, 84, 96, 99, 102, 107, 112–13, 120, 126; translations of, 29, 66, 130
Vossius, 42

Walpole, Sir Robert, 124
Ward, Addison, 123
Waterland, Daniel, *Advice to a Young Student*, 24–25
Watt, Ian, 11, 72, 105, 129, 132–35
Watts, Isaac, 23, 26, 30
Weinbrot, Howard, 119–20, 122, 124–25
Western, Aunt, 85
Western, Sophia, 71–73, 75, 79, 82, 85, 94
Western, Squire, 79, 85

Wild, Jonathan, 82, 84, 87–88, 124
Wilkins, Deborah, 72
Williams, Parson (in *Shamela*), 79, 82–83
Wilson, Mr. (in *Joseph Andrews*), 80–81, 90
Winchester Cathedral library, 37–38
wits, use of classics by, 80, 84, 91
Woffington, Peg, 44
Wolfius, translation of Demosthenes by, 45
women, classical learning of, 28–29, 80, 85
Wood, Thomas, 35

Xantippe, 93
Xenophon, 24, 29, 34–36, 38

York Cathedral library, 37–38
Young, Edward, 121
Young, William, 43, 45, 54–56

Zoilus, 116